D1570625

ABOVE THE THUNDER

ABOVE
–THE–
THUNDER

Reminiscences of a Field Artillery
Pilot in World War II

Raymond C. Kerns

The Kent State University Press
Kent, Ohio

© 2009 by The Kent State University Press, Kent, Ohio 44242
Library of Congress Catalog Card Number 2008040098

ISBN 978-0-87338-980-8

Manufactured in the United States of America

Library of Congress Cataloging-in-Publication Data
Kerns, Raymond C., 1921–2008.
Above the thunder : reminiscences of a field artillery pilot in World War II /
Raymond C. Kerns.
p. cm.
Includes bibliographical references and index.
ISBN 978-0-87338-980-8 (hardcover : alk. paper)∞
1. Kerns, Raymond C., 1921–2008.   2. World War, 1914–1918—Aerial operations,
American.   3. United States. Army—Aviation.   4. World War, 1939–1945—
Campaigns—Pacific Area.   5. World War, 1939–1945—Artillery operations,
American.   6. World War, 1939–1945—Personal narratives, American.
7. Air pilots, Military—United States—Biography. I. Title.
D790.2.K47 2009
940.54'4973092—dc22
[B]
2008040098

British Library Cataloging-in-Publication data are available.

13 12 11 10 09   5 4 3 2 1

This book is dedicated to Dorie, my wife
and my inspiration for every good thing I've done
since I met her on 25 June 1940.
And to our children, Carol and Noel,
and our grandson, Grant Raymond Kerns.
And to my parents.

Thunder across the land!

Thunder! We take our stand.

Thunder! And we are the ones

Who watch above the thunder of the guns.

—RAYMOND C. KERNS, *"Watch above the Thunder"*

(A Song for Army Aviation)

CONTENTS

ILLUSTRATIONS

A NOTE ON THE LANGUAGE

This book faithfully records a time in American history when certain terms were commonly used that may now seem offensive. Words like "Jap" and "Nip" were soldier shorthand for Japanese and Nipponese, and also came into widespread use among civilians.

Racial epithets were used in the highly charged atmosphere of the war, and no doubt there were some who intended these "shorthand" terms as insults, but it will become evident to the reader that Raymond C. Kerns was not among them. He deeply respected all mankind, including the "enemy," and for him, these terms carried no hint of racism.

We are very proud that in this book about war, the author's great love for humanity shines through.

The Family of Raymond C. Kerns

PREFACE AND
ACKNOWLEDGMENTS

If you're looking for macho, fighting-man talk, you've picked up the wrong book. As you may guess when looking at my photos, I'm not that kind of fellow. And you won't find lurid romance or exaggerated dramatization of fairly ordinary events—I hope. Not that I don't like drama, I just can't write it.

This is just an honest narration of some of my experiences, observations, thoughts, and acquaintances during my service in the U.S. Army between 1940 and 1945, during first years of what became a new branch of the Army: Army Aviation.

If I'm not a very remarkable fellow, why do I bother writing my story? Well, while I was not the first, I was among the earliest pilots in the Army Ground Forces organic air observation program that began in 1942, proved itself of great value on the battlefields of World War II, and eventually evolved to the highly sophisticated combat and logistical element that it is today. Few of my contemporaries have written their personal experiences, so not many people know what we really did to earn our pay. Therefore, I think that I, who probably was a fairly typical Army pilot, can and should help give the public some idea of what it was like. Besides, I enjoy telling my little stories.

I was born in 1921 on a small tobacco farm in Nicholas County, Kentucky. We were very poor people, and times were hard all over when I was growing up. My parents divorced when I was eleven, and I dropped out of school before completing the ninth grade. After working on various farms and in two or three futureless small-town jobs, I enlisted in the Army on 6 September 1940 for duty with the 8th Field Artillery at Schofield Barracks, Oahu, Territory of Hawaii, where I arrived in December. A year later, I was there as a radio operator when the Japanese attack opened our full participation in World War II. That's where this book begins.

★

It was Lew LeGrand who tracked down former members of the 89th and brought them together into an informal organization called the 89th Field Artillery Battalion Association. My wife, Dorie, and I attended its annual reunions in the late eighties and through most of the nineties, and I served as publisher of *Thunder,* the association's newsletter. It was good to be in contact with these old friends, and I am deeply grateful for their kindness and friendship. In many cases, they helped make it possible for me to recall and record the experiences in this book.

My recollection of events, names, and dates was often refreshed by reference to Sanford Winston's *The Golden Cross,* a history of the 33d Infantry Division in World War II. Rafael Steinberg's *Return to the Philippines* provided some background information on Russell Volckmann.

Don Vineyard of Mansfield, Missouri, my partner in the 122d Field Artillery Battalion, read and critiqued the manuscript for this book and prompted my memory of some adventures we shared. Floyd Erickson of Pleasant Hill, California, was a former flying friend whose own L-4 exploits would put mine to shame if he had ever written them down. Floyd put me in touch with Tom Baker of Tijeras, New Mexico, a flying son of Don Baker, another old artillery pilot. Tom read and critiqued my manuscript as well, then put the whole thing in order and submitted it for publication. It would never have seen the light of day without Tom's personal dedication over a period of several years.

I'm also grateful to Tom for writing the introduction to this book, which establishes some historical context. At this writing, Tom and I have never even met face to face, yet I count him among my closest friends.

—Introduction—

THE HEROIC LIAISON PILOTS OF WORLD WAR II AND THE AMAZING PIPER CUB L-4

TOM BAKER

Lt. Col. Raymond R. Kerns has written here what I believe to be one of the finest memoirs to come out of World War II. He witnessed and participated in some extraordinary events, including the Japanese attack on Pearl Harbor, and he has the writing skills to bring them to life for us. One of the historians who reviewed the manuscript for the publisher said it would make a good movie, and I said it before he did.

Raymond Kerns was a young enlisted man in the Army before the start of the war, stationed in Hawaii, and when the Japanese attacked Pear Harbor on 7 December 1941, he was at Schofield Barracks and fired back at the attacking aircraft with an automatic rifle that he hastily grabbed from his barracks arms room, and thus began his eventful participation in the conflict. Later in the war, as an artillery liaison pilot, he was involved in many more exploits that he vividly recounts for us in this book, as U.S. forces battled the Japanese Imperial Army back across the Pacific, dislodging it from New Guinea and the Philippines as they hammered their way ever closer to its homeland.

Kerns has given his fellow Americans a rare gift in this book, one that will be increasingly valued as future generations study that greatest of all armed conflicts in the history of mankind, which is over sixty years

U.S. Army liaison pilot wings (Photograph by Tom Baker).

gone already and fast receding into history. There is a little something here for everybody: students of human nature, warfare, aviation, World War II buffs, and even (in its descriptions of native Pacific islanders) anthropologists. Like all good books, it will mean something different to everyone who reads it. For me, it brings to life all those young men whom the war took away from the farms, offices, schools, and factories of America and sent to fight in distant parts of the world, places with strange names most of them had never even heard of, some to die there, and some whose bones, like those of big John Durant and his comrades (see chapter 4), lie there still.

Most of those young men returned home after the war and raised families (my generation, the baby boomers), eventually became grand-parents and great-grandparents, and now have grown old or passed on. The book is special to me, not only because I am privileged to be a friend of the author but also because my father was one of those young men, and in many ways this is his story too. Like Kerns, my father flew the small Army observation planes that wreaked such devastation on the enemy through the artillery fire they called in upon the battlefields. This book provides the reader with some idea of what those men thought and felt as they found themselves far from home and family, locked in life-and-death struggles with wily, brutal foes. It is those insights that give this book its greatest importance.

On a secondary but still important level, Kerns's memoir illuminates the history and beginnings of U.S. Army aviation, for much of what he writes about occurred while he was piloting the small, unarmed, low-flying observation aircraft of the artillery assigned to the support of the infantry. Beginning in 1942, these so-called liaison airplanes were assigned directly to the Army ground forces, not the Air Forces (that is, the Army Air Forces or Army Air Corps, which became the independent U.S. Air Force after the war), and unlike the Air Forces pilots who flew the fighters and bombers that the public usually associates with World War II aviation, the Army pilots of the ground forces interacted closely and continually with the foot soldiers who slugged it out with the enemy face to face. These liaison pilots, or L-pilots, thus had experiences much different from the pilots of fighter or bomber planes, and, indeed, L-pilots lived in a different world from Air Corps pilots.

Air Forces pilots were normally based with their fighters or bombers at airfields away from the fighting front, or (in the case of Navy and Marine pilots) on aircraft carriers at sea, and only saw combat infantrymen, if they saw them at all, when they attacked assigned targets in some proximity to them. They rarely had any personal interaction with foot soldiers. At the end of each flying mission, Air Corps pilots returned to their relatively civilized quarters (the envy of all infantrymen in their muddy foxholes on the battlefield) in barracks or tents adjacent to their airfields.

By contrast, the Army liaison pilots of World War II were essentially flying soldiers, who lived, ate, slept, and otherwise spent their daily lives alongside the infantrymen they supported. Each infantry division had its attached division artillery (Div Arty), and each battalion of artillery was allotted two small airplanes with their pilots, observers, and ground crews. Rather than having each artillery battalion's two aircraft acting independently, Div Arty centralized control in an air section, usually commanded by a major who coordinated the activities of all the battalion pilots for the division. Thus, when an infantry division moved, its attached Div Arty with its air section and aircraft moved with it. This infantry/artillery/aviation team, with its activities tightly coordinated, remained together throughout the campaigns. A division's bulldozers scraped out airfields for its planes at every change of location, as the Army maneuvered about the landscape.

The primary duties of an artillery pilot and his observer (if he took one along) were, first, to direct daily artillery fire on the enemy from their aerial observation posts (air OPs) and, second, to assist the ground forces in any way possible—and they found many ways. The armies of World War II maneuvered under the protection of massed artillery barrages, and to be effective, this cannon fire had to be delivered with the greatest possible precision. Although the infantry always had artillery forward observers on the ground with it for this purpose, the air observation posts proved to be so much more effective, because of their wide aerial view of things, that the aircraft ended up doing most of the artillery fire direction work. (In the Pacific theater, the pilots usually flew alone and did the fire-direction duties themselves, while in Europe they more often took up trained observers who directed the fire missions.)

But it bears repeating that these Army pilots were always and ever an integral element of the ground forces; their airplanes were listed as artillery equipment (officially they were even listed as vehicles, like jeeps), and the infantry divisions they were attached to took care of them, greatly appreciated them (in most cases cherished them), and considered them their own. According to *The Golden Cross,* the official history of the 33d Infantry Division, to which Lieutenant Kerns was attached:

> Few people had more friends in the 33d than the artillery liaison pilots. Eleven in number, they accomplished the work of fifty men. They dropped supplies to small patrols operating well in front of the Division line. Whole battalions on the move were oriented by pilots providing "protective" cover. Platoons in the attack received immediate information on strength and disposition of enemy forces occupying their objectives.
>
> Commanded by Major Richard F. Bortz, the Air Section exemplifies cooperation between infantry and artillery. Battalion and company commanders planning an advance were always given a chance to first survey the terrain from the air. Patrol leaders received the same consideration. Engineering parties, dispatched on reconnaissance for prospective road or bridge sites, had their leaders ferried over the hills via L-4.

More beneficial than anything else, however, was the Air Section's effect on infantry morale. To riflemen up front, the sight of a Cub plane cruising overhead was cause for rejoicing. It meant immediate relief from Japanese artillery fires. Enemy gunners, realizing that operations in the face of this observation could only bring counter battery fire, promptly ceased activity. Mountain guns were hastily wheeled back into caves and outside camouflage buttoned into place. Nip barrages thereafter were generally reserved for dawn and dusk—before the L-4s came out or after they had retired for the night.

Every pilot in the section received the Silver Star and Air Medal; awards in which the infantry heartily concurred.[1]

Infantrymen never forgot the help provided by the artillery pilots and observers during desperate encounters with determined enemies. In March 2008, Kerns received a letter from former 33d Division infantryman James McNicols, a man he had never met or heard of, thanking him for directing artillery fire on Japanese troops on Luzon on 5 and 6 March 1945, while the 33d Division was pushing up the Tubao-Agoo Road toward Baguio against heavy resistance. McNicols had researched Army records to find out who was in the L-4 above him during those two days, directing the gunfire that lessened the enemy pressure on him and his comrades. Sixty-three years after the event, he sent his thanks to the pilot. The division history goes on to describe the many photo missions flown by the pilots, which were often conducted so far beyond the range of the artillery that the enemy had no fear of shooting at the Cubs, and the planes often came home with their cloth skins ventilated by bullet holes.

The airplane referred to, the Army L-4 (L for "liaison"), was the type usually flown by these pilots throughout the war in both the Pacific and European theaters. The L-4 was actually just a slightly modified civilian J-3 Piper Cub, a small (thirty-five-foot wingspan) airplane designed in 1930 for low-cost pleasure flying and basic flight training (see appendix for diagrams, full specifications, and a detailed history of its civilian development). A Cub carried two people, shoehorned into the cramped cockpit one behind the other (in tandem), and seemed an unlikely candidate for a warplane, which is no doubt why the Army brass dismissed out-of-hand the idea of using it in warfare when it was first proposed. And yet, in one of those strange twists of fate, the little Piper Cub ended up becoming the most effective warplane of the Second World War.

By 1942, the Piper J-3 Cub had been in production for nearly a dozen years, thousands had been sold to the public, and it had become so familiar to the average American that "piper cub" had become a generic term for any small airplane. Painted yellow with a black stripe down the side, a Cub was mechanically the simplest of airplanes, of light yet rugged construction. It weighed only 680 pounds empty and consisted of a deceptively flimsy-looking skeleton of welded steel tubing and aluminum formers to give it its shape, with wooden spars of Sitka spruce passing through aluminum ribs to form its wings. This whole framework (except for the aluminum sheet-metal cowling around the engine) was covered with a cotton cloth skin that was stiffened and made airtight by several coats of a special kind of paint, called "dope" (from the effects of its fumes on the painters). Within that cloth skin, the plane was mostly air, accounting for why Liuetenant Kerns could fly one home from a mission with forty-seven bullet holes in it—most of them being merely holes in the fabric, and the bullets had hit nothing but air in passing through.

Except for its engine, a Cub had few moving parts, so there was not a great deal to go wrong with it as long as its engine kept running, and the engine itself was a simple, reliable, air-cooled four-cylinder power plant (an O-170-3/A-65-8) manufactured by the Continental Engine Corporation. With only sixty-five horsepower turning the propeller, though, the airplane barely made seventy-five miles per hour at cruise, and at slower speeds, against a stiff headwind, it might hover—or even travel backward—over the ground (some pilots did this just for fun on windy days). But this slow speed also made the airplane ideal for aerial observation and allowed it to land practically anywhere—a road, a stretch of beach, a meadow, anywhere a little reasonably flat open space could be found. It could also be fitted with skis to fly off snow, pontoons to fly from water, or (with a hook fixed above its wing) could snag a cable and land without even touching the ground. And the plane's simple construction rendered it easy to maintain and repair in the field. Cloth patches could be applied in minutes to any rips or tears in its fabric skin (my father once flew one temporarily repaired with adhesive tape and Kerns writes of one patched with hankerchiefs). The tubular steel framework of a Cub's fuselage, landing gear, or tail, if bent or broken, could be hammered back into shape or welded with motor-pool equipment, while a damaged wooden propeller, in a pinch, could be whittled back to a functional shape with a pocketknife. The low-compression engine was not fussy about fuel and could burn automobile or truck gas when necessary.

Thus, rugged in all the ways that counted, stable and easy to fly from its civilian sport-plane heritage, the Piper Cub in war became an aerial jeep of tremendous utility to the Army. As Kerns notes in this book, the Cub proved itself to be the most cost-effective weapon in the Allied arsenal (a Piper L-4 cost the government only $2,800). As the eyes in the sky of the artillery, commanding the massed firepower of battalions of field guns, the Cub frequently became the most important asset on the battlefield. Gen. A. D. Bruce, commander of the 77th Infantry Division, was quoted after the war as saying, "The secret weapons of the South Pacific War were the Piper Cub L-4 and the bulldozer."[2]

When called to war, the J-3 Cub shed its yellow paint for military OD (olive drab) camouflage green, was provided with some extra cockpit glass to aid aerial observation, plus a platform behind its rear seat on which to mount the bulky radios of the day, and was thereby transformed into an airplane that some rightly came to call "the most lethal warplane in the world"—the Army L-4. Though it sounds like a joke, the description was entirely accurate, for the pilot of an L-4, in radio contact with battalions of artillery, could quickly call down so many tons of high explosive onto a target that even flights of heavy bombers could not equal its destructive power. Someone once calculated that a single artillery battalion could fire fifty tons of shells in an hour, and the pilot or observer of an L-4 could direct the fire of *several* battalions at once onto a target if need be.[3] Furthermore, he could deliver this tremendous firepower on call, with greater precision than bombers, and keep it up for as long as necessary to destroy the target, even following moving targets if necessary. After a few demonstrations of this awesome ability, both Japanese and German guns quickly learned to fall silent when a Cub appeared in the sky, so as not to reveal their locations and invite such deadly retribution. As mentioned in the 33d Division history, this, of course, endeared the Cubs and their pilots to ground troops everywhere. Army inductees might initially have been surprised to see the little Piper Cubs of their hometown airports going to war with them, but when they entered combat, the troops, as well as their commanders, soon came to rely on the Cubs in a myriad of ways. (One of my father's friends, then captain Brenton A. Devol Jr., suffered the indignity of being shot at by the U.S. Navy during the North Africa landings by ships' gunners who mistook his Cub for an enemy aircraft. Another Cub flying with him was shot down. The Navy gunners later explained, ruefully, "If you were at sea and saw a Cub putt-putting by, would you believe it?"[4])

In addition to directing artillery fire, as Kerns relates through his own experiences, L-4 pilots, flying anywhere from a few feet to a few hundred feet off the ground and communicating with ground troops by radio, even exploited their bird's-eye view of things to assist individual soldiers and infantry patrols in maneuvering in close combat with the enemy. On their own, in often-unauthorized private wars, high-spirited and aggressive Cub pilots and passengers often took on the enemy directly, shooting rifles and pistols at enemy troops and dropping hand grenades or other improvised bombs on them, reminiscent of the earliest days of wartime aviation in World War I.

Among the noncombat activities of liaison pilots was ferrying war correspondents and photographers around the war zones (correspondent Ernie Pyle and photographer Margaret Bourke-White were two of the most famous); USO entertainers such as Bob Hope and other movie stars who came out to entertain the troops were flown by L-4 into difficult locations where larger aircraft could not operate. Hope, who with other members of his troupe once rode L-4s over sixty miles of water to entertain soldiers on a remote Pacific island, quipped that an L-4 "was a Mustang (fighter plane) that wouldn't eat its cereal."[5] With all these advantages light aircraft provided the Army, it is startling to note that just before World War II began, the U.S. Army had no light planes at all in its inventory, nor any plans to acquire any. Army leaders at that time were simply ignorant of what light aviation could do for them. How, then, did the ground army gain its own close-support air arm, distinct from the Army Air Forces?

The chain of events began in 1940, after Hitler's armies had smashed into Poland, but before the attack on Pearl Harbor. A board was convened in Washington to consider how the existing American aviation industry could be converted to wartime production, should such become necessary. Attention was focused on the manufacturers of large aircraft, not light planes. However, representatives of the light plane industry, including William T. Piper of Piper Aircraft, were also in attendance, hoping to persuade the brass and the bureaucrats that they could make a contribution to the war effort with their small, slow airplanes. In *Mr. Piper and His Cubs,* Devon Francis quotes an Army general on this board telling them: "Light aircraft are impractical for military use," and the sentiment was then seconded by an admiral of the Navy. It was a disappointing experience for the makers of light civilian aircraft and an example of just how shortsighted and hidebound the military brass can be. William Piper grew so frustrated at their reluctance to hear him out that he finally remarked, only half in jest, "We'd like to explain our side of the picture to somebody, some sergeant or corporal, maybe."[6] He was turned away.

Undaunted, the light plane manufacturers, Piper, Aeronca, and Taylorcraft, refused to accept the negative verdict of the military leadership and made an end run around the Washington bureaucrats by offering the use of their aircraft—free of charge and complete with civilian pilots—directly to generals conducting war games in the United States, hoping thereby to demonstrate what small aircraft were capable of in tactical military situations. Since there was no law against it, several Army commanders in the field accepted the offer. One of them, then colonel Dwight Eisenhower (later supreme commander of Allied Forces in Europe), was already a licensed pilot and welcomed the chance to try light airplanes in a military environment. Gen. George Patton also had a pilot's license and even owned a small airplane himself, and both he and Eisenhower soon became staunch advocates of the Army acquiring its own light planes.

At prewar military exercises at Camp Forrest, Tennessee; Fort Bliss, Texas; and Camp Polk, Louisiana; the civilian Piper Cubs, Aeroncas, and Taylorcrafts ferried officers around the mock battlefields and to conferences, gave umpires bird's-eye views of the action, unsnarled traffic jams—directed by Gen. Walter Krueger, Third Army commander, by bellowing orders out the windows of a Cub through a bullhorn (the general figures later in Kern's story)—delivered messages and supplies, landed and took off from practically anywhere a truck could go, and generally demonstrated their extreme usefulness to ground forces in these "liaison" roles, not to mention their potential for directing artillery fire. The Fort Bliss exercises in July 1941 were typical: ten civilian J-3 Piper Cubs, two Aeroncas, and two Taylorcrafts participated in the biggest war games ever undertaken by the Army in the desert, flying in 115-degree heat, landing and taking off from roads, dry lakebeds, and strips hastily scraped out by Army bulldozers, and sticking close to the troops wherever they went. Tony Piper, the factory owner's son, piloted one of the demonstration Cubs, and Henry Wann, a Piper employee who later became an Army pilot and a friend of my father's, flew another. Eisenhower borrowed a Cub every evening during the desert war games and took it aloft to relax and cool off a little.

In all these prewar training exercises, as the unofficial little civilian airplanes demonstrated what they could do, officers on the ground who had previously been unfamiliar with light aircraft learned what they were capable of and had some eye-opening experiences. One of these was crusty old cavalryman Gen. Innis P. Swift, commander of the 1st Cavalry Division. Swift became another convert to the cause of the liaison planes and added his voice to those putting pressure on military authorities to adopt them. According to legend, one day Gen. Swift saw a Cub bouncing around in the grass during a difficult landing and remarked, "Why, it looks just like a grasshopper!" and from that point on, whenever he wanted a liaison plane, would bark, "Send me a grasshopper!" However the name was acquired, it stuck, and thereafter all liaison aircraft, but particularly the Piper Cubs, were commonly referred to as grasshoppers, and many L-planes thereafter sported impromptu grasshopper logos on their cowlings or fuselages.

The praises of its high-echelon officers in the field finally persuaded

Liaison pilot Capt. Donald A. Baker with an L-5 Stinson, Luzon Island, Philippines, 1945. Note the grasshopper logo painted on the cowling (Photograph courtesy of Tom Baker).

the War Department to relent its initial position, and on 6 June 1942, it allocated small aircraft directly to Army and Navy units "organically," military jargon for "under the command and control of those forces." The name of the Piper Cub was even mentioned in the authorizing document.[7] Thus was Army Aviation born, growing over the years and wars into the powerful combat force it is today. Immediately after it acquired airplanes, the Army set about recruiting pilots to fly them from within its ranks, awarding them the distinctive L-wings to wear on their uniforms upon successful completion of their training.

That is how my father, Donald A. Baker, who had never been near an airplane in his life before he entered the Army, came to be—like this author of this book—one of the most highly skilled flyers in the world: an Army artillery liaison pilot. His story is a fairly typical one and will serve to illustrate the experiences of many others who became L-pilots in World War II. Like my father, many of them had been ground-bound civilians before the war, with no thought of becoming aviators. When the war began, my father was a warehouse clerk in a furniture store in Omaha, Nebraska, preoccupied with playing semipro softball in the city leagues, and had never even been up in an airplane, much less considered piloting one. If you'd told him in 1941 that he'd soon be on the other side of the world, flying airplanes over jungles filled with hostile Japanese, he'd have thought you were crazy. But thus does war suddenly change the fortunes of young men. Not many months after he entered the army, the shipping clerk who had seldom been out of Omaha found himself thousands of miles from home, sleeping in a jungle on one of the Philippine Islands with a .45 pistol close at hand in case marauding Japanese discovered him. Nearby, as he slept, two large, fierce, but friendly (Japanese-hating) Igorot tribesmen stood guard around his airplane all night with spears. He had been forced to land in Japanese-occupied territory when his plane ran out of fuel. Eventually he located friendly troops, begged some truck gas for his airplane, and got out of there safely.

When the Army put out a call to its troops for volunteers for flight training, many men like my father who had never thought about aviation were suddenly confronted with the opportunity to become airplane pilots. As a newly minted second lieutenant at the Army Artillery School at Fort Sill, my father noticed the call for volunteers on a bulletin board. On impulse, he signed up for the flight school—mainly to escape the monotony of running a motor pool, he said. His mother, who was deathly afraid of airplanes, having witnessed their formative and crash-prone years, was never told that her son had become an aviator, since it would have distressed her terribly—she just knew that airplanes always crashed and killed their pilots sooner or later. "My flying was one of the best-kept secrets of the war," my father chuckled years later.

Lieutenant Kerns, however, had harbored an ambition to become a pilot since childhood, ever since seeing Lindbergh's *Spirit of St. Louis* pass over his family farm in the late 1920s. He had even taken civilian flying lessons in his spare time while he was a radio operator in the prewar Army in Hawaii. In fact, as a private, Kerns narrowly missed being in the air in a little Interstate Cadet trainer plane when the Japanese attacked

Pearl Harbor. He was just getting ready for his lesson that morning when the bombs began to fall. For him, the Army's call for volunteers for flight training was heaven-sent.

Soldiers who were accepted for flight training, like my father and Raymond Kerns, were first sent to one of several civilian flight schools around the country that came under contract with the War Department to give servicemen their primary flight training. My father went to Pittsburgh, Kansas, while Lt. Kerns attended one in Denton, Texas. These civilian schools trained their students in L-4 Cubs and L-3 Aeroncas, with civilian flight instructors operating under the supervision of Army Air Forces officers. After they successfully completed basic flight training and won their Air Forces wings, the fledgling aviators reported to Post Field at Fort Sill for their tactical Army aviation training, where the real fun began.

From what my father and his friends have told me and from what Kerns has written in this book, I doubt that there ever has been, or ever will be, again, such rigorous or unconventional flight training as pilots received in liaison aircraft at Fort Sill during World War II. Upon reporting to the school, the students were immediately ordered to remove their brand-new Army Air Forces wings from their uniforms and told they were going to have to earn them all over again, as Army L-wings. They were also informed, "We are now going to teach you to do things with an airplane that you have always been told that you should never do, and you are going to do them very well." Some of the training maneuvers seemed wild and dangerous to ordinary pilots and, in fact, broke all civilian flight regulations, but they were designed to develop the extraordinary piloting skills necessary to operate airplanes from unusual locations and promote survival under combat conditions.

Teaching these skills at Fort Sill were handpicked flight instructors from all over the nation, many of them civilians, some of them former barnstormers—and in their dealings with their students they were tough, demanding, and unforgiving. Although they might be friendly enough when off duty, my father said that they would shout orders like maniacs from the backseat of a Cub during flight training, deliberately adding mental pressure to the physical (it was necessary to shout anyway over the roar of the engine), and occasionally banging him over the head with rolled-up maps to emphasize a point if he made the slightest error. Anyone who failed to please these instructors would soon find a pink slip of paper on his bunk, ordering him to report to the commandant's office, and thereafter was seen no more in the school. Mediocrity was not tolerated, and students who did not demonstrate a strong aptitude for flying were soon washed out of the program. It was simply too dangerous to allow marginal pilots to fly to the very limits of what an airplane can do. The Army wanted only the very best liaison pilots, and that's what it got.

Some ninety classes were trained at Fort Sill between 1942 and the end of the war. Each class underwent sixteen weeks and two hundred hours of tough training, both on the ground in classrooms and in the air as pilots. In addition to their flying, they learned basic maintenance and repair of their airplanes. Near the end of the course, they were taught to direct artillery fire from the air by radio.

For the flight training, primitive practice airfields were scraped out all over the Fort Sill military reservation and became known to sweaty-palmed student pilots as Rattlesnake Field, Rabbit Hill, Geronimo Field, and Apache Field, to name a few, each one presenting unique flying challenges. Students landed and took off uphill and down, over and around obstacles, with the wind blowing in any direction. My father often spoke about the hair-raising, extremely short-field landings he was required to make and how he was taught to do them. After first "dragging" a prospective landing site, that is, flying slowly only a few feet above it to inspect it closely for any hidden dangers, the student then went around and landed using a slow, mushing, nose-high "power approach" instead of a glide, a technique designed to provide the absolute minimum of landing roll. To do this, a pilot holds his airplane in the air at critically low speeds by the precise application of engine power, "hanging on the prop," so to speak, and whenever he needs to get a look ahead (since the airplane's nose is sticking up in front of him blocking his view), he kicks rudder a little to slew the airplane around sideways just enough to see forward. Flown this way, an airplane is actually semistalled, and its rate of descent is controlled by the throttle and "feel," or seat-of-the-pants instinct. When he arrives at his chosen touchdown spot, being only inches above it by that time (if all is going well), he chops the throttle and the airplane drops to the ground and rolls to a short stop, sometimes in hardly the length of a tennis court. This kind of a landing took a lot of practice, but after a pilot mastered it he could set a Cub down nearly anywhere. The Piper Cub, with its long, thick, high-lift wing, forgave such transgressions of ordinary flying safety, and obediently did as it was asked, while other planes, such as the Taylorcraft L-2, might whip over into a stall and kill a pilot who tried such things (which in fact occurred, so that the L-2 was eventually shelved as an Army trainer).

Student pilots had to fly for miles one foot above the ground. They took off and landed on one wheel, while turning, and around corners. Pilots began short, maximum-performance by first towing the airplane back to the very end of the strip, to gain every inch of takeoff room, then revving up the engine to full throttle while holding the wheels braked, then releasing brakes for the quickest possible acceleration, and horsing the airplane off the ground at the lowest possible flying speed.

During part of the training, collapsible barriers of lightweight poles were erected, and students had to make both landings and takeoffs over them without knocking them down. At higher altitudes, they practiced sudden turns and reversals of direction as defense against attacks by enemy fighter planes. My father said the instructors called these maneuvers "rapid descents," and one such trick involved quickly rolling the airplane over almost onto its back while simultaneously turning in the opposite direction, a "split-S" stunt that faster airplanes attempting pursuit could not follow. The L-pilot then dove for the ground and when close to it would bleed off excess speed built up in the dive by fishtailing or skidding the airplane right and left with rudder to expose its fuselage to the relative wind, which quickly slowed it to landing speed. Once on the ground, the pilot was taught to exit the airplane with all possible speed and seek cover (and if he got the chance, he was also to drag his airplane to cover as well).

For many an L-pilot, all this push-to-the-limits training paid off handsomely on the battlefield. Lt. Joseph Gordon Furbee, for example, who flew with the Allied spearhead into Germany after the D-Day Normandy landings, was shot down by a German FW-190 fighter plane that peppered his Cub with machine gun bullets and shattered its propeller. He landed, unhurt, on a street in a German town. After his mechanics drove a half-track truck to the crash site, patched up the Cub, and then used the truck to knock down any obstacles to his takeoff, he was faced with the task of flying his L-4 out of a small open field in the town. He managed to get the plane airborne from the muddy field, but then:

> Less than a hundred yards ahead was a two-story building which I had no hope of clearing. . . . I banked to the left, the left wing barely cleared the ground as I made a 90-degree turn and leveled out for a climb up. I missed the building, only to find myself staring into a line of electric wires on poles along a railroad track. No way could I clear over them, so I eased the stick forward to glide under, skimming just above the railroad. Luck was with me—there were no boxcars on the track. The terrain fell away downward ahead, so I was not forced into climbing at once. My airspeed increased and soon I was free as a bird flying at any altitude desired.[8]

It was all in a day's work for an Army L-pilot.

The J-3/L-4 Cub was well suited to such hijinks because it was light, nimble, and exceptionally well designed aerodynamically. Piper had designed it to be the safest possible civilian trainer and sportsplane, suitable for pilots with even minimal skills, so its handling was inherently forgiving. A Cub just naturally wanted to fly, and it was difficult to stall one out even at the very slow speeds and crazy attitudes into which liaison pilots often forced them—it would never stall, in fact, without first shivering emphatically to warn its pilot that he'd better get the nose down a little. Because it had such benign flight characteristics, it was harder to make fatal mistakes with a Cub than with nearly any other airplane ever built. It was so stable, in fact, that it was difficult to force into a spin or to hold in the spin once begun, and a pilot could exit a spin just by letting go of the controls—the plane would soon right itself. It could turn on a dime, wheel in amazingly tight circles, and practically hover over a battlefield to observe the tactical situation and direct artillery fire. In the hands of a highly skilled pilot, a Piper Cub could do astounding things. It remains one of the best aircraft ever designed, and it's a pity they aren't made anymore, but most sports plane pilots today demand more powerful, faster, quieter, and more comfortable airplanes. Its final version, the Super Cub, was produced up until 1981, and those still flying today are in demand as bush planes in Alaska and other rugged parts of the world.

It was these stellar flying characteristics that resulted in the L-4 being chosen by the Army over its competitors for use overseas (for simplicity's sake, and to standardize overseas shipments of planes and parts, the Army wanted to settle on just one aircraft), while the Taylorcraft L-2 and L-3 Aeronca remained mostly stateside in training roles.

While a Cub could fly off of wheels, skis, or pontoons, at one point during the war it was flown without the need for any landing gear at all. This was the "Brodie System" of landing and taking off from cables strung along the side of a ship or between poles on land. Landing on a cable fifty feet above the ground or on the deck of a ship looked like a circus stunt, but it proved to be a practical solution to some vexing tactical problems that had arisen during the war, situations where there was no space available for normal takeoffs or landings.

Navy lieutenant James H. Brodie, on assignment to the Office of Strategic Services (the OSS, forerunner of the CIA), figured out a way to attach hooks to the top of liaison airplanes' wings, so pilots could fly these hooks into nylon loops connected to cables and thus both land and take off from the cables when they were installed on ships (or anywhere else, for that matter).

Lieutenant Kerns, who attended one of the early flight-training classes at Fort Sill, went to the Pacific with the 33d Division before this method was invented, so he never encountered it, but my father completed his flight training a little later, as the device was coming into use. After winning his L-wings at Fort Sill in 1944, Lieutenant Baker was sent to Hawaii, where he was trained to land and take off this way in an L-4, without the airplane's wheels ever touching the ground (or a ship's deck). This method had first been envisioned as a means to launch and retrieve liaison planes from ships in the mid-Atlantic, so that they could orbit around convoys to spot the German submarines that were causing great losses to Allied shipping during the Battle of the Atlantic. But as the war went on, and the U-boat threat diminished, the idea was transferred to another seaborne task: providing air cover for amphibious assaults, with the invasion of Japan ultimately in mind.

The ships employed for this mission were modified LSTs (for "Landing Ship, Tank," although many crew members swore it meant "Large, Slow Target"). The problem the Brodie device solved in this case was how to bring small aircraft in close to shore and launch them so that their pilots could direct (by radio) naval gunfire on enemy installations on shore, and later, after a beachhead was established, artillery fire. If they were launched from regular aircraft carriers far out to sea, the Cubs, with their single twelve-gallon gas tanks and relatively short range, didn't carry enough fuel to be able to fly to shore, spend the necessary time over the beachhead, and return. They needed to be launched (and retrieved) closer to the scene of the action.

As improbable as it seemed, the Brodie system, fit the bill admirably and proved quite successful the few times it had the chance to be used in combat before the war ended. The special LSTs were fitted with long booms projecting out over the water fore and aft, with a three-hundred-foot-long cable strung between them down the side of the ship. To land on the cable, an L-4 (or -5) was flown slowly and carefully toward it, using the same sort of nose-high power approach as used for short-field landings on land, until the hook projecting from the top of its wing snagged the cable, or more accurately the loop of nylon webbing hanging from a trolley on the cable. As the captured airplane then slid down the cable, it would be braked to a stop by the trolley, dangling in midair. From there, the plane was lowered to the deck by a crane. To take off, it was lifted up and hung back on one end of the cable with its engine running. The pilot then revved the engine to full power, the airplane was released to run down the cable, and when he neared the end of the cable, the pilot unhooked his airplane by pulling a lanyard hanging from the roof of his cockpit (which reminded my father of the overhead chains used to flush old-fashioned toilets) and flew away.

It took some finesse (and some nerve at first) to land and take off from cables this way, but after a little practice L-pilots did it almost casually. In fact, remembered one Fort Sill instructor, some students practicing on a Brodie rig set up at Fort Sill got so good at it they became bored with ordinary straight approaches to the cable, and when they thought no one in authority was watching, they invented more interesting ways to snag it. One pilot would do a loop and hook the cable at the bottom of the loop. Another would shut off his engine a thousand feet above the cable and glide down onto it deadstick. Yet another thought it was fun to bounce his airplane off the ground and up into the cable. They all eventually got caught. "My punishment was to ground each of them for a week," the instructor remembered, "but secretly I admired their skill."[9]

My father, an athlete with quick reflexes, was a natural for this stunt. The only thing that made it a bit tricky at first, he said, was that there wasn't much separation between the top of the propeller arc and the hook above the wing, and the nose-high approaches pilots made to the loop narrowed it even more. Another complication arose when the flat-bottomed LSTs rocked in the sea, for then the booms supporting the cables could swing up and down vertically in an arc of as much as twenty or thirty feet. In that situation, the pilot had to gauge the rhythm of the swinging booms and conform to the motion, approaching the cable porpoise-style. During practice sessions on dry land, with the cable stretched between towers set in the ground, Dad saw one Cub hit the loop with its propeller instead of its hook, ending up dangling by its nose with the loop wound around the prop (the pilot, although unharmed in the "landing," tried to jump to the ground rather than wait for assistance, and broke his leg in the fall). Another exciting moment could occur, he said, when you thought you'd snagged the loop, but actually hadn't, so when you chopped the throttle, expecting to hang from the cable, the airplane would just drop, requiring a very quick hand on the throttle to avoid dropping into the sea (or plopping onto the ground). Fortunately the plucky little Cubs could almost instantly get flying again, so such mishaps were rare. The most common accidents only resulted in broken propellers.

The Brodie system of landing liaison planes on cables strung down the sides of ships. Here an L-4 has landed by hooking the nylon loop hanging from a trolley on the cable, has been braked to a stop, and is hanging suspended from the cable. Next it will be lowered to the deck of the ship, an LST (Photograph courtesy of the Aviation Historical Society).

It would have been interesting to read the famous war correspondent Ernie Pyle's account of being launched from a Brodie device, for the Cub that flew him to the island of Ie Shima took off that way, and he surely would have written about it, as he did everything else he saw or experienced in the war, but Pyle was killed by a sniper's bullet on that island shortly after he arrived there.[10]

For all its Rube Goldberg appearance, the Brodie device proved its worth in the assault on Okinawa, where Brodie-equipped LSTs brought their Cubs in close to shore and launched them to direct deadly accurate naval fire on Japanese shore defenses, and retrieved them to refuel and relaunch. A Brodie apparatus and its operating crew could also be transported in a C-47 cargo plane (the civilian DC-3) and set up on land, and thus be used in areas where regular landing fields had not been built, or for some reason could not be. When camouflaged, the towers and booms could not be seen from above by an enemy the way a graded runway could. But the war ended before many LSTs could be equipped with the Brodie device, and it therefore never realized its full potential. Thus many liaison pilots on the war fronts, like Lieutenant Kerns, never even got to see it. The dropping of the atomic bombs on Japan and its subsequent surrender made the assault on the Japanese home islands unnecessary (otherwise I might not be here to write this, since Dad told me that casualties among the liaison pilots were expected to be very high, and he may not have survived the invasion), and after the war the advent of helicopters made the Brodie system obsolete.

Before the invention of the Brodie device, another method to launch liaison aircraft at sea during an invasion was found, and this one also involved LSTs. In this case, the ships were converted into mini aircraft carriers by the addition of takeoff platforms about seventy-five yards long made of timbers and planks. On some of these ships, several Cubs could be carried on either side of the short runway, with their tails toward the runway and their rudders removed to gain extra clearance. Such pocket aircraft carriers showed what they could do during the invasions of Sicily, Anzio, and southern France. However, unlike with the Brodie system, the airplanes could not return to land on the flight decks, because they were too short for landings. On at least one occasion, during the invasion of France, a Cub could not find anywhere to land ashore and had to come back and ditch in the water beside its LST (the ship then tried to winch the airplane back aboard, but wrecked it in the attempt).

In his book *Grasshopper Pilot,* Bill Cummings of the 3d Infantry Division related how he took off from one of these improvised aircraft carriers off the coast of Sicily on the morning of the Allied invasion of that island, 10 July 1943.[11] It was his first-ever takeoff from an LST, but his L-4 hopped into the air just fine, and with that worry out of the way he headed toward the beach, weaving among the landing craft and nervously remembering how other Cubs had been shot down by their own side in the earlier invasion of North Africa. It was Lieutenant Cummings's first combat experience, he was ill from the effects of malaria and dysentery, and he was alone in the airplane and unsure what to expect. When he reached the shore, he climbed up to fifteen hundred feet amid all the invasion activity and roamed across the beachhead and beyond it, radioing what he saw happening below to the commanders of the landing forces on their flagship at sea and replying to their questions. He thus became their eyes in the sky that morning and enabled them to direct reinforcements to locations where they were needed most.

When Cummings saw Allied troops on the beach being shelled by German defenses, he flew inland, spotted the enemy guns by their smoke and muzzle flashes, and called in naval gunfire that destroyed them. In another place, he saw naval shells landing too close to American Rangers advancing inland, and called a cease-fire there that allowed them to continue their advance. He kept the commanders apprised of the location of the front line as it moved forward from the beachhead and reported on the progress as it occurred. When he ran out of fuel that afternoon, he landed his Cub on a road near friendly troops and begged some truck gas, refueled his plane, and was back in the air in short order, continuing his mission. His efforts that day saved thousands of Allied lives and made a major contribution to the success of the invasion. At the end of the day he landed his L-4 near the beach, climbed out, and fell into an exhausted sleep on the ground for the night. The next day, he was called to the tent of his commander, Gen. L. K. Truscott Jr., and, to the cheers and applause of the staff officers, was awarded the Distinguished Service Cross by order of Gen. George S. Patton, while everyone toasted his health.

Cubs rarely flew at night, since they had no cockpit lights, nor were artillery airstrips in the war zones provided with landing lights, since they were situated so near the front lines that blackout conditions were the norm after the sun went down.[12] Therefore enemy artillery felt safe to shell Allied positions at night, when there were no Cubs up to see where it was coming from and call in counterbattery fire. Lieutenant Cummings, however, discovered that he could fly his L-4 in Italy on moonlit nights and thereby gained tremendous popularity among infantrymen in the area, for when he was aloft and his engine could be heard overhead in the darkness, the Germans would not fire their guns, aware that he would be able to see the muzzle flashes. When his ground crew heard him returning from one of these night flights, they put a few splashes of gasoline in empty C-ration cans on either side of the airstrip and ignited these little flares for a few moments to show him where to land. (Lieutenant Kerns and his fellow pilots made similar flares from soda-pop bottles, placing a single one on the approach end of the field and two at the other end.) Cummings wrote that soldiers often stopped by his airstrip to thank him profusely for making it possible for them to get some sleep at night, blissfully free from German shelling.[13]

After D-Day in Normandy, as the Allies pushed across France and into Germany, L-4s rode shotgun on Patton's hard-charging armored columns and ranged out ahead of them to locate German positions and artillery targets. In this campaign the Cubs gained the nickname "Maytag Messerschmitts," and as a sideline some pilots mounted bazooka rocket launchers on their L-4s and went hunting German tanks. ("All of us Grasshoppers enjoyed chasing enemy tanks around," wrote Cummings.[14]) Strictly speaking, this was against regulations, for before the war the Army Air Forces, after initially protesting the scheme to give the ground army its own airplanes, had agreed to go along with the scheme on the condition that the liaison aircraft not be armed—Air Corps brass insisted that they retain control of all armed aircraft. The Army dutifully complied, issuing orders forbidding liaison planes to mount weapons. Pilots were allowed to carry only a pistol in a shoulder holster, as an aid to survival in case they were forced down, but that was the extent of an L-4's official armament. This led one war correspondent to write, accurately, that when a passenger armed with a pistol climbed into a Cub, its firepower was doubled.

But at various places and times during the war, the rule against arming L-planes was broken by individual pilots eager to engage the enemy with something more than sidearms or whatever they could drop out the windows. For example, Lt. Don Vineyard and his friend Lt. Raymond Kerns welded a discarded machine gun from a bomber to the landing-gear struts of Vineyard's L-4 and shot up Japanese patrols and installations with it, and Kerns used it to destroy a Japanese fuel dump. Unfortunately (or perhaps fortunately for the Japanese) their commander found out about the gun and made them take it off.

But when some Cub pilots mounted bazookas on their airplanes during the Allied drive across Europe into Germany, a few Army commanders (especially Patton) were willing to look the other way. The most famous of these was Maj. Charles Carpenter of the 4th Armored Division, a former high school history teacher, who mounted six bazookas on his L-4—three on each side—and named his Cub *Rosie the Rocketer* (a play on Rosie the Riveter, the fictional female factory worker who symbolized the six million American women working in U.S. factories building ships and airplanes during the war; Lieutenant Kerns's fiancée, Dorie Lane, was one of them). Major Carpenter was Gen. John Wood's personal pilot, and this fact, plus his having a little more rank than most Army pilots, meant that he was not often burdened with artillery-spotting duties and thus had more time to devote to his own private war. It was rumored that the death of his brother in combat gave him extra motivation to strike at the enemy.

Newspaper correspondents dubbed Carpenter "Bazooka Charlie" in their dispatches home, and the bolder ones begged rides with him on his aerial hunts, though he preferred to fly solo because the extra weight of a passenger cramped his style. Carpenter veered around buildings and trees to get shots at tanks and was finally credited with six panzer kills—two in a single day—and he also knocked out several other armored vehicles. From the air, he could spot enemy tanks in their camouflaged positions when the infantry on the ground could not. Even when he missed a tank with his rockets, he took solace in the fact that he'd at least revealed its location to the ground troops, who could then deal with it themselves.[15]

Generals Patton and Eisenhower, among the original proponents of liaison aircraft, were two of the many commanders who moved around the battlefields in liaison planes. Another one, Gen. Mark Clark, wrote after the war that the Cub "was often indispensable to the commander requiring firsthand knowledge of the battlefield." Clark had his own L-4 equipped with pontoons during the Italian campaign, since the Italian Peninsula is surrounded by salt water, and he could thereby land anywhere on the coastline. "I don't know what I would have done without my little puddle-jumper," he wrote. One day on takeoff a heavy wave knocked the Cub's pontoons loose, and Clark's pilot, Maj. John T. Walker, seeing the pontoons dangling crazily beneath the plane, realized that it would be impossible to land that way. "Where would you prefer to crash, Sir?" he asked the general. "How about Sorrento?" replied Clark. "It's a pretty place." In the surf at Sorrento, owing to Walker's skill and the slow landing speed of an L-4, both men waded away from the wreck unhurt.[16]

Allied commanders were not the only ones who came to appreciate the advantages of an aerial view from "puddle-jumper" aircraft. On the enemy side, Gen. Erwin Rommel was frequently aloft in Germany's version of a low-and-slow, unarmed liaison aircraft, the Fiesler Storch (Stork). One German solder in North Africa remembered how Rommel's troops would suddenly find him overhead, dropping orders scribbled on scraps of paper. He often directed his famous tank battles from the air.[17] The German Storch was a larger and faster airplane than the American L-4 Cub, more complex and expensive to build, but it was less nimble and was never used to such good effect as the Cub. In what almost seems like a symbolic demonstration of the Cub's superiority, in one of the last (and surely the most unusual) aerial combats of World War II in Europe, Cub pilot Lt. Duane Francies and observer Lt. William S. Martin engaged a Storch in aerial combat, using their pistols. Banging away like Wild West cowboys at a range of about twenty feet (Francies noted the German pilot staring at them with "his eyes as big as eggs,") they fired their Colt .45s out the Cub's windows as fast as they could pull the triggers, aiming at the German airplane's windshield. The Storch spiraled down to the ground and crashed in a meadow, and its lightly injured crew jumped out of the wreckage, only to be captured by Francies and Martin, who had quickly landed their Cub nearby. Later in the day, the two lieutenants posed proudly for cameras beside their trophy, the wrecked Storch, and one historian has noted that they are the only airmen ever known to have brought down an enemy aircraft with a pistol.[18]

In Europe, Cubs were so effective in directing artillery fire on the enemy that the German High Command offered several days of leave to any soldier who could manage to bring one down. German fighter pilots were awarded more points than they received for downing an Allied fighter plane if they could shoot down a Cub, which they were seldom able to do, unless they could catch one by surprise, since wily Cub pilots made it very hard for faster airplanes to follow them in turns. I am aware of two confirmed instances (and several more are mentioned in wartime literature) in which a Cub pilot turned the tables on a pursuing enemy fighter pilot by luring him down into a ravine or canyon that only a tight-turning L-4 could get out of, causing the attacker to crash.[19]

In the Pacific, as the U.S. Army and Marines island-hopped toward Japan, wresting each island in turn from the Japanese in seaborne assaults, the artillery air sections attached to infantry divisions typically brought their aircraft ashore in the holds of the amphibious LSTs, rolling them out the bow doors of the ship onto the beach on their own wheels or strapped into the beds of two-and-a-half-ton trucks, in either case with their wings detached and stacked or strapped beside them. Once they reached a suitable location to fly from, mechanics would reattach the wings and the airplanes took to the air. Brand new L-4s straight from the factory would be delivered by cargo ship to the supply docks in their shipping crates and from there trucked to the airfields. After the airplanes were assembled, the big empty crates came in useful as sleeping quarters for a couple of men or as supply sheds.

Workers at the Piper factory in Lock Haven, Pennsylvania, eventually built 5,703 L-4s for the Army, that were used in both the European and Pacific theaters. At the height of wartime production, an L-4 was rolling out the doors of the factory every twenty minutes. The L-4 was later joined overseas by the L-5, the Stinson Sentinel, a military version of the civilian two-seat Stinson 105 Voyager, a somewhat larger and heavier airplane than the Cub and with a more powerful (180 horsepower) engine (see the photo of Captain Baker on page 11). Being able to lift more, some L-5s were specially constructed as ambulance ships, with built-in stretcher bays. Seeing their usefulness to the ground army, both the Army Air Forces and the Marines acquired liaison aircraft of their own to use as aerial taxicabs and to evacuate wounded (the Marines also directed navy and artillery fire with them). My father told me, however, that Army Air Forces pilots, accustomed to flying larger and heavier airplanes, rarely acquired Fort Sill–style flying skills, so that he and his fellow artillery pilots could always tell at a glance whether a liaison plane approaching their airstrip was being flown by another artillery pilot or by an AAF one, just by the way it was being handled—Air Forces pilots didn't have "the touch," he said. They merely flew the airplanes, while Army liaison pilots wore them like extensions of their own bodies, and to an experienced eye the difference was readily apparent.

After the war my father, like many other Army pilots, went on to make a career of Army Aviation, serving, as Kerns did, through the Korean and Vietnam Wars. As our family moved from one Army post assignment to another during that time, my brothers and I grew up around these ex–World War II liaison pilots and heard some of the stories they told, although we kids, being kids, thought little of it at the time. We just assumed everyone's fathers had done such things. It wasn't until we grew up—and started flying airplanes ourselves—that we realized what amazing things liaison pilots had done with their light aircraft during the war.

Long after my father had retired from the Army to civilian life, I continued to hear of the World War II exploits of liaison pilots from him and his old friends, and I decided to collect and record these stories and perhaps turn them into a book (which, like so many good intentions, never came to pass, but former liaison pilot Bill Stratton has done a good job of collecting L-pilot stories in his two volumes of *Box Seat over Hell* and has formed an International Liaison Pilot Association online). I pumped Dad and his friends for more stories whenever I got the chance. Thus it was that one day in the late 1980s, as I sat in a restaurant with my father and his old flying buddy Floyd Erickson, it wasn't long before Erickson had me convulsed with a hilarious story of his trying to land a crippled L-4 in the Philippines during a combat offensive. He told us that just as he neared the ground, one of the airplane's wings struck a tree with such force that he was thrown out the door of the cockpit, and he ended up riding along outside on the wing struts for a while, as the pilotless airplane went through some wild gyrations before finally diving into the ground. The mental image he drew of a man clinging grimly to the wings of an out-of-control airplane as it careened around the sky, and then dove into the ground, nearly had me falling out of my chair. Fortunately, he said, the crash did not injure him much—in fact, he hurt himself more in scrambling over rocks and brush trying to get away from the wreckage, for he feared the Japanese might beat the Americans to the scene.

Pilotless airplanes running wild seem to have been a particular bane of then lieutenant Erickson, for on another occasion a Cub ran away from him while he was trying to prop (hand-start) it. Since a Cub had nothing so exotic as a self-starter, not having any electrical system to run one, it was normal procedure to hand-start an L-4 by flipping its propeller. If the pilot had no helper to do it for him, he did it himself, after first chocking a wheel (or jamming his boot under one), and then when he had the engine running, he kicked the chock away and climbed into the cockpit. Lieutenant Erickson had accidentally left the throttle of this particular L-4 wide open while he propped it, and to his astonishment the engine came to life with a great roar, knocked him down, and the Cub began to take off without him. With "Eric" (as his friends called him) running frantically in the airplane's wake, like Buster Keaton in one of his silent comedies, the unoccupied airplane left him behind in a cloud of dust and headed for the wild blue. Fortunately, just as it was taking to the air, one wheel dropped into a pothole, causing the propeller to hit the ground and stop the engine, to the immense relief of its pursuer.

Erickson had a great fund of such stories, preferring the funny ones over the tragic, and I urged him to write them down, or at least speak them into a tape recorder and let me do it for him, but he pooh-poohed the idea. "If anyone needs to write down his WWII memories," he said, "it would be Ray Kerns. You should hear some of the things he did." This was the first I had heard of Kerns, although my father said the name sounded familiar to him and he believed they had met socially on at least one occasion (most of the World War II L-pilots who stayed in the Army after the war seemed to have met each other at one time or another). Erickson, as it turned out, was as good a friend of Kerns as he was of my father, even though my dad and Kerns barely knew each other. So, with Eric as the middleman, I contacted Ray Kerns, whom I learned had flown Cubs with the 33d Infantry Division against the Japanese in the Pacific, earning both the Silver Star and the Air Medal. To my delight, Kerns told me that he was already writing his World War II memoirs. As the editor of a postwar publication called *Thunder,* dedicated to maintaining contacts and arranging reunions with former Army friends in the 89th Field Artillery Battalion, he had begun writing some of his memories as articles for that publication, which had given him a good start on his book. He sent me a complete set of the magazines, and a glance at his writing was all I needed to tell me that here was one of the best writers I had ever encountered.

"But," he said with the modesty I always encountered in my father's generation of gentle warriors, "Eric's stories would put mine to shame, if he'd only write them down." Whether that was true or not would never be known, for Erickson was deaf to my entreaties. My father, too, insisted he had not seen enough combat to fill a book (though I did succeed in getting him to write his memoirs for our family). This left me aiming a barrage of badgering at Kerns to finish getting his memories down on paper, so that I could enjoy them all the sooner, and not only did he endure my prodding without protest, but he did me the honor of letting me read each chapter as it was completed. I thus played the part of proofreader, a superfluous service since his daughter, Carol, can spot a misplaced comma at a hundred paces, and Kerns's writing is impeccable to begin with, but it did give me an excuse to keep asking for more of his memoirs.

When the book was finished, with Kerns's permission I sought out publishers for it, but in the 1990s we met with no success. Unaccountably to me, no press I contacted seemed interested at that time. Perhaps I approached the wrong ones or gave up too easily, but, to my shame, I became discouraged, set the book aside amid a pile of rejection slips, and allowed a decade to slip by. Then one day I picked up the manuscript again, reread it, and decided it could not be allowed to languish. Some publisher, somewhere, surely had the sense to recognize a great work when he saw it, and I would find that publisher no matter how long it took.

And this time, to my surprise, interest in the book was immediate and widespread. Somehow, in the intervening years, the situation had turned around 180 degrees. World War II had become a hot topic. Bookstores now contained volumes on all aspects of the war, a World War II memorial had finally been built on the Mall in Washington, videographer/historian Ken Burns had produced a documentary on the war that was viewed by millions on TV, and I had been hearing veterans of World War II being interviewed on radio talk shows and rightfully thanked for their service. It seemed that America was finally waking up to the great debt it owes the veterans of World War II, and it was in this atmosphere, happily, that I was now offering one of the best memoirs ever written about the war. Enticed by a few excerpts, this time several publishers expressed keen interest in the manuscript, and Kerns was actually able to choose among them. He picked Kent State University Press, partly because Ohio is part of his old stomping grounds, near where he grew up, and partly because in its director, Will Underwood, we found a helpful collaborator.

Kerns's book now joins the all-too-few volumes written by and about the heroic Army liaison pilots of World War II. (See the list of additional readings at the end of this book for some of these.) Probably from ignorance of the roles and accomplishments of the L-pilots, many authors of supposedly comprehensive histories of World War II hardly mention the "organic" Army Aviation of that war. The L-4 Cub may indeed have been "the most lethal aircraft of the war," but that didn't make it the most famous, or even very well known, probably because it was the least glamorous—it was "the little airplane that could"—and for many years its stellar role in the winning of the war has been largely unknown or ignored by a public more interested in the bigger, sexier, and more powerful fighters and bombers.

There were many thousands of liaison aircraft used by the U.S. Army in World War II—nearly six thousand Piper L-4 Cubs alone—and Joseph Furbee Gordon, author of *Flying Low,* has estimated that there must have been around four thousand Army liaison pilots who flew them.[20] Very few seem to have written their experiences down, unfortunately, and thus their stories have remained in only their memories or related only to immediate family. And when the owner of such a memory departs for better worlds, as both my father and Floyd Erickson have done now, the stories they did not tell or write down are gone forever. To those such as Raymond Kerns, who have gone to considerable effort to write their memoirs down for us, we should be very grateful. They have given us a part of our American heritage.

As this book was going to press, Raymond Kerns was struggling with the final stages of a long illness, and after putting the finishing touches on the manuscript, he passed away on 6 February 2008, two months before his eighty-seventh birthday. He thus joined his good friend Floyd Erickson; my father, Donald A. Baker; most of their fellow L-pilots; and the fast-lengthening list of other World War II veterans who can no longer tell us firsthand what they experienced in that great global conflict of the twentieth century. This book was his final accomplishment and his gift to history.

I think General Sherman was not entirely correct when he said that war is hell and you cannot refine it. War certainly is hell, but there are some respects in which we can refine it—if our hearts are so inclined. Nevertheless, so long as leaders and nations remain ambitious, greedy, callous, uncaring about human beings, the wars, with all their inhuman cruelties, will come. As Sherman further observed, "You might as well appeal against the thunderstorm."

—RAYMOND C. KERNS

PROLOGUE

One summer afternoon in 1927, when I was six years old, I was playing under some black locust trees just across the dusty pike from our farm home near Buzzard Roost in Nicholas County, Kentucky. (Well, the legal name of the little crossroads was Sprout, but since early settlement times it had been called Buzzard Roost, and so it is to this day, and it's on my birth certificate.) Anyway, my little brother, Bobby, was taking his nap, and Dad was at work somewhere in the fields. I was playing in the dirt and listening to Mom singing as she did her housework.

And then there came another sound, a thin droning that I knew at once had to be an airplane, although I had never seen or heard one before. It took a lot of searching, but finally I saw them, not one but three airplanes, almost directly overhead. They were flying in a "V" formation. The leading plane was a monoplane that looked white and almost transparent, so that the sky seemed to be a blue liquid flowing right through its wings. The other two planes appeared smaller, were dark in color, and were biplanes.

It was many years before I learned that the white monoplane I saw that afternoon was the most famous airplane in the world, flown by the whole world's hero, Capt. Charles A. Lindbergh. The others were Army pursuit ships escorting him as he toured the country after returning from France.

Lindbergh's solo flight from New York to Paris in *The Spirit of St. Louis* in May 1927 inspired many a boy to dream of flying, and I was one of them. I filled my schoolbooks and pencil tablets with drawings of biplane fighters, dirigibles, Civil War cannon, and riflemen firing over earthworks and knocking down straight rows of stick figures. As I thinned corn or hoed tobacco or worked a team of horses, I was always dreaming of airplanes. Unfortunately for me, I grew up skinny and awkward, dropped out of school in the ninth grade, and when I tried to enlist in the Army Air Corps in 1940, they turned me down for lack of a diploma. I became a radio operator in the 8th Field Artillery at Schofield Barracks, Oahu, Territory of Hawaii, where I arrived on 10 December 1940 aboard the U.S. Army Transport *Hunter Liggett.*

Except for a ten-minute ride in a Kinner-powered Waco biplane with a barnstormer in 1939, I had never flown. But I was conscientious, believed in keeping my nose clean and doing what I reasonably could to make the folks back home proud, so I did well as a soldier. By October 1941, I was financially able to get some flight training at John Rodgers Airport, located where Honolulu International is today. I got thirty minutes in a Fleet biplane, but at $16 dual (tandem controls) it was too much for my $66 a month salary (a buck private drew $30 a month in those days, but I was a private first class with a specialist third-class rating on top of it), so from there on it was $8 dual in an Interstate "Cadet."

Wednesday afternoon was recreational time for us lucky redleg GIs at Schofield. I had usually spent it at Soldiers Beach at Haleiwa, but for Wednesday, 3 December 1941, I scheduled an hour with my instructor in the fifty-five horsepower Interstate. That would make the required eight hours of pre-solo dual, and my hopes were high. We went up over Keehi Lagoon, between the airport and Honolulu, and McVey had me do spins to the left and spins to the right, one turn, two turns, one-and-a-half turns—all that good pre-solo stuff they used to do and should still do.

After about half an hour of that, he told me to give him a spin to the

PFC Raymond Kerns in the carefree prewar summer of 1941, aboard the yacht *Ebb Tide* about forty miles south of Oahu. A group of soldiers had rented the craft for deep-water trolling. It was owned and operated by a Captain Salazar, with his daughter as crew.

right and hold it until he told me to pull out. "And when you come out," he said, "I want the nose right on Diamond Head."

The Cadet was a very light airplane, and it would spin a lot of times in the 4,500 feet we had beneath us. We must have spun more than a dozen turns before he gave me the word. I reversed the rudder, let off the stick, and got out of the spin, then started pulling up and putting on power. Diamond Head? I had no idea where it was.

"What in the hell are you doing?" asked McVey.

"Getting the nose up to the horizon, sir. Returning to level flight."

"Horizon, hell! You're about to stall out on top of a loop."

After he got the plane back to a suitable attitude he gave it to me and told me to climb back to 4,500. Halfway there, he asked how I felt. I told him I felt just a little woozy, and he said, well, there was no need for us to do more spins if I was feeling bad, so we might as well call it a day. He asked when I was scheduled next.

"Sunday at 9:30, sir."

"OK, Sunday we'll do a few more stalls and spins, and if you don't get sick I'll let you solo."

Sweeter words I had never heard. "Thank you, sir!"

★

The old Hawaiian Division had just been broken up to make the new 24th and 25th Infantry Divisions, and my battery had become Headquarters Battery of the 89th Field Artillery Battalion, 25th Division Artillery. On Thursday, we went into the field to reconnoiter new positions in the Kailua-Kaneohe sector on the eastern side of the island, our old position at Pearl City to be ours no more. We returned to Schofield at noon on Saturday, which, in the staggered payday system then in effect, happened to be our day for the eagle.

After being paid and getting dressed in our slacks and sports shirts, Bill Gibson and I walked over to Wahiwa and saw a Japanese-language movie in which a father, from a distance, shot his daughter with a rifle to prevent her leaping from a high cliff. Then we attended a carnival on the post, where we saw an interesting demonstration of hypnotism—you know, all the hell-raising things that tough, rowdy soldiers do on payday night. And just about the time the bugler of the guard was playing "Taps," we arrived outside our barracks and said goodnight. Gibson was going to play golf next morning, he said, and I was going to make my flight schedule.

Then we'd get together and think of something to do Sunday afternoon.

– One –

THE
PINEAPPLE SOLDIER

According to accounts I've read, he was Lt. Akira Sakamoto. I can envision him pulling his flying goggles down over his eyes, hastily rechecking the "ready" switches for guns and bombs, and rolling his Aichi-99 into a howling plunge toward Wheeler Field. Behind him twenty-five more dive-bombers from the Imperial Japanese Navy's aircraft carrier Zuikaku began peeling off to follow him down in line astern. Higher up, the Zeros of their fighter escort, encountering no American opposition, prepared to join in the attack.

It was Sunday morning, 7 December 1941. My watch told me it was 0740 hours, but most people think it was nearly 0800 by the military clock. At that moment, few Americans, if any, knew that several hundred Japanese warplanes were streaming over the Island of Oahu, intent on destroying the U.S. Navy's Pacific Fleet where it lay at anchor in Pearl Harbor. Surprise was essential for success, and the attackers had achieved total surprise, seeming to drop out of nowhere—but actually coming in from a large carrier force some two hundred miles north of Oahu. Another essential was early destruction of the planes and facilities of the United States Army Air Force on Oahu, which had as its primary mission defense of the naval base at Pearl Harbor. Wheeler was the Army's principal fighter base in Hawaii, and Sakimoto's task was to nip reaction in the bud.

As his bomber slanted downward, Sakimoto could see rows of Curtiss P-40s and P-36 fighter planes tied down, wingtip to wingtip, on Wheeler. There was no hostile activity in evidence. He could see some strollers, an automobile here and there, a few people on the golf course, and soldiers moving between barracks and mess halls. It was evident that neither Wheeler nor adjoining Schofield Barracks had been alerted. Sakamoto's heart must have raced in exultation and excitement as he concentrated on aligning his sights on what had suddenly become, by orders from Tokyo, enemy aircraft there below.

As the howl of Lieutenant Sakamoto's diving plane rose in pitch and volume, it finally intruded on my consciousness and that of a few other men in the latrine of our barracks. With my razor poised in midair, I gazed silently at First Sergeant Regan of Service Battery. We stood there staring at each other, wondering if the pilot would be able to pull out. The howl suddenly ended in a thunderous, building-shaking crash.

Pvt. Burnis Williamson yelled, "He's crashed in the quadrangle!"

It sounded as if he had, but when we rushed out to the third-floor porch and looked into the grassy square surrounded by concrete barracks like our own, we saw nothing unusual. And now we became aware of continuing howling and crashing and shuddering, so we ran to the east windows of our room.

We could see smoke already boiling up from Wheeler, nearly a mile away. Planes were trailing each other in from over the mountains of the Waianae Range, dropping their bombs on the airfield, then pulling up and banking around toward our left to sweep across Schofield with their machine guns chattering.

Since we had no mandatory formations on Sunday, most of our men were still in bed; my personal schedule had gotten me up early. I was expecting to make my first solo flight that day at John Rodgers Airport, which was where Honolulu International is now. I wanted to get breakfast before the mess hall closed at 0800, and then I'd ride the bus to the airport. But many of our men, tired from a long Saturday night

This 1950s aerial view of a part of Schofield Barracks is much as it must have appeared to the attacking Japanese pilots. The quadrangle is the enclosed area between the buildings and is similar to the one referred to in the text (Photograph courtesy of Tom Baker).

after payday, lay like logs in their bunks. Only "Pappy" Downs rose up on an elbow and growled, "What the hell is going on, anyway?"

Pappy was one of my colleagues in the Radio Section. His real name was Maurice, but he was in his late twenties, which made him seem old to most of us boys, so we called him Pappy. I replied to him, "Somebody's bombing the hell out of Wheeler Field!"

Beside me at the window, Sergeant Regan smiled. "No," he said, "they're not really bombing. It's just a mock air raid. Funny they didn't let us know about it, though. They usually do."

"Sergeant," I said, "if it's just a mock air raid, where is all that smoke coming from?"

"Smoke bombs," he explained. "They always use them."

"Sergeant, I don't believe smoke bombs would shake this building from that far away."

He snorted derisively (as they always say in books). "What's the matter, Kerns? You scared?"

I wasn't exactly scared, just very concerned and becoming excited, but I said to him, "You're damned right I am, Sergeant!"

I pointed to one of the planes as it pulled up and banked sharply, silhouetted against a gray cloud.

"You see the elliptical shape of those wings? I don't know whose planes those are, but I know we don't have any planes in the islands that look like that."

Regan still was not convinced, but the matter was quickly settled when bullets began breaking windows of the NCO (noncommissioned officer) rooms on one side of the barracks—one of them being Regan's own room—and one of the planes broke into view directly overhead, no more than seventy-five feet away, its guns now spewing bullets into the buildings beyond ours. On its gray and dull yellow wings and fuselage we could clearly see its markings: the big red Rising Sun.

"Hot damn! Japanese! It's the damned Japs! Oh, those little yellow bastards will be sorry for this!" Sergeant Regan may have been the originator of that term we so fondly and universally used in reference to our Pacific enemy during that war. Seeing how things are all these years later, I hope they don't hold it against us.

The men now rolled out with alacrity, crowding to the windows and porch to see for themselves what was happening. From the porch, I watched a man caught in the middle of the quadrangle moving from side to side along a small, low structure there as strafing planes came from different directions. He finally got a break and ran for better cover. A man in cook's whites took a look around the corner of a kitchen across the quadrangle just in time to catch a bullet. He dropped and lay still.[1] A machine gun stitched a stream of lead in front of Pvt. William Cancro, and, as the man from "Joisy" later reported, he "toined" and ran another way. However, seeing a man fall with several bullets in his body, Cancro "toined" again to help Privates First Class Clarence Compton and Charles Dahl carry the man into our dayroom and place him on a pool table. PFC Warren Harriman, narrowly missed by a flurry of bullets, ran through a screen door to the first floor of the barracks and pounded up two flights of stairs, arriving breathless and bleeding from a small cut on his cheek to announce to us: "They're shooting real bullets! They're killing people downstairs!"

He was so right. Men caught in the open sought cover from the machine guns while an exodus of the curious from mess halls sometimes prevented others from getting back in. Pvt. Walter R. French was killed; PFC Claude E. Phipps took two bullets in the body but made it to cover in a barracks corridor before he collapsed; Pvt. Leo R. Eppes was outside his mess hall when a bullet from a Zero nailed him in the leg; Cpl. John E. Robinson was hit in the hand, and Pvt. Stephen A. Kitt went down wounded. First Lieutenant Charles G. Cassell, a former Army Air Corps bomber pilot who had recently joined our battery and was still quartered at Hickam Field, ran outside to bring a neighbor's little girl to cover when the attack started there. He was shot through the face.[2]

In the midst of the furor, PFC Van Swaney, of Calf Creek in McCulloch County, Texas, bugler of the guard for the 25th Division Artillery that day, marched to the bugler's post near the guardhouse and played "Alert Call"—twice, in the prescribed military manner. He never hurried or missed a note. I think that if a monument is ever erected to the Pineapple Soldiers of Pearl Harbor Day it should be a statue of Van Swaney in campaign hat, wool olive-drab (OD) shirt with khaki tie tucked in, khaki trousers and canvas leggings, his bugle to his lips, calling the nation to war. Like the others, Van did just what he was supposed to do: his assigned duty. If there was failure that day, it was not in the lower echelons.

Officers and NCOs not living in barracks were alerted in various ways, usually by hearing the bombs, and made their way as quickly as possible to their units. Capt. John Ferris was probably typical of our battery commanders. He arrived at his orderly room no more than ten minutes after the attack began. Breathless from running, he used the squawk box to announce that the attacking planes were Japanese: "This is no drill. This is no drill. This is a real air raid. I want everyone on the ground floor. Stay inside, stay in the corridors. All men to the ground floor. This is no drill."

We had been so fascinated with watching the planes that few of

Pvt. Leo Eppes, seen here clowning for the camera in front of Schofield Barracks, took a bullet in the leg from a strafing Japanese plane during the attack on Pearl Harbor. Beside Eppes is Pvt. Allison Murphy (Photograph courtesy of Henry Hazelwood).

us had started to dress, and now the men began heading downstairs, grabbing a garment or two, many of them wearing only the shorts and undershirt that are a soldier's pajamas as well as his underwear. I yelled to the general assembly that we should at least take helmets and gas masks, but few paid any attention to me. I was just a PFC. So I soon found myself alone in the room where about forty men had been before. An occasional bullet zinged off the concrete floor as I hastily donned my field gear. I had recently read of the German airborne assault on Crete, and I had no desire to be caught out in some guava thicket in my underwear fighting enemy paratroopers. Finally, I laced up my leggings and headed for the stairs. And I fell flat on my face. I got up, took one more step, and fell again. Then I sat on the top step, took off my leggings, and put them on the proper legs so the strings of one would not catch on the hooks of the other and hobble me.

On the first floor at last, I ran down the porch and turned toward our supply room, gun in mind. I stepped over Claude Phipps as he lay bleeding on the floor and continued on my way. I helped PFC Leo Magnan and another man break in the supply room door, and there we got tools and further broke through the iron bars of the arms room, wondering where Sgt. Kenneth McCart was with the keys. (We later learned he was at the motor pool with Cpl. Adolph Otto Mann, shooting out-of-focus 8 mm movies of the Japanese planes.)

Although assigned a 1903 Springfield rifle, I grabbed a Browning automatic, commonly called a BAR, and hastily loaded three twenty-round magazines of ammo. Then I ran out to the quadrangle and waited for a target. Very soon one of the strafing dive-bombers came low across our building, firing into the building across the quadrangle. I brought up my BAR and let go a burst at him, but within about three seconds he had disappeared beyond that building, his rear gunner throwing lead back at our barracks as he went. I waited a few minutes for another, but none came near. And then I remembered that Captain Ferris had ordered us to stay inside, so I went into the dayroom, from which men were being dispatched in small groups to proceed to the motor pool, gun park, and section rooms to start loading out for the field.

So far as I know, I was the only man in my battalion to fire at the Japanese planes that day, with one exception. Our battalion commander, six-foot four-inch Lt. Col. (later brigadier general) William P. Bledsoe, a veteran of World War I, reportedly was seen out in the open, stomping and cursing as he fired his pistol at the planes.

The dayroom was still crowded with men, and the wounded man on the pool table lay moaning softly, his white undershirt soaked with blood. Amid the babble, I recognized the high-pitched voice of Pvt. Carl Bunn asking, "How in the hell do you get this thing to fire automatic?" Immediately afterward he accidentally fired a burst from his BAR into the dayroom ceiling, bringing down plaster over everything, including

As Japanese airplanes sprayed Schofield Barracks with bullets, Capt. John Ferris (right) announced over the squawk box, "This is no drill, this is no drill!" Ferris is seen here two years later, in 1943, when he was Colonel Ferris, battalion commander of the 89th Field Artillery, on the Solomon Islands. At left is Capt. W. D. "Doug" Baker, who was later killed in action on Luzon, and Col. William W. Dick, G-3 of the 25th Infantry Division (U.S. Army photo).

the wounded man. Bunn was a droll young radio operator with innumerable friends, a special fondness for oranges and beer, and a passionate devotion to Columbus Grove, Ohio. But he was never to see his beloved hometown again. In little more than three years, he would die beside his radio in a fight at Binalonan on Luzon. Burnis Williamson's Springfield left a bullet hole above the screen door that was still visible when he visited forty years later.

Some of the boys were already on the move. A bullet slammed into the backseat of Pvt. Elmer Darling's command car, just missing his shoulder. Maj. James Carroll, the battalion exec, en route to the ammo supply point, kept yelling, "Faster! Faster!" His driver, PFC Robert D. Schumaker, floored the accelerator but was frustrated by the engine governor that limited the vehicle to 35 mph. When Capt. Gavin L. Muirhead saw PFC Carl Koon frantically typing vehicle dispatches, he yelled, "We don't need dispatches now! This is war!"

In less than an hour our battery—Headquarters Battery (HQ Btry)—was dispersed over a large field in Area M, between Schofield and Kolekole Pass, waiting for its turn on the roads to move to our island defense position. Some of us had grabbed little paper cartons of milk before leaving the barracks area, but few of us had eaten that morning. Now our mess sergeant, S.Sgt. Lorenzo Silvestre, formerly of the Philippine Scouts, assisted by cooks Charles Dlusky, George Kimball, and Michael Drapczak, came around handing out apples and sandwiches made from roast beef that had been prepared for Sunday dinner.

Radio operator William A. "Billy" Mulherin, who had spent the night at the YMCA in Honolulu, made his way to Schofield as quickly as possible, and now joined us in the dispersal area. He had passed along the edge of Pearl Harbor, and in his Georgia drawl, he gave us our first word of the disaster that had struck the Navy there.

Also arriving, smiling happily and not at all angry with the Japanese, were two young soldiers named Robert Trayer and James O'Donnell who, a few months earlier, had stowed away on the Matson Liner Lurline and got almost to San Diego before they were caught. Like all but the most serious offenders, they had just been released from Schofield Stockade—the one made notorious by James Jones's novel *From Here to Eternity*.

Meanwhile, fire continued to billow from Wheeler Field's planes and hangars, casting a gloom of dark smoke that mixed with the broken clouds. Under those clouds, circling bravely in a loneliness that was both dramatic and pathetic, was a P-40 in camouflage paint with an unpainted silvery P-36 flying on its wing. They were the only American planes I saw aloft that morning, but there were a few others, piloted by devoted young lieutenants who used their private cars to reach their planes and take to the air, ill armed, against odds of twenty to one or worse, while their own air base was under attack, their own quarters blazing. They destroyed a number of Japanese planes. For example,

Two good men: Privates Carl Bunn and Bill Williamson. Bunn survived the attack on Pearl Harbor only to die three years later beside his radio on the Philippine island of Luzon.

only weeks out of flight school, Lieutenants Kenneth Taylor and George Welch took down two and four, respectively. There were a few others. As I have said, if there was a failure that day, it was not in the lower echelons of the command.

There was, however, at least one exception: the lieutenant who dismissed a radar report of large numbers of unidentified aircraft approaching from the north and took no action. He had been informed of a flight of twelve B-17 bombers arriving from the States for refueling, and he assumed those were what he had seen on the radar.

But the truth is that things looked rather bleak at that juncture. They didn't brighten much when Captain Ferris told us that, according to higher headquarters, the Japanese had landed parachute troops and set up roadblocks to delay or prevent our deployment. They were described as dressed in blue coveralls with the Rising Sun insignia on the left breast pocket. All this was in error, of course, but we thought then that it was true; therefore, Captain Ferris wanted an automatic weapon on each of the battery vehicles. Noting my BAR and the 140 rounds of ammo I now carried, he gave me the responsibility for one of the radio section's weapons carriers. If we ran into a roadblock, he said, we would open fire with all weapons and run through at top speed, stopping for nothing.

It was the first time I had ever been given charge of anything other than a sentry post or a range guard tower. Getting the weapons carrier ready for defense, I called on other radio section men to help: Ralph Park of Akron; Willie Waldsmith, the jockey from Massachusetts; Billy Mulherin, the Georgia boy; Salvatore Crupi of Brooklyn. Those men would have laughed at me yesterday if I'd tried to give them orders, but today they responded with goodwill and helped roll the canvas up to the front bow so I could stand behind the cab, steadying myself and the BAR against the wooden bows as we traveled. When I assigned them directions to watch and to fire, they gave strict attention and took their positions in the truck. Like the other radiomen—Burnis Williamson, William Cancro, Carl Bunn, Pappy Downs, James McAndrews, and George Williams, our section chief—they were all Regular Army men, proud of their country, its flag, and the uniform they wore. In this time of crisis they wanted only to be given orders. Thanks to my BAR and Captain Ferris, I was temporarily privileged to give them.

It was a critical time in my life, in a way. Although I loved soldiering, I had always had a conviction that if anyone ever fired at me he would hit me, and that would be the end of it all. Now, visualizing all the possible ambush points along the familiar route to our field positions, I felt that I had practically no chance at all to survive the trip. It was disturbing, thinking that within a couple of hours at most, I would be dead. Was there any way to avoid it? I could think of no way at all that would not disgrace me before the other soldiers, my friends back home, and all my family. I remembered how my folks had always admired and respected those who had honorably served the nation in war, how proud they were of one of Kentucky's counties—Breathitt, I think—where not one man had to be drafted for the First World War. In their minds there was nothing more honorable than to die in service under our flag.

So I had to go forward, so to speak. I resolved to do so gracefully, and I resigned myself to dying that morning. I actually thought of how proud the family would be when they got the word, and with what respect they would mention my name in years to come. So, being thus mentally resigned, I felt no fear that might have interfered with performing my duty, and I was prepared literally to defend that truck to the death. Of course, I got not a scratch that day, and, strange to say, I never thereafter had any doubt—for longer than a few seconds at a time—that I would survive the war.

While we were getting the truck ready, the second Japanese attack came in. It didn't hit us, but a formation of eighteen bombers passed directly overhead, not far above the now scattering clouds, droning toward Pearl Harbor. I looked around for our two fighters but could not spot them. Then, far above the neat enemy formations, I noticed a flash, a small movement far up in the sky above it, and down came two planes, a dark one in the lead, a silver one following. Like hawks dropping toward their prey, the two fighters came almost straight down through the midst of the enemy. They began firing, and the bomber gunners responded in kind, the crisscrossing tracers looking pale in the morning light. After a brief delay the thin, ripping sounds of the guns drifted down to us.

The two fighters continued their dive together until they had passed through and below the Japanese formation, and then the silver plane pulled up and turned away to disappear behind a cloud. The dark plane shallowed its dive a little but kept coming down, and smoke began streaming out behind it. I thought then that the dark plane was the P-40 I had seen shortly before, so I kept urging the pilot to pull out, pull out, but it appeared that he did not try to do so. I guess he was already dead or unconscious. The plane exploded in a burst of flame and black smoke in a pineapple field a short distance from us, and for the first time that day, I got that empty, weak-kneed feeling that comes with being just a wee bit shaken up. The enemy bombers continued on their way, apparently unperturbed.

Since then, I have read several accounts of American fighter losses during that affair, and it seems that none occurred in that particular locale just south of Schofield; thus, I must have witnessed the silver P-36 shooting down a Japanese fighter, meanwhile passing through the bomber formation and being fired on by them.

Immediately after the plane came down, we got the order to move out. We went along the southeast edge of Schofield, passed the smoking wreckage at Wheeler, and went out the Wheeler gate onto the Kamehameha Highway toward Honolulu. Rolling down the long, gentle slope through fields of pineapple toward the cane fields at lower levels, we looked down on Pearl Harbor as on a game being played in a stadium.

From the vicinity of Ford Island in the middle of the harbor and from Hickam Field on the far side of it, black smoke boiled upward, adding to the volume of a huge cloud that spread and drifted slowly southwestward. Around that smoke Japanese planes swirled and dived and zoomed like night bugs around a light, and the air was alive with dark puffs of antiaircraft artillery shell bursts. Within the smoke pall, the bursts flashed dull red. As we drew nearer, we could see the battleships burning and many small boats moving about the smoky harbor that, although we didn't know the numbers then, was the fresh grave of some two thousand officers and sailors, many of whose bodies would never be recovered. I stood in the back of our truck, holding my BAR and marveling at the scene of death and destruction. Any personal fears I might previously have felt were completely forgotten.

Following the main highway as it was then, we passed very near the water's edge at Aiea. There I could have reached out and almost touched the bow of the naval repair ship *Vestal,* which had been run up on the beach, its afterdeck blasted and smoking. In the immediate background the USS *Arizona,* whose sunken hull is still the tomb of a thousand men and is part of a national memorial, was burning fiercely. Beyond that and to the right and left, other ships, hangars, and buildings were going up in smoke and fire. Not far away we could see the Aiea dock, where numerous vehicles of various kinds were taking on loads of wounded from small boats, then speeding away toward hospitals. Sgt. James Carney, of HQ Btry, was in the Schofield hospital recovering from a broken leg sustained in football, and he was able to assist in handling the wounded men brought there, most of whom were from Wheeler or Schofield. He said that the corridor floors became slippery with blood.

Leaving the shoreline of Pearl Harbor, we passed a large number of huge storage tanks that I had been told held most, if not all, of the reserve fuel for the Pacific Fleet, and even I, in my massive ignorance of such things, wondered why the Japanese had not bombed them. Maybe they would be hit in further strikes later in the day. In fact, though, they were not, although it would have required small effort and would have been a truly devastating blow to the crippled fleet. Adm. Husband E. Kimmel later observed that destruction of the fuel reserve would have forced withdrawal of the fleet to the American West Coast. But it appears that high-level Japanese planners of the strike had failed to include the tank farm on the target list, and the Japanese fleet commander, Vice Adm. Chuichi Nagumo, having hit his assigned targets, withdrew his forces instead of exploiting his incredible success.

We went on through Honolulu, past Waikiki and Diamond Head, and around the cliffs at the southeast end of the island, where I had thought we would surely encounter, amid the jumbled boulders and steep slopes, one of the reported roadblocks. We stood to our guns grim and ready, fully expecting to meet our doom. Nothing happened, and we proceeded on past Bellows Field and Waimanalo and then, in a dismal drizzle of rain, we pulled off into a guava-thicketed field below Nuuanu Pali. Two of our firing batteries, armed then with British 75 mm howitzers, took positions from which they could support the defense of the Kailua-Kaneohe Bay sector. The other firing battery, Btry A, was temporarily assigned to man two large coast defense guns of 240 mm bore. They labored long and hard to get those two pieces far up into the narrow confines of the dead-end Kalihi Valley and emplace them on concrete Panama mounts, which provided a 360-degree traverse capability. Service Battery was busy all day and night getting ammunition and other critical supplies to all battalion units.

During a recent field exercise I had lost my raincoat. It had not been replaced, and the overcast, drizzly afternoon there on the windward side of Oahu was chilly, so I sought out the supply truck and asked Sergeant

McCart if one was available. He invited me to see what I could find. He had piled supplies into the truck with more haste than order, but I dug out a short overcoat, wool OD. It bore the taro-leaf shoulder patch of the old Hawaiian Division, the patch to which the new 24th Infantry Division had fallen heir. I put the short coat on over my wet khakis and, having no immediate task, did what every good field soldier does when he gets a chance: I lay down in the supply truck and went to sleep.

It was late afternoon when Sgt. Edward Bylotas woke me. He said I was to go with him as radio operator to establish an observation post, which would be taken over by Btry C as soon as that undermanned unit could get a crew together and lay a field telephone line out to the position. Pvt. Ernett Onderdonck would drive our half-ton command car. We took off northwest along the highway, the top down on the clumsy vehicle. I sat bolt upright in the rear seat, wearing my short coat and my old-style World War I British helmet, cradling my BAR across my knees, feeling quite powerful and dangerous.

In gathering darkness, we concealed the vehicle in bushes near the highway and carried our BC-scope (battery commander's telescope, a periscopic binocular observation device mounted on a tripod) out to the beach on Kualoa Point, at the northwest end of Kaneohe Bay. The tract of land, covered with coco palms, was unoccupied except for one darkened, modest dwelling, which we carefully avoided.

Eddie started setting up the BC-scope in the trees at the edge of the sand, and Onderdonck and I immediately began pointing out to him what he certainly could see for himself: it was a hell of a poor place for an OP. We were at the water's edge, where the first Jap ashore could take us out of action if a prelanding bombardment didn't beat him to it. We were at sea level, where our range of vision was most limited. And my SCR-194 "walkie-talkie" radio would not even consider raising its voice to the one back at the battalion command post (CP). But, said Eddie, this was where they had told him to put the post.

While we were discussing this, a light suddenly appeared outside the single house nearby, and we could see a man carry a lantern out to the beach and hang it on a tree. He then went back into the darkened house. Although we had no instructions regarding such matters, we took it upon ourselves to enforce the blackout to which we ourselves were subject. Onderdonck and I walked over to the house and knocked on the door. A man who was obviously of Japanese ancestry opened the door a few inches and looked at us, a dim light glowing behind him in the house. We asked him the reason for the lantern on the tree, but he gave no reply, just stared at us as if wondering where we had come from so suddenly. We told him to take it down immediately. Without a word, he took down the lantern, carried it into the house, and closed the door.

When we got back to Eddie, he had taken down the BC-scope. We would go back to the CP and recheck our instructions, he said. He asked me to go with him this time. When we arrived, Lt. Jay D. Vanderpool pointed out on a map the desired location, on the nose of a ridge that jutted out about the middle of Kaneohe Bay's shoreline, between Libby-ville (now called Kahaluu) and Heeia. It was about four miles from our first spot.

None of us three had eaten since the apples and roast beef in the dispersal area, so we felt our way around the blacked-out bivouac until we found the kitchen tent. Supper had been served while we were gone, and there was nothing left but coffee. George Kimball, hopping back and forth across a torrent of muddy water running through the middle of his work area, filled our canteen cups with hot black coffee, and we stood out under the dripping guava trees and drank it gratefully. Then we were off again, blundering down the road with the doubtful aid of the command car's slitted blue blackout lights.

A narrow paved road rounded the nose of our OP hill, and beside it we again concealed the car. Then we climbed up to the military crest of the point and set up the BC-scope. We had no entrenching shovels, shelter halves, or blankets for protection from the rain and the wet ground. Our post was just where we flopped down beside the BC-scope. I extended the aluminum antenna of the notoriously inadequate SCR-194 radio and managed to contact the CP to let them know we had arrived.

Kaneohe Bay was totally dark, all the marker buoy lights having been extinguished for security reasons. Across the bay, buildings were still smoldering at the Kaneohe Naval Air Station, and a narrow path of light from that source shimmered on the water to the foot of our hill. By chance, our base point (a point on which our batteries would register to obtain accurate firing data and from which they could transfer fire to any targets we might locate for them), the tip of a small island in the bay, lay in that path of light; otherwise we could not have seen it. We could see nothing else, except that once during the evening we saw flashes through the clouds over the Koolau Mountains and heard heavy firing from the direction of Pearl Harbor. I heard later that this was our own antiaircraft batteries firing at planes coming in to Ford Island from the American carrier *Enterprise*. Several were shot down.

On a schedule of two hours on and four off, Bylotas took the first watch of the night. Onderdonck and I lay down to sleep on the wet ground. At 0200 hours, Bylotas woke me up and I went on duty. I heard boat engines down in the bay at about 0230 and soon made out that several craft were moving about in the darkness. I could only think of one explanation for them: they had to be enemy landing boats assembling, preparing to put troops ashore at daybreak. I awakened Bylotas, and he agreed that it sounded mighty suspicious. As we talked, Ernett woke up and the three of us discussed it.

Although the 25th Division had three direct support artillery battalions, of which our own 89th was one, it then had only two infantry regiments, the 27th, Wolfhounds, and the 35th, Cactus. The third regiment, which the 89th was supposed to support, was a Hawaiian National Guard regiment, and it had not been fielded. Thus, ours was a field artillery battalion with no close combat troops in front of it. If the enemy had come in at Kaneohe Bay that morning—and missed the few shot-up sailors and Marines at the naval air station—their welcoming committee would have consisted of Bylotas, Onderdonck, and Kerns— backed, of course, by the eight British 75s of the 89th's two light batteries. We agreed that in such event we would remain in position and adjust artillery fire on them until it appeared they were about to cut us off from retreat, then we would withdraw along the ridge toward Btry C, using our small arms whenever we could. I was glad for the 140 BAR cartridges I carried in seven heavy magazines in my ammo belt.

I had been able to communicate with the battalion fire direction center (FDC) and inform them of the boat engines. They calmly said, "Roger. Keep us informed." Meanwhile, they twice relayed to us very interesting but unverified (and later proven false) reports of enemy landings, one at Waimanalo Bay to our right, the other near Kahuku Point to our left. That was enough to keep us on our toes.

One of the boat engines sounded much larger than the others, and as we sat talking we heard it come in very close to the beach just below us. Then, shockingly, a searchlight came on and began sweeping the shoreline directly below our OP. I worked the bolt on my BAR and drew down on that light. Another second and I'd have blasted it, but Eddie said, "No, no! Don't fire until we check it with the CP."

I fumed and fussed but called the CP. "Do not fire," they replied. "Just keep us informed."

Then all three of us fumed and fussed. The light went out and the unseen boat moved slowly away.

A short time later, probably about 0400, we saw two long boats slide slowly into view in the streak of light from the burning hangars. Just beyond them was our base point, from which we could easily and quickly transfer fire. They were heading toward the beach, side by side, and our imaginations extended them into a long line of troop-laden landing craft moving toward us through the darkness. Bylotas, certain that this time we'd get fire, dictated a fire mission to me and I relayed it to the FDC. The response was, "Roger. We will not fire at this time. Keep us informed." Were Bylotas, Onderdonck, and Kerns going to have to defend Oahu's northeastern coast without even artillery support? It had begun to look that way to us, and we were highly teed off.

At last, gray dawn began to herald a new day, Monday, 8 December 1941. As the light spread over Kaneohe, we started to see them. Just as we had suspected, there they were, dozens of Japanese landing boats scattered over the bay. Again we cranked up the radio to send a fire mission. Surely they would give us fire now!

But wait—just a minute—those look like—oh, hell! They were U.S. Navy PBY Catalina amphibious patrol bombers that had been dispersed about the bay for better security from any further Japanese attacks. During the night, as we learned, Navy people in small boats had been moving about the bay, servicing the Catalinas in preparation for patrols to be flown on Monday. Lacking the usual navigation aids, one crew had become disoriented and had used its spotlight to scan the beach for a moment. It was then that I had almost gone to war with our own Navy.

After daylight, Onderdonck, a big former merchant seaman from Galveston, and I went looking for food and drink. Without using our truck to gad about or go to the battery—which would have been the sensible thing, though we did not then feel at liberty to do so—we could find only green bananas and warm Coca-Cola, which we purchased from a roadside vendor near our position. We carried that loot to our aerie, and that's all we had to eat and drink on Monday and Tuesday.

On that Monday, Capt. "Nick" Carter's Btry B of our battalion pulled one of its howitzers out of position and took it down to Waimanalo Bay, where it was bore-sighted on the periscope of a Japanese miniature submarine that had become stranded on a reef. But, according to Lt. Philip Grimes, one of the battery officers, orders to fire were never received. The submarine's crew of two abandoned it. One of them drowned in the surf. The other, Ensign Kazuo Sakamaki, was captured by personnel from nearby Bellows Field, becoming the first POW taken by the United States in that war. He was the sole survivor of the ten young officers who manned five midget subs that took part in the Pearl Harbor attack. The Navy salvaged the submarine and it toured the continental United States in a war-bond sales campaign.[3]

I remember the men discussing an alleged argument between Colonel Bledsoe and an Army Air Force officer at Bellows who wanted us to hold fire and let his people bomb the sub. By the time the argument ended, the whole affair was over. However, on 31 January 1942 one of the 89th's OPs reported two submarines off Manana (Rabbit) Island, and the AAF marked their location with flares. Btry B then fired twenty rounds, the first ever against the enemy by the 89th. Effect, if any, on the submarines was not determined.

About 2100 hours on Tuesday evening, the long-awaited telephone line and observation team from Btry C finally arrived and relieved us on the OP. They told us we were to go to Btry C for the rest of the night, then return to HQ Btry on Wednesday morning. We drove back to the highway, then found a narrow gravel road that led a half mile or so back toward the mountain wall to a patch of woods in which, we had been told, was Btry C's position. We were met by the first sergeant, the only man we actually saw that night. He told us, apologetically, that there was no way we could get anything to eat or drink until morning. He said that the battery commander (BC) was asleep in his tent and had posted outside it four guards, who would have no relief during the night. Two cooks were permitted to sleep until 0400 hours, at which time they would start preparing breakfast. Everyone else was out on the defense perimeter and required to be awake and alert all night. Only he, the first sergeant, was permitted to move about. He told us we could choose to either sleep in our vehicle or join his men on the perimeter and said it was rumored that a group of sailors from a sunken Japanese ship had made their way ashore and were operating as a guerrilla force, making sneak attacks against American units and installations. It was another completely unfounded tale, of course, but it was apparently a nerve-shattering fact to the Btry C commander. That particular officer did not long remain in a command position.

For three nights we had been out on the ground with no cover or bedding of any kind except our clothing, so even the command car was a welcome prospect. But there was another problem: mosquitoes! Neither on Oahu nor anywhere else have I ever seen them more numerous or voracious than they were at Btry C that night. Onderdonck pulled his shirt up over his head and snored peacefully, but neither Bylotas nor I could sleep. Every bit of exposed skin throbbed and burned and itched, and the night was filled with the high-pitched whine of thousands of humming wings. Already exhausted and our nerves on edge, the two of us slapped and scratched and floundered about and cursed. At one point, for the only time in my life, I gave serious consideration to suicide, just to be free of those infernal insects. The loaded BAR was a great temptation. But then Bylotas said, "Hell, Kerns, we may as well go out on the perimeter. It can't be any more miserable than this."

Leaving Onderdonck asleep in the truck, we walked down the road to the bend where the first sergeant had said the perimeter crossed. There we lay down on the road itself with our rifles pointed through a closed farm gate toward a hillside that sloped gently away in the star-light. It was much better there; there was a slight breeze and few if any mosquitoes. My morale began to rise a bit.

Then there was a shot somewhere down the woodline to our left. Then another somewhere else—and another—and two or three together. Soon the entire perimeter was rippling with rifle fire as the tired and disgusted soldiers released their tension. I asked Bylotas if I might fire, too, and he said hell yes, he'd join me. We aimed our weapons at the hillside and blazed away.

Immediately, from right under the muzzle of my BAR, there arose a loud outcry of pain and anger. There in the ditch, unseen and unheard by us until then, were two Btry C troopers whose ears had been slapped by the muzzle blast of our guns. We apologized and held our fire, but the rest of the troops went on firing for quite a while. We heard that a dead cow was found on the hillside next morning.

But we were not present to see the dead cow. As soon as dawn made our departure legal, Bylotas, Onderdonck, and Kerns, Inc., wasted no time in vacating the premises of Btry C. Home had seldom looked so good to us as it did that morning, with good chow, our own friends and officers, the issue of blankets and canvas cots, tents to sleep in, and our barracks bags with clean clothing. And there was the friendly Lister bag with plenty of water to drink. We were soldiering properly once again, with mosquito bars in place.

Before the week was out, Burnis Williamson and I were sent to Kalihi Valley, where there was a pair of 240 mm guns on 360-degree Panama mounts that had been assigned temporarily to Btry A of the 89th for coastal defense on our side of the island. Pending installation of wire lines, communication was a problem, the puny SCR-194 radios being totally unable to reach over the mountain wall at the head of the valley. Williamson and I were to use an SCR-178 low frequency continuous–wave (CW) radio-telegraph outfit to handle communication of fire commands and other essential data between Btry A and the 89th's FDC.

Kalihi was not at all bad, although it did have its drawbacks. Today there are a highway up the valley and tunnels through the mountain to the Kaneohe side, but in 1941 the pavement ended far down toward

Honolulu, and Btry A's position was at the end of a dirt track, still a considerable distance from the head of the canyon. The canyon was a dead end, nearly always clouded over and usually raining. If the rain ceased, a sure way to start it was to fire the 240s. Williamson and I shared a pup tent floored with several copies of the Honolulu papers, which soon became soaked and moldy, as did our blankets. Our feet were always muddy and wet, so our practice was to crawl into the tiny tent, put our muddy feet on the mosquito bar to hold it down, and seldom take off our shoes and leggings. Like the other men, we ate standing out in the perpetual rain, occasionally draining the rainwater out of our food—along with numerous gnats. But we solved the communication problem and proved our worth to Colonel Bledsoe.

The last house up Kalihi Valley was the home of a family named Militante, and Williamson and I made friends with them. This paid off most handsomely when Christmas came, because they invited us to a luau-style Christmas dinner—which we enjoyed while sitting at a table inside a house, just like civilized people. We were envied by the other boys, with whom, incidentally, we also enjoyed the Army's usual holiday turkey and trimmings. It was a memorable Christmas for us.

By the time we returned to HQ Btry, soon after Christmas, it had moved to a location on the Maunawili Ranch in the Kailua area. Maunawili is the famous beauty spot where, according to tradition, Queen Liliuokalani was inspired to compose the classic Hawaiian song, "Aloha Oe." Battalion headquarters was in the main ranch house, while HQ Btry was around the modest residence of the ranch manager, a Japanese American whose name, as I recall, was Iwanaga. The battalion FDC was some distance down the road in a dugout lighted with the first fluorescent tubes I ever saw. The radio section occupied a camouflage-painted shack under a huge mango tree in the manager's yard and, to the envy of the rest of the battery, was given access to the cold-water showers in his separate bathhouse. Life wasn't at all bad for us there.

But there was much to be done before Oahu could be secure. The 25th, like its sister division, the 24th, was at only about 60 percent of its authorized combat strength. Much of its equipment—such as our old radio sets—was obsolete. Before the end of December, our ancient French

Privates Ralph Park, Burnis Williamson, and Maurice "Pappy" Downs, Oahu, 1941.

75s were replaced by new 105 mm howitzers. We had never seen one of the new quarter-ton jeeps that were to become ubiquitous, nor the new FM (frequency modulated) radios. We still used the blue denim fatigues and barracks bags, still had the flat British helmets, still depended on the AAF for aerial observation. We had no prepared positions for our CP, our weapons, our OPs, and the many other facilities needed for island defense against invasion.

We worked hard at supplying the deficiencies, including training new men who came in with only basic training, knowing nothing of any special function. We began receiving more elaborate equipment, more modern materiel that made necessary varying degrees of retraining of experienced soldiers and officers. Meanwhile, internal security remained a matter of serious concern, and most men spent at least a couple of hours on guard duty each night after a long, hard day of work.

At some point, Williamson and I shared another choice assignment. With only an SCR-194 for communication, we established a temporary special OP on the narrow nose of a ridge overlooking Kailua. Our principal duty was to observe and report at five-minute intervals the position of any object we spotted at sea. With our carefully oriented BC-scope, we were to measure horizontal and vertical angles to such objects, while back at the FDC the chart operators would translate those angles into the actual positions of the objects. The most interesting thing I can recall our having sighted was a badly listing aircraft carrier that proceeded very slowly southeastward to round the island toward Pearl Harbor.

About a hundred yards below our OP was a house built on a large rock formation in which our ridge terminated. A day or so after our arrival, a young girl came up from the house and told us that her mother would like to have us locate our post inside the house, a proposition that sounded very good to us. We found that the house had a large section of windows in an arc that surveyed perfectly our area of interest. Inside the windows was a long, cushioned window seat, and there we set up and reoriented our BC-scope. From our viewpoint (in every sense) it was ideal.

We learned that the husband and father was a broadcasting executive

From left: Sal Crupi, Ralph Park, Billy Mulherin, and "Pappy" Downs, in front of the camouflaged shack in the Maunawili Ranch manager's yard.

in Honolulu and, because of gasoline rationing, was staying in the city except for occasional visits; therefore, only the mother and daughter were at home. The house was built to conform to the natural formation of the rocks, some of which projected through the floors or walls and served as furniture. On one of these rocks was a large guest book and, beside it, the largest candle I've ever seen, surrounded by a massive accumulation of drippings. They told us that the candle was placed there and burned for one hour on the day the house was first occupied and again on each anniversary of that date. The guest book contained signatures and addresses of many famous people whose names I recognized—one, I recall was Pearl S. Buck. Williamson and I felt honored at being asked to sign.

But our enjoyment of the plush OP was short-lived. Because of the triangulation requirements, it was necessary for us to inform FDC of our

The author copying Morse code received by SCR-161 radio, 1941.

new location and altitude above sea level. It didn't take long for one of the officers at the FDC to notice the change, and it was back to the ridge for Williamson and Kerns. We soon returned once more to the HQ Btry area.

Colonel Bledsoe had retained a couple of his old French 75s and mounted them on two trucks. He called them his roving guns. Whatever their limitations, these improvised self-propelled pieces with their ancient ammunition were useful in training officers in the conduct of fire. Impact areas on Rabbit Island and offshore rocks were designated, and service practices were conducted.[4]

During one of these firing sessions, Ralph Park and I were detailed as radio operators to relay fire commands from the OP to the gun position. In charge of the firing was Major Ferris, the former HQ Btry commander, who had been promoted and made battalion S-3 (operations and training officer). After all the officers had fired, Major Ferris asked Colonel Bledsoe if he might let Private First Class Kerns fire a problem. The colonel appeared just as surprised as I was, but he said, "Why, certainly. If he knows the procedure, let him fire." Major Ferris designated a target for me and I stepped up to the BC-scope just as if I knew what I was doing.

But I didn't. Major Ferris knew I had picked up some knowledge of

gunnery, but I think he gave me credit for more than I knew. The procedure for this practice required the observer not merely to sense where
the rounds landed relative to the target but to measure the deviations
with the scope, carry out a rather complex mental calculation using
several factors, and come up with fire commands that went directly to
the guns without the intervening services of an FDC. I had never done
such a thing before. But I had heard and, in many cases, repeated into
a microphone, the commands that had been sent to the roving guns
that day. I had remembered the adjusted data for many of the targets
out there on Rabbit Island, and my target lay between two of those.
Standing at the BC-scope, I mentally interpolated between the adjusted
elevations and deflections for those two targets, respectively, and came
up with data for my target. I fitted this into an otherwise fairly simple
command sequence and called it out confidently to Park. He relayed it
to the guns. The two bursts that resulted bracketed the target for range,
deflection correct.

Knowing that, to save ammunition, there would be no fire for
effect, I hesitated a few seconds. Major Ferris asked, "What is your next
command?"

"Repeat range, fire for effect," I replied.

"Cease fire, mission accomplished," said Major Ferris. "Are there any
comments?"

One of the captains stood up and said, "Yes, sir. He changed his
method of conducting fire when he said 'repeat range, fire for effect.' He
should have said 'battery so many rounds, elevation such-and-such.'"

He was right, and I knew it, but before Ferris could reply to the
captain, Bledsoe said, "Damn it, Captain, sit down and shut up! That's
the best mission that's been fired out here today."

There was another time, not long after that, when I successfully fired
a mission, and this time I knew what I was doing. Those occasions were
to pay off later in ways of which I never dreamed.

Soon after my experience with the roving guns, Major Ferris had me
transferred to a job in the FDC as a chart operator and battery computer.
This gave me further opportunity to learn gunnery—and it also gained
me the status of "jawbone" sergeant, an acting sergeant, granted the

authority and privileges of the grade but still drawing the pay of a PFC, specialist 3d class. I moved into an old shack near the FDC, sharing a room with my new boss, Tech. Sgt. John W. Stone. Under his guidance and with the friendly encouragement of Lt. Robert Bernard, our personnel adjutant, I made important advances in my understanding of the sometimes mysterious ways of artillerymen.

I'd been in FDC about two months, I guess, when my new BC, Captain Snow, called and asked whether I thought I could handle the radio section. He said he had busted George Williams for overstaying a pass. I moved back to the section that day and was immediately promoted to sergeant. A month later—about the first of June—I was further promoted to staff sergeant, the grade called for by my position as radio section chief.

Captain Snow had told me that Colonel Bledsoe, a firm advocate of radio instead of wire as the prime communication means for artillery, wanted the radio section put into top shape, and I set out to do the best I could at that task. We had received several draftee replacements and two or three men transferred from other assignments in the battery. I put Corporal Downs, the assistant section chief, in charge of making radio operators out of these new men while I concentrated on coordinating all other activities of the section and helped as I could in improving radio communications in the firing batteries. Driving around the sector in my command car with long whip antenna waving, I received the salute of many a sentry who thought I must be someone important, so I just returned the salutes and went on.

As the new men progressed with their training, there came a day when Pappy Downs advised me that one of them, Leroy Ryder, in order to complete his training, needed to work for a while with an experienced operator on one of our major stations. I put him on our station in the division artillery (Div Arty) command net, and that led to my first little difficulty as section chief.

I considered Burnis Williamson and Ralph Park the best operators we had, and the Div Arty command-net station had been theirs for a long time. To get better contact and to avoid pinpointing the headquarters for enemy radio direction finders, the station was located some distance from the battery area, and the two operators lived there, coming to the battery only for meals. They had built themselves a comfortable shack out of scrap materials and had run a power line in from the road a hundred yards away. They had even built themselves a transformer so they could use the line power to run their radio, thus avoiding the onerous task of cranking the generator while transmitting. They were proud of their work and quite happy with their situation.

Park answered when I phoned the station.

"Park, I'm going to send Leroy Ryder up there tomorrow to work for a while to get experience in the net. Either you or Willie will have to come down to the battery. I don't care which one, you can decide that between yourselves."

Ralph was beside himself with outrage. He objected strongly and in very positive terms, and I appealed to his own understanding of the need for training the men to get him to accept the inevitable. But he raised the devil, nonetheless.

"Willie and I work our fingers to the bone to build this place up, and now that we've got a good setup you send these Johns from the States— these damned handcuffed volunteers—up here to get all the gravy!" he yelled.

"I know you've worked hard and you deserve what you've got, Park, but you can see the position we're in. Besides that, I need a top-notch operator down here to take over the 193 from Crupi."

I thought that would soften Ralph a bit, and it did. The SCR-193 was by far the biggest and most powerful set we had. It was mounted in the back of a command car, and any operator would have been pleased to get it.

"Well, OK," said Park, grudgingly, "I won't even mention it to Willie. I'll come down myself."

There was no more trouble about it.

One night, as sergeant of the guard, I was returning from checking the sentries around the area when, passing the little garage building that was our orderly room, I heard a typewriter in operation. I stopped in to see why Private First Class Rupert, the battery clerk, was working so late and found that he was typing applications for Officer Candidate

School (OCS) that, he said, had to reach Battalion Headquarters early next morning to meet a quota deadline. I sat down to talk with him. As he finished the last application, he asked me why I hadn't applied for OCS.

"Oh, it wouldn't do any good. I'd never make it."

"Why not? You have as good a chance as any of these guys who are applying. What's your IQ score?"

I didn't even know I had an IQ score, so he looked it up in the files.

"Why, this is the best score I know of in the battery. Look, why don't you let me type up an application for you. The BC will sign it in the morning and it can go up with the others. Maybe you can at least get back to the states."

That last part sold me. A few days later I went before a board of officers at Schofield. I was called into a large room with windows along one side. Before those windows were a couple of small tables, at which sat two majors and two captains, one of whom, Capt. Claude Shepard, I knew. In the middle of the room, facing them, was a straight chair in which I was instructed to be seated. On a wall some distance to my left was a large map of the island of Oahu. Otherwise, the room was empty.

The officers took turns asking me questions while I sat stiff and straight in the chair, with no place to hide. I could barely see their faces, the backlight from the windows making them little more than silhouettes. The questions covered a wide range of subjects—my personal background, my duty assignment, various aspects of my duties, current events and my opinions regarding them, military organization and chain of command, and so on. Seldom was I allowed to complete an answer before another would interrupt with a question on some unrelated topic. Occasionally, after I had given an answer, the officers would sit silently for a short time and look at each other as if appalled at my ignorance. Then the quiz would be resumed.

One of the questions they popped at me was, "How far is it from here to Haleiwa?" I remembered the map off to my left. I glanced at it for a few seconds and counted the grid squares between Schofield and Haleiwa. Noting that the direction cut diagonally across the squares, I made an allowance for that and told them it was approximately so many thousands of yards. That seemed to please them.

Eventually, without a word to me, they all got up and exited through a door to their left. I remained seated. Occasionally, one of them would come back, open the door, gaze silently at me for several seconds, then close the door again. After about ten minutes, they filed back in and sat down. One of them said, "Sergeant Kerns, we note that you have only an eighth grade education, that you have never studied geometry or trigonometry, and that your education in mathematics is generally quite limited. Mathematics is very important in artillery, as you may know. Therefore, it is the opinion of this board that if you go to OCS now you run a very high risk of failing. Having failed once, you may never get another chance. So we, the board, recommend that you return to your battery, study algebra and trigonometry, and apply again after a few months."

My heart sank, of course, and my dream of seeing home again before the end of the war crumbled to dust. But the major wasn't finished.

"However, we have received letters of recommendation for you from your BC, Captain Snow; your battalion S-3, Major Ferris; and from your former battalion commander, Colonel Bledsoe, now the Div Arty chief of staff. On the strength of these recommendations, we have decided to leave the decision up to you. Either stay and study, as we have recommended, or go now and take your chances, as you may choose. You may go outside now and think it over for a few minutes."

"Thank you, sir, but I can decide right now. I'd like to go and take my chances."

"Very well. You're dismissed, Sergeant. Good luck."

Out of fourteen applicants from the 89th who were examined that day, five of us passed that artillery board. Of those five, I was the only one who then made it past the medical examination. Within two weeks, I was on a ship for the U.S. of A.

Some historians claim that the morale of the U.S. fighting forces was extremely low in the months following the attack on Pearl Harbor. I don't believe it, not for a minute. We firmly believed in our cause, we were angry with the enemy for having attacked without warning or a declaration of war, we wanted to strike back, and we had not the slightest doubt that, ultimately, we would win the war. True, we were rather astonished at the Japanese strength relative to our own, but the typical American fighting man was determined, like First Sergeant

Regan, that "those little yellow bastards" would be sorry for what they had done. We took pride in such things as the words of Marine Corps major James Devereaux just before his tiny garrison at Wake Island was finally overwhelmed by vastly superior numbers of Japanese troops. The brave commander refused to accept the certainty of defeat, and his last message reported: "The issue is still in doubt."[5]

There was frustration, of course, among the ground troops who had to sit on guard and wait for an enemy that might never come, while the sea and air people were going out to find and fight him wherever they could. The average man was genuinely eager for an active combat role in the war, and a few of our ground troops found it by getting transfers to the AAF as radio operators and gunners. Others who tried and failed were bitterly disappointed. My friend Ernett Onderdonck was one of those whose request for transfer was refused, and he went to the stockade for striking Major Carroll, the acting battalion commander, with his fist. Some of our men went to Kaneohe in their free time and got rides with dive-bomber pilots on their training flights just to feel a little closer to the war. Men who are eager for closing with the enemy are not in low morale, and the sight of damaged planes and casualties returning to Oahu during the Battle of Midway did nothing to cool their ardor.[6]

There may have been senior officers and civilian officials who held doubts and fears—people such as my onetime hero, Col. Charles A. Lindbergh, who thought the Germans invincible—but the lower echelons, technically ready or not, did not share them.[7] As the Pearl Harbor disaster united the people of the country and brought their support for the war, so it fired up the fighting forces to go after the enemy. When the time was finally right, they went and they conquered.

I'm proud to have been a Pineapple Soldier. I'm proud to have had even a minor role in the events of that tragic day when this nation was plunged into the greatest of wars, and in the preparation of one of that war's finest artillery units for the outstanding combat record it would earn on Guadalcanal, New Georgia, and Luzon. In the process, I learned something of the technicalities of field artillery, but still more important, I believe, I came to understand the basic philosophy of the artilleryman, the redleg soldier who is there to provide the best possible fire support for the most admirable of all soldiers, the infantry rifleman, who must close with the enemy and fight him face to face.

When I left the islands for OCS in August 1942, I looked back from the ship at the sunset to see Mount Olomana faintly silhouetted against the backlighted Koolaus, and I could envision the scene there at its foot on Maunawili Ranch where the HQ Btry men would be straggling down to the mess tent, joking, laughing, their mess kits jangling, somebody's radio playing "Maria Elena." I knew it was the end of a phase of my life, that I could never be back there again, and I couldn't keep the tears out of my eyes. I wish that I could roll away the years and be back there with them right now.

– Two –

NINETY-DAY WONDERS AND
FAIR-HAIRED BOYS

In 1942, soldiers didn't jet about the world in plush seats, waited on by lovely stewardesses. They carried their duffel bags up a gangplank and down into the dank depths of some ship that had been fitted out to accommodate the maximum number of men with minimum consideration of comfort, and that smelled like somebody's dirty socks. We spent about a week between Honolulu and San Francisco. While we cruised northeastward toward home, Marines were fighting a desperate battle against the enemy on Guadalcanal, Rommel was attacking El Alamein, Australians were holding against Japanese assaults at Milne Bay, Germans and Russians were locked in a tremendous battle for Stalingrad, and Churchill visited Stalin to discuss possibilities for a second front to ease pressure on the Soviet forces.

The trip itself has left little impression on my mind. I recall being at Fort McDowell on Angel Island, because I sent from there a wire to a certain girl asking if she would marry me.

And I recall being on a train that stopped in Lordsburg, New Mexico. An old Indian came alongside the train selling tamales at five cents each. Reaching their arms out the open windows, soldiers bought them by the handful and began eating. It was my first taste of a tamale, and my immediate reaction was to ridicule those who had told me they were hot. But after about five minutes my mouth began to burn. I headed for the place at the rear of the car where you could get a weak trickle of tepid water in a thin paper cup that held about two tablespoonfuls. There was a long line and everyone was in a hurry, so there was much puffing and blowing and yelling for the guy at the spigot to move on. I learned about really hot tamales from that.

★

Suddenly, I was at Fort Sill, Oklahoma, home of the U.S. Field Artillery.[1] Off came all the insignia of grade and on went the OCS patch, sewn to the left breast pocket of our shirts. We moved into tar paper shacks, called "hutments," built on concrete slabs in long rows. At the end of each two rows was a latrine building with showers. The hutments were numbered, of course, and each held six candidates, assigned alphabetically by last name. In my hutment were Everett Kelley, Donald Kellogg, Earl "Bud" Kelly, Howard Kenyon, and Bernard Kipley. Each of us had a steel cot with cotton mattress, a shelf with rod for hangers, and a few square feet of floor space to call our own. There were one or two bare bulbs hanging from overhead and a small oil heater.

Discipline was necessarily quite strict, because the amount of material to be covered made the OCS period a rather frantic thirteen weeks. The miracle of the "Ninety-Day Wonders," it turned out, was that they survived. There was little time to be wasted. After First Call, played by a record over a very scratchy loudspeaker, we had fifteen minutes to be ready for our first formation. In that time we had to make it to the latrine—shave, brush teeth, and all that kind of thing—make bunks, sweep out the hutment, and be dressed in proper uniform of the day.

The first formation was a roll call followed, during part of the course, by "voice culture." The latter consisted of repetition of commands in unison as directed by a senior candidate from another class. This was often varied by being made a "Simon Says" drill just to keep us awake, and sometimes individual candidates were called on to demonstrate the proper voice and inflection for various commands. After that was the morning meal, for which, like all other meals, we were allotted thirty minutes. Those detailed for table waiter duty got no special consideration. They served the meal and ate, they hoped, before the half hour was gone. Food discipline was very strict, too. We were told: "Take all you want, but eat all you take."

And then we hit the classroom or the range. We might be learning to fieldstrip different small arms (sometimes blindfolded) or driving six-by-six trucks cross-country or studying the dry regulations pertaining to supply or solving problems in gunnery or survey or adjusting fire out on the range. In the gunnery and survey problems, I came up against the challenge of which the OCS board at Schofield had warned me. I had to study a little more than most, I guess, to overcome my total ignorance of the methods of trigonometry, but I carried my tables of trigonometric functions and logarithms and I made out OK. The fun part was the classroom, when all twenty men in the section would be at blackboards working on the same problem. There were occasions when the instructor would come up behind me and begin, "Well, now, Kerns, you seem to be having a little trouble there. Let me . . . Well, you have the right answer there—but I don't see how you got it. How did you do that?"

I'd explain to him and he'd say it was OK, but he'd like for me to show on the board more of the reasoning process. I had to tell him I did not know how. Looking around at other boards, I was utterly mystified as to the reason for all the algebraic procedures that filled them. Using just simple arithmetic, supplemented with a lot of thinking that I didn't know how to show, I wrote much less. But I got the same results.

Out on the firing range, however, I was a champion. I don't suppose I was the best in the class, but I was certainly the best in our twenty-man section. During the five-week gunnery period, each student had to fire at least twelve problems of certain types, and he had to compute initial data for the 228 other problems fired by his section mates. So we sat out there on top of some barren ridges, swept by the icy winds of late November and December, at ease in our chilled steel folding chairs, each with a clipboard on his lap, gazing with teary eyes across a shallow valley or two at a shell-pocked area in which numerous nondescript pieces of obsolete materiel lay scattered about. In front of us, two BC-scopes—

one for the instructor, one for the students. Behind us, radio operators to relay our commands or sensings to the guns.

"All right, gentlemen, your target. Take as a reference point the Blockhouse on Signal Mountain.[2] Go nine zero mils right and at a greater distance to a lone tree at the head of a small ravine. Two-zero mils farther right, at a still greater distance, is a piece of materiel in the middle of a beaten area. That is the target. Is there anyone who does not identify the target? Very well, compute your initial data."

Twenty frozen students were hastily consulting maps, measuring angles by use of previously calibrated fingers and fists, making hasty calculations, writing down factors, sticking up hands to show when they were ready. At some point in this process, the instructor would designate a candidate to fire the target.

"Kerns, take the target under fire."

It was my twelfth and last required problem, and it was of the most difficult kind, the "Large-T," in which, because of the large angle between the gun-target line and the observer-target line, a range error was seen by the observer as a deflection error, and deflection was observed as range, thus involving factors not present in computing data for other conditions of observation. But I had never failed to do well, and I got up to the BC-scope without one twinge of nervousness. I surpassed even my own high expectations, and when I sat down the instructor said, "Now, gentlemen, that's the way a Large-T problem should be fired." I swelled with pride and confidence but was happy to realize that I'd completed the course requirement and didn't have to risk my reputation again.

He designated another target. I computed initial data for it and stuck up my hand, at the same time noting to myself that I was first to do so. Without hesitating for a second, the instructor said, "Kerns, take the target under fire."

I was surprised, since I had just fired, but again I lay my clipboard on my chair and walked to the BC-scope. I'm sure my voice sounded firm and confident as I called out to the radio operator, and I soon heard him report, "On the way." I watched the target area to catch the burst.

I watched and I watched. And I watched. And I saw nothing. Must be down in that swale in front of the target area, I thought, and I gave it some more range. Still no burst. Well—must be on the other side of the ridge, I said to myself, and I knocked off twice as much range as I'd added before. No burst. Well, shucks! Where the devil was it? Maybe it was off to the left, mixed in with the bursts where another section was firing. I sent a deflection change but the instructor called "Cease fire" and told me to be seated.

"Do you know where your rounds were?" he asked.

As I sat down, I picked up my clipboard on which I had noted my initial data, and I knew then where my rounds had gone. I had remembered the base point elevation wrong by 100 mils, and my rounds had gone far beyond the target area. In fact, the instructor said, I had almost hit the reservation boundary. It was my thirteenth mission and my first "U" for Unsatisfactory. I was thoroughly embarrassed, to say the least. It was the classic "hundred mil error" that is the dread of all artillerymen.

Field Artillery OCS candidates at Fort Sill received only two grades: "S" for Satisfactory, "U" for Unsatisfactory. In addition to that miserable fire mission, I got one "U" on a pop quiz based on a very long, boring reading assignment in supply regulations. The only man in our hutment who had any serious trouble was Howard Kenyon, a good old country boy from Nebraska who had come down from Alaska as a corporal. When Howard got something through his head, he never forgot it, but he was slow to learn. He worked very hard, and some of us, especially Kellogg and Kipley, helped him each night until lights out at 2100 hours. Then Kenyon would go to the study hall and remain there until 2300, every night. Nevertheless, with only three weeks left to go before graduation, he was put back into an OCS preparatory course. Long after the rest of us had gone on to our first assignments as second lieutenants, Kenyon was still there, finishing the prep course and going all the way through OCS again. He graduated, he was commissioned, and as a second lieutenant he was killed in action in Belgium.

There was a demerit system in effect at OCS, and I suppose there was some limit on the number of demerits a candidate could get and survive. I got a few, all out of two incidents, neither of which I could reasonably have avoided. In one case, I was the hutment orderly, responsible for being certain all was secure, lights out, heater turned off, floor clean, all in spic-and-span order, before we left for the day's activities. Kenyon, having joined another class but still living in our hutment, asked me to leave the heater on for him, since he had another half hour to study before his first class. He forgot to turn it off, and I got some demerits. In the other case, I got a standard GI haircut on Saturday afternoon, and on Monday morning a tactical (administrative) officer coming through our classroom gigged me for needing a haircut. I think the trouble was that I just didn't look handsome enough to be a lieutenant.

There was never any doubt about my academically passing the course, but I did manage to almost get kicked out, which certainly would have changed the course of my life. Dorie, who is now my wife and who then was the girl who had answered yes to my telegraphic proposal, came out to Sill to visit me. She arrived on a Tuesday and would have to leave within a day or two, back to Ohio and her job repairing radios at a plant in Columbus. There was no possibility for me to spend any time with her off the post, since OCS men could get passes only on Saturday evenings— until 0100 hours on Sunday morning. There was nothing to do on the post except to sit in the midst of hundreds of soldiers at the enlisted men's club and drink Coke or beer. So, in desperation, I took the OCS patch off of one of my shirts and sewed on my staff sergeant chevrons and, after duty on Tuesday, off to Lawton I went to see my betrothed.

All went well. No one questioned me, since NCOs were normally able to get passes on Tuesday night. Some of them even had quarters in town and commuted. So about 2330 hours I got a taxi and started back to the post, allowing plenty of time before the 0100 pass deadline.

As the cab approached the Military Police (MP) post at the main gate, the taxi driver said, "You're going to be in trouble, aren't you, Sergeant?"

"I don't think so, why?"

"Well, it's a little bit late for you to be getting in."

"Oh, no, I have plenty of time before one o'clock."

"Remember, though, this is Tuesday, not Saturday. You should have been in by eleven o'clock if you were coming in at all."

"Oh, hell! You're right. Take me back to town."

He made a U-turn right in front of the gate and took me back to the historic old Keegan Hotel, the yellow-painted, weather-boarded inn where Dorie had a room. I knocked on her door, explained the situation, and told her I needed a place to stay until I could safely return to post in the morning. Dorie was rightly skeptical, but after a great deal of hesitation on her part and earnest reassurance on mine, she agreed to let me sleep in the chair in her room, where I remained a perfect, if uncomfortable, gentleman. (Today, over sixty-five years later, Dorie is still shy about my telling that story.)

Next morning, I caught the first bus going to the post. It stopped at the gate, and an MP came aboard, spot-checking passes. He didn't ask for mine. I slipped into our hutment and into a proper uniform barely in time to make roll call.

I was just lucky. If the taxi driver hadn't spoken, I'd never have gotten an Army commission. A classmate named Johnson did the same thing one night, except that he got married while he was in town. A few days later, a brief notice of the wedding having taken place at 9:30 on a certain evening appeared in the Lawton paper. One of the tac officers saw it, recognized the name, and Johnson was thrown out of the school. Others were disqualified for breaches of the high standards set for candidates, and I've always been humbly grateful to that cab driver, the MP who did not check my pass, and to the kind Fates that protected me in this as in so many other aspects of my life. And I want to assure you, an American citizen, that this incident does not accurately represent the standards of honor and ethics I maintained during my service, either before or after the incident.

★

Instruction in gunnery lasted five weeks, and the fourth week was known as "The Bloody Fourth." Not only was it a week in which there were notoriously difficult exams that sent many a candidate packing or back to a less advanced class or even to a prep course, as in the case of Howard Kenyon, but during that week each candidate was required to turn in to the administrative office his written appraisal of each of the other nineteen candidates in his section. These reports served several purposes. For one, they gave an indication of each candidate's ability to evaluate the character, capabilities, and shortcomings of other men and to express his evaluation in writing. The evaluations of each candidate could be boiled down to an appraisal that could hardly be anything less than honest, and it might be favorable or not. An individual who tried to use the evaluation to injure someone against whom he held a grudge was very likely to be readily spotted, and the resulting injury would be to himself. And so there was many a candidate who was academically strong but lost out by having impressed most of his associates in some unfavorable way or who betrayed his dishonesty to the tac officers by his appraisals of others. Our class was slimmer after The Bloody Fourth.

One day early in December, the class was interrupted by a visit from two officers who briefed us on a new program for providing an organic air observation capability to field artillery units. The general idea was to give each field artillery battalion and division artillery headquarters a couple of light airplanes to be flown by artillery officers organic to the units. The training program was already in progress and needed volunteers for pilot training. It was emphasized that the pilots would be artillery officers first, aviators second. The planes were merely a means for getting into position to observe the targets and adjust fire. Volunteers from the class were asked to apply at Post Field.

In the hutment that night, I announced my intention of volunteering for flight training, and I started trying to sell my hutment mates on going with me. A day or two later, Bud Kelly, Everett Kelley, and I went together over to the field and applied. Col. Rollie Harrison, the first and, at that time, only flight surgeon involved in the program gave us physical and psychological evaluations.

The last big event before graduation of FAOCS Class #44 was Reconnaissance, Selection, and Occupation of Position (RSOP) 12. It was a three-day exercise, employing actual troop units, with candidates occupying certain critical positions in each. Each candidate's duty assignment was changed frequently so he could gain experience and have his performance observed in a variety of situations. In one phase, I was in charge of conducting a survey on which an actual division artillery concentration was later fired. Again, I filled the role of an enlisted telephone operator, and in one of the most interesting problems, I was commander of a battery of four 105 mm howitzers that, on a road march behind advancing infantry, had to go quickly into position to put down covering fire for the infantry's withdrawal in front of an attacking enemy armored force, then to fight the tanks with direct fire. I managed to get satisfactory solutions in all cases—but, of course, barring some unimaginable catastrophe, my graduation and commissioning were already assured. My best memory of RSOP 12 is of the frosty, moonlit nights out on the ranges with coyotes yapping and howling on the hills after our bivouac was quiet.

We arrived back in quarters after RSOP 12 early in the evening the day before graduation. Most of us were up until after midnight, getting all in order for the big day, which started early with our formation for the graduation ceremonies in the post theater. There was the traditional tossing of the caps, discarding the enlisted man's scarlet artillery braid for the black and gold of the officer corps, and then we hurried back to our hutments to change into our new officers' "pinks and greens" before lining up for payment of our $250 initial clothing allowance.

But I had a wee bit of a problem. My new uniforms had come in by Railway Express, COD, and were over at the Fort Sill railway station waiting to be picked up. I didn't have enough money to pick them up until after I received my clothing allowance. I was far back in the slow-moving line, and already it was almost time for the departure of the special bus on which I had a ticket to Oklahoma City. In desperation, I asked Bud Kelly if he could loan me $80 to pay for the uniform, so I could pick it up and return by the time the end of the line reached the little shack where the pay office had been set up.

With Kelly's money in hand, I began trying to get a taxi. So did everyone else. By the time I finally got back from the station, the pay line was gone and they told me I'd have to go to the main finance office on the old post to get my uniform allowance. But the guards were being taken off the hutment area, so all candidates had to have their gear out of there. The buses were mostly loaded, some had already left, and Bud was delaying his bus, hoping to get his $80 back. I hastily explained and told him I'd mail it to him. Then I hurried to our hutment, changed into my new lieutenant's uniform, grabbed my suitcase, and started hurrying over to the old post—a good quarter of a mile away.

As I left the hutment area, I encountered the sergeant in charge of the security guard, which he had just relieved. He greeted me with a big smile and a salute, the first salute for my gold bars. I returned it and gave him a dollar, in accordance with tradition, and he stuffed it into a bulging pocket.

I lugged my heavy suitcase across the post as fast as I could, and the finance people were glad to see me—now they could close out the special payroll. I hurried back toward the OCS area, but just as I turned a corner and came into view of the street where all the buses had been lined up, I saw the last one pull out and turn down toward Gate 3, on the way to Oklahoma City. I set my suitcase down and stood beside it, just about exhausted, discouraged, and cursing in a most ungentlemanly way. I had missed the bus, and that would cause me to miss the train, which would cause me to miss at least a day of the first leave I'd ever had in my twenty-seven months of Army service. And I had my ticket for that particular bus in my pocket. One other minor detail: it was Christmas Eve 1942.

A civilian car stopped beside me and a sergeant driving it asked me whether I needed a ride. I was in the car faster than I can tell about it. I told him there was a bus going down toward Gate 3 and up the highway to Oklahoma City. I asked him to catch it for me, and he did. About two miles up the highway, he pulled alongside and I waved my ticket at the bus driver. He stopped. I left $3 on the seat of the sergeant's car and boarded the bus.

Going into Oklahoma City, the bus was ascending a grade up to a bridge over several railroad tracks when it suddenly stopped. After a quick check back in the engine compartment, the driver told us he would call for another bus from the downtown terminal to come out and get us. The wait seemed interminable, but the new bus finally got there and we were mobile once again.

As I hurried into the railway depot, I was aware that I barely had time to get my ticket before my train would depart. There was only one person ahead of me at the window, a most fortunate circumstance, except for one thing: she was an old lady with a ticket as long as her arm, and the agent had to explain to her each change she'd have to make and answer innumerable questions about every aspect of her trip. The minutes, and then the seconds, ticked rapidly away. The time came for my train to leave. At last, I got my ticket in hand and ran for the boarding platform, still carrying my heavy suitcase. The train was starting to roll, the conductor already aboard and hooking the chain across the platform between cars. I ran to catch up, he unhooked the chain for me, and I was on my way to Columbus, Ohio.

Most of the passengers—maybe all of them—in my car were military, either on leave or en route to new assignments. Some were from my OCS class. In the usual juvenile manner of young men away from the constraints of normal society, there was much loud talk, much parading up and down the aisle, much passing of bottles, and much singing and laughing that went on and on through the night as the train rolled eastward. There was little chance to sleep, and I'd had practically none for the past three nights. So when I arrived in Columbus late the next afternoon to be met by Dorie, I was not the sharpest kid in town. By the time we caught another train and rode to Xenia, the greetings by Mom and my sisters, Carolyn and Peggy, seemed wrapped in a dreamlike haze of unreality. And there was my younger brother, Bob, who insisted on calling me "Lute." When my best friend, Buzz Perkins, came around next morning, I still felt numb in mind and body.

And then there was a bus trip to Kentucky, rain and mud and riding bareback on a wet horse across a flooded creek to reach Dad's house, visits with various aunts and uncles, introducing Dorie to my Kentucky relatives, and then it was back to Ohio once more. Before I knew it, Dorie and I were on a train and headed for Denton, Texas, in compliance with orders I had received at Fort Sill.

The floods were widespread, and damage to bridges and culverts and long stretches of track was extensive all along the line, so the train never ran fast, usually creeping along, actually stopping at each culvert until trainmen could examine it. So our entire trip was by the traditional "slow train through Arkansas." But we arrived in time for me to report to Capt. Roy Marrs, commandant of the 25th Liaison Pilot Training Detachment

(LPTD), U.S. Army Air Force Gulf Coast Training Command, at Denton, in full compliance with my orders.

Tommy Calvert, a red-faced, square-jawed young Dallasite and a fine fellow, was my first flight instructor, as well as a good one. We took off in an Aeronca (nicknamed "Air-Knocker") L-3, right into a blinding snowstorm. Tommy made a hasty circuit of the field and landed; we logged five minutes. That was my orientation ride and my first government flying time. It was 4 January 1943.

The next day there was a wedding in Denton, and Dorie and I moved to 1112 North Highland Street, where we and Bud and Marie Kelly had rented rooms. It was conveniently near the campus of North Texas State Teacher's College (later to be North Texas State University), but we were there for only a few days before moving to a more suitable room with a fireplace and a private bath in the large Victorian home of a Mrs. Lomax on West Oak Street.

Like a great many places in this country, Denton has grown a lot since 1943. Then it was just a small town centered on the courthouse, its economy primarily agricultural but significantly augmented by two colleges: the North Texas State Teachers College and the Texas State College for Women. If it had any fame, it was as the onetime home of the Old West outlaw, Sam Bass. But it did have the red-brick Southern Hotel, where several of us had found temporary lodging while reporting to the commandant of the 25th LPTD and getting administratively squared away.

We were required to maintain quarters on the campus of the teachers college, which was to teach the ground-school subjects in our course, and we were authorized to use the college's on-campus cafeteria. From there, Army trucks would transport us to a sod field about four miles from town, at which Harte Flying Service, under contract with the government, would provide the actual flight instruction. Captain Marrs, the military commandant, had a small administrative staff, and all of our check rides would be given by Army Air Force officers brought in as required.

The class of twenty students, alternating with another class, spent half of each day in ground school, half in flying. I was surprised to see in the class ahead of ours a familiar face from the prewar Schofield Barracks and from my OCS board experience, Capt. Claude Shepard.

During the cold weather, the trip to the field in the open trucks called for everyone to wear the heavy sheepskin flying jackets and caps such as were issued to bomber crews in those days; and the padding, the chilly weather, and the youthful high spirits of the students made the steel bed of the truck a sort of wrestling arena. There was much horseplay and much fun to be had between Denton and the field. When we piled out in front of the little operations building, we were warmed up and ready to go.

Meanwhile, back in the classrooms, ground school opened some new doors for most of us. The school introduced us to the theory of flight, pilotage, dead reckoning, flying rules and regulations, and aviation weather. Basic though this education was, it still was rather thick for some of us farm boys, few of whom had more than a high school diploma.

A teaching trick used by one instructor, a middle-aged man, impressed me. I think he must have used some kind of hypnotic spell to get his points across to us. He taught theory of flight, and he explained each principle to us just once, no more. His explanation would at first leave many of us students totally in the dark. But then he would stand up there in front of the twenty students, his bald head glistening, round face beaming with good humor, and fix his mild blue eyes on each of us in turn, raising his eyebrows and saying to each, "See? See?" I never knew it to fail.

Physical training was a minor part of our schooling there, and as far as I was concerned, totally unnecessary. Having never had a muscle to my name, I hated calisthenics, and at Denton they made it worse by using the PT period almost exclusively for tumbling practice. The instructors laid out long mats on the floor and expected us to do all sorts of utterly impossible things. But I tried, and they didn't press me too much. To be perfectly honest, I envied those superior SOBs who could lie on their backs and flip up to their feet without using their arms.

Don't let me be too modest about my achievements as a student pilot at Denton. Perhaps I should say no more than that I was probably not the hottest student in my class, but I had no trouble with either flying or the related ground school. The first few hours were a repetition of the instruction I had received in Hawaii more than a year before, so I breezed through it easily and soon came to the point at which, when I had seven hours and forty-four minutes of government dual instruction in my log (yes, we did log time to the minute then), Tommy, with no advance notice, had me stop the plane in midfield on a landing roll, and he got out. He fastened the belt over the empty front seat of the Piper L-4 and said, "Shoot me three three-point touch-and-go landings unless I wave you in. OK, go!"

I refuse to become poetic about my first solo. Millions have done it and it requires no superman to achieve it—just great courage and supreme self-confidence with a modicum of aviating skill. However, without Tommy's bulk in the front seat ahead of me the plane looked much longer. This was partially compensated for by the fact that now, for the first time in flight, I could see the instrument panel, albeit something like five feet away. As I accelerated over the sod I could feel the unusual lightness of the plane, especially the nose. I remembered that Tommy had rolled the elevator trim forward a bit when he fastened the seat belt, but I hit it another turn or so. Then I flew three very easy patterns and good landings, and that was my solo.

The condition of the airplanes we were using left much to be desired. They were not very old, but they were much used and little protected from the elements. Their fabric was weathered, Plexiglas yellowed, crazed, and warped so you had to pick the best spots to see through. Aging transparent tube fuel gauges in the wing roots of the Aeroncas were often so coated with fuel residue inside that they were useless. Some of the engines were weak from many hard hours of flying. The tires were thin, bungees soft. Props were nicked and flaking off varnish, sometimes with reinforcing fabric starting to fray. Cowlings were battered and loose fitting. On one of my first flights with Tommy, the cabin door came off our Aeronca and bounced off the tail surfaces. It might have discouraged a pilot, but as a student pilot I thought little of it.

It was such a plane that I was flying on one of the first occasions when I was permitted to go solo out of sight of the field. I was going along at about four hundred feet above the North Texas plains when I suddenly remembered something Tommy had done during one of our dual flights. It seemed to me he had suddenly thrown the stick over and back and shoved in a rudder pedal, and the plane had flipped quickly around in a neat horizontal spin—a snap roll. He did it a couple of times. Then he looked around at me and grinned and said, "Don't ever try that when you're out here solo."

And so, without taking even one second to consider my altitude and my very doubtful ability to accomplish a snap roll, I tried to do what Tommy had told me not to do. What I did—I think—was a horizontal half-roll followed immediately by a diving half-roll and a wing-straining pullout about ten feet above a cow pasture. If there'd been even a bush at that point, I'd have hit it. A tall cow would have been endangered. If anyone outside the plane had seen it, I'm sure they'd have covered their eyes.

I did an equally stupid thing—after Tommy Calvert had told me not to—one day when I was practicing stalls at what we called high altitude, about forty-five hundred feet. I throttled back to do a power-off stall, and just as the stall broke, the engine died. In that plane, a dead engine meant a motionless prop, and there was no starter. I had once asked Tommy about the possibility of diving one of these little planes to a speed that would turn the six-foot wooden prop and start the Continental engine. He was horrified at the idea. In those old planes, he said, you'd tear apart in midair and kill yourself before you ever got one started. He told all his students, most emphatically, "Don't try it!"

But I had forty-five hundred feet and was close to the field, so naturally I decided to try it. It's hard to hold the nose of an L-4 straight down, but I did my best. The airspeed, normally about 65 miles per hour in those tired ships, passed 100, 110, and then the redline speed at 120. It was shuddering and fluttering somewhere well above that when the prop finally ticked over and the engine caught. I pulled out carefully to level flight at two thousand feet, feeling a bit proud of myself. Tommy would never have known it happened had it not been that someone saw my long dive and reported it. Tommy suspected it was me, and I couldn't lie to him. He gave me hell about it.

One day when I came in from a solo period and parked an old

Aeronca, I noted that the fuel truck was coming down the line, servicing planes as it came. I went into operations, where Tommy told me that Everett Kelley, who was scheduled up next in that plane, was sick. He told me to go back out and get some more time if I wanted to. When I got back to the plane, the fuel truck had already passed, so I got someone to pull the prop for me and off I went.

After another hour of tooling around solo, I was ready to quit, so I headed in, like a good student, on my forty-five-degree entry to the downwind leg of the pattern, flying at exactly five hundred feet above a big patch of woods below. I was over the middle of the woods when the engine quit. No warning, no stuttering, it just flat quit. In accordance with my training, I immediately established the best glide speed and then considered my situation. It was apparent that my only hope to get out of the woods was to go straight ahead, downwind, and pray for the wind to blow harder.

I barely cleared the last trees and sat down with no trouble in a field where several cows looked at me with mild interest and then resumed their grazing. I knew I was out of gas, although you couldn't prove it by that old glass tube in the wing root. I got out and sat down to await developments. We had no radio, but I knew that one of the pilots passing over in the same entry pattern would report me down. Soon a Harte pickup truck stopped on a nearby farm road and Mr. Cates, the senior civilian instructor, came sauntering over.

"What's the trouble?"

"Out of gas, sir."

"How do you know?"

"Well, I . . ."

"Did you check it?"

"Well, no, sir, I didn't . . ."

"Then how do you know you're out of gas?"

"Well, sir, I just assumed . . ."

"You don't make assumptions about airplanes, Lieutenant, you check. Do you know what Form 1 is for?"

"Yes, sir."

"Did you check it before you took off in this plane?"

"No, sir, I had just flown the plane in and . . ."

Standing on the left wheel, he had removed the wing-top fuel filler cap and stuck a dry weed into the tank.

"But you're right, you're out of gas. If you'd checked the Form 1 before takeoff you'd have known the plane had not been fueled. You're lucky it didn't turn out worse."

He flew the plane back to the field on gas he had brought in the truck, and I rode the pickup. Tommy was unhappy that I hadn't checked the Form 1, but he was pleased that I'd successfully handled a forced landing and learned a lesson.

Toward the end of our Denton training we had to get in our night landings. For that, three highway pot flares were placed in a line down the middle of one lobe of the heart-shaped field and a big bonfire was lighted about fifty yards off to one flank. These were our only visible points of reference on the moonless, overcast nights when we flew. Around the bonfire the instructors and the waiting students gathered to keep warm, roast hot dogs, and talk while the others were flying.

It was kind of scary, crawling into that little airplane in the flickering light of the bonfire and taxiing out to take off all alone into pitch blackness. Our planes had no lights of any kind, inside or out, except the built-in phosphorescent glow of the meager instrument array, like a Mickey Mouse watch. Our instruments were an altimeter graduated in intervals of two hundred feet, an airspeed indicator, a tachometer, and a magnetic compass. There were gauges for oil and cylinder head temperatures, too—and that was all. No attitude instruments.

The approved technique for night landing involved lining up parallel to the flares and flying the plane down toward the unseen surface of the field until the main gear touched the sod and bounced away. At that point, the pilot cut the power and placed the plane into a three-point landing attitude. Then he waited and hoped that the next touchdown would be on the three wheels and soft enough to stick without bouncing again.

Since pilots in the pattern could not see each other or communicate, one of the instructors was detailed to keep them safely separated by waving one over to the fire if he seemed out of time with the plane ahead. Then it usually would be necessary to wave all three of them in before the spacing could be reestablished.

Harte's contract required him to have given each graduating student at least sixty hours of flying time. One out of our class of twenty did not graduate. "Der Vroeg," Lt. Arend Vroegindewey, was a little, scrubbed-looking guy with a thin, sharp face and pleasant blue eyes. I don't think he was ever enthusiastic about flying, but he was such a very nice fellow that he was quite popular among the students. One day when his instructor gave him a simulated forced landing, the engine failed to pick up for the recovery and they ended up in the top of a tree. Neither was badly hurt, but Der Vroeg quit the course. I think he was our only loss at Denton.

A Lieutenant Blondelle gave me my last check ride at Denton while I still had a few hours' time to fly. And I well recall the day Tommy sent three of his students out solo to simply put in enough time to complete the contract. There was a low, ragged, indefinite overcast. Tommy told us to practice high air maneuvers if we could get to sixteen hundred feet; if not, we were to come down to five hundred and fly ground patterns.

When I taxied out to take off, Everett Kelley was in front of me and Gordon Lilly behind. I followed Kelley until, at a thousand feet, he vanished into the clouds. I leveled off just below the ceiling, and within five seconds he dropped out very close to my right wing. I banked violently to the left to get away from him. As I rolled away, I saw for the first time a plane that had come up close on my left. To avoid turning into him, I continued rolling until I was inverted, then pulled the nose toward the ground as if completing a loop, thus reversing my direction. I came right on back up until the altitude and airspeed were right and then I kicked around in a wingover, expecting to see the two planes ahead. But there was only Kelley, and I discovered that the other plane had followed me through my maneuver and was close on my tail.

"Aha!" I thought, "Old Lilly thinks he's pretty sharp, following me like that. Well, let's see how sharp he is." And so I proceeded to try to shake him off my tail. But there was no way. It was as if I were towing him, the way he hung on. I finally had to admit that he could outfly me, and I flew along straight and level to let him come alongside. But when the plane pulled up again on my left, it was the bald head and red face of Mr. Cates that I recognized in the cabin. He had the door open, and as he glared at me across the rushing air he jabbed a finger toward the ground. I headed for home.

It turned out that Mr. Cates was chasing in solo students because the weather was rapidly lowering. He had nabbed three of us. Besides Kelley and me, he also had Billy McPhail on the carpet before Lieutenant Bechtel, executive officer to Captain Marrs. When Bechtel asked what the trouble was, Mr. Cates told him with anger that seemed quite sincere.

"McPhail was doing loop after loop, right in the traffic pattern. Kelley was playing leapfrog in and out of the clouds. Kerns—well, I'm not sure what he was trying to do. It looked like an amateur dogfight."

Nice, easygoing Lieutenant Bechtel told us all we should know better than that, and fined us five stars each. Mr. Cates snorted in disgust but said nothing. A star cost only one nickel donated to the class's graduation party fund, and we felt greatly relieved. But at that most unpropitious moment, Captain Marrs walked in.

"Well, what's all this about?" he asked Bechtel. Bechtel told him.

"What punishment have you given them?" asked Captain Marrs. Bechtel told him.

"Five stars! Five stars! A hundred stars!" quoth Captain Marrs. "And you are all restricted to quarters except for duty—for the remainder of your time at this post. Let me see the records of these three."

His face looking like a thunderstorm about to break, Marrs carefully went over our school records.

"Well, all of you have clean records up to this point," he said. "If you had just one bad mark against you before this, I'd kick you out of this school!"

Still in my 201 file there is an order signed by Captain Marrs that confined me to quarters under the 104th Article of War for violation of local flying regulations, the only recorded punishment I got in nearly thirty years of Army service. It actually amounted to just overnight, for we shipped out to Fort Sill next day.

The first words we heard at Fort Sill were, "GET THOSE WINGS OFF!"

"But . . . sir, we have orders . . ."

"You have Army Air Force orders, but you do not wear wings with Field Artillery branch insignia until you have Army Ground Forces orders, and you won't get those until you have satisfactorily finished the course of instruction here at the Department of Air Training. Any questions? Take 'em off."

And so as humble wingless wonders, we started a new daily routine that began each morning at Post Field, Fort Sill, Oklahoma, with mass takeoff of scores of little OD-painted planes with the old-style red-centered white star.[3] The big sod field would reverberate with the multiple mini-roars of Continental engines and Sensenich props.

At the same time, half of the student pilots would be in ground school classes, learning all about the simple systems of the Cub-type airplane; how to service and maintain it—the Army way, of course; how to patch or replace fabric; how to make field expedient repairs; how to uncrate, assemble, and rig a new plane; and how to tear it down and recrate it for shipment. We practiced refueling from five-gallon cans through a chamois fastened over a grounded funnel—which would be our normal method of refueling once we joined our units.

In case you've never seen a Piper L-4—the type I flew most of the time in training—maybe I should tell you that it was statistically not very impressive. It was a tandem two-place high-wing taildragger built of metal tubing and covered with linen fabric. It weighed about 680 pounds and was supposed to carry 370. The four-cylinder, sixty-five-horsepower, Continental O-170–3 engine (the "O" stood for "opposed") was fueled from a twelve-gallon tank mounted just ahead of the instrument panel and would drive the seventy-two-inch Sensenich laminated birch propeller at 2,150 rpm for about one and a half hours of cruising at approximately seventy miles per hour. The main wing spars were of wood (spruce). The main gear had heel brakes, and the tail wheel was steerable with the rudder pedals. Its wingspan was 35 feet 2½ inches; overall length, 22 feet 3 inches; height, 6 feet 8 inches. Entry to the cabin was by means of a split door hinged at top and bottom on the right side. The seats were of canvas over tubing; the plywood floorboard was painted gray. There was 360-degree visibility, as well as overhead, through the windshield and extensive canopy. Both sections of the door could be left open in flight, as could a window on the left, which was hinged at the top and swung up to snap to a fitting under the wing. It had a plain, straight, removable stick with a simple black rubber grip, front and back, and the throttle was at the window ledge on the left. There was a magneto switch and a carburetor heat control on the panel and an elevator trim crank a foot or so below the throttle. In front of the windshield was the filler cap for the gas tank, and through the cap extended a wire with a crook on its end. That wire was attached to a cork float in the tank and constituted the fuel gauge.

The L-4 had no wing flaps, no gyro instruments, no turn-and-bank indicator, and very little of anything that was not absolutely necessary. The redline airspeed was 120, and the plane would land at about forty miles per hour on its slick balloon tires. (See the appendix for more information on Piper Cubs.)

Besides the Piper L-4, the Department of Air Training of the Field Artillery School (DAT-FAS) also used the Taylorcraft L-2 airplane. The L-2 was a slightly faster plane than the L-4, because of its thinner wing. It was also just a little heavier, as I recall, and a little better looking, having a well-formed Plexiglas canopy, whereas the L-4 had just plain Plexiglas panels covering the frame above the level of the window ledge and back to a little aft of the trailing edge of the wings. Because of its added weight and thinner wing, the L-2 was less forgiving of clumsiness in the maximum-performance flying we had to do every day. Those first assigned to the L-2 on arrival at DAT-FAS flew nothing else while they were there, and the rest of us flew it not at all. Bud Kelly trained in the L-2, while Everett Kelley and I were in L-4s. The only serious accident in our class was when an L-2 stalled out and spun in, killing a member of our old Denton group, a Lieutenant Darling, and his instructor.

I almost got it myself once on a max performance approach. Several of us were in the pattern at one of the stage fields, practicing solo. I was maybe two hundred feet up and trying to get the proper aspect of the barrier lined up for my final descent when the L-4 suddenly dropped out from under me. If it had been an L-2, I probably would have been done for, but I caught the dropping left wing, threw on the coal, pulled out over the pasture short of the field, then climbed over the barrier. At that point, I cut the power and landed safely. The next student in the pattern behind me was so shaken by having observed my close call that he went around.

On another day when the wind was pretty high and we students were shooting approaches solo over the barrier, a group of instructors stood near the barrier watching us, each waving his student around if he thought the approach was getting into a dangerous condition. On one of my approaches, I got the plane coming down in a steep approach like a helicopter, perfectly lined up, feeling as steady as an L-4 ever feels. I was sure I had an excellent landing made, but every instructor on the ground began frantically waving me off. It wasn't like me, but I completely ignored them and came on in. I cleared the barrier, touched down gently, and stopped in about the length of the plane—actually short of the panel that marked the intended touchdown point. My own instructor turned and walked off, shaking his head, while the others laughed. I have no idea what he might have said that I couldn't hear. I do have an idea what would have happened if the wind had suddenly died or shifted direction.

Except when we carried an SCR-610 (one of the new FM radios) for ground contact when adjusting fire, we had no radio in the school ships. And so one day when a long string of us on a cross-country orientation flight went fluttering into Sheppard Field at Wichita Falls, we knew nothing of local conditions except what we could see. There was an instructor leading the flight, but most of us were solo students. We followed him in with no problem—except one student. He had gotten a bit behind on the way in and he didn't see the rest of us land, so he came in the wrong way, downwind. The tower had to cause a B-17 (a large American bomber) on short final to break off and go around. The high and mighty AAF people were outraged, of course.

At some point in the program, there was a cross-country buddy ride. Billy McPhail and I were together on one of these single-plane trips. Billy's hometown was Comanche, Oklahoma, which happened to be near the route we were expecting to fly, and we deviated just a little to fly over his mother's house. She came out into the back yard and waved at us, and Billy decided to drop a note to her. Looking around for something with which to weight the note, he found a ten-inch crescent wrench. He fastened the note to it, I lined up on the McPhail homestead, and Billy let fly. I'm so very, very glad to be able to report that the wrench missed Mrs. McPhail by about three feet before burying itself in the Oklahoma soil.

★

I got through Stage A in good shape. Staff Sergeant Wilkerson was my instructor, and it seems to me that most of our flying was west and south of the Fort Sill reservation. This country was formerly part of the reservation for the Kiowa and Comanche Indians, and it was fairly flat, laid out with straight north-south and east-west roads at one-mile intervals. Each of these 640-acre sections was divided into quarter sections by trails at half-mile intervals that made a cross in the exact center of the section, and it was on these crossroads that our ground patterns—S-turns and rectangular course, wind-drift 8, elementary 8, two-bank or parachute 8—all in the "Five-hundred-Foot Series"—were oriented.

The "Thousand-Foot Series" consisted of a sequence of turns: ninety-degree left turn with thirty-degree bank (90L/30), 90R/30, 180L/45, 90L/45, 360R/70, and 360L/70. Sounds easy, I suppose, but with a nit-picker sitting up there yelling about every (estimated) degree of bank, every (sensed) foot of altitude variation, and every (eyeballed) degree of heading error, it could really wring the sweat out of a student. There was no instrument to measure bank, you could lose fifty feet before the altimeter registered a change (the student, in the backseat, had to lean around the instructor to see it anyway), and the oscillating, lagging magnetic compass was useless during a turn.

We did stalls at two thousand feet—power on and power off, partial, complete, and full oscillation; spins from three thousand feet, once to right and once to left, two revolutions each. And we practiced chandelles and wingovers at any altitude above fifteen hundred feet. But all that was just review and refinement of what we'd been doing at Denton. It was in Stage B that we got into the more interesting part of the DAT-FAS program, in which we were expected to learn to maintain and service our planes in primitive front-line environments and routinely operate from unprepared fields and roads under conditions requiring maximum performance of the aircraft. Mike Strok, who was instrumental in establishing the course at DAT-FAS and was himself one of the very early graduates of it, says that the emphasis was on "learning by practicing the extremes to which the pilot can push the aircraft and himself." The training included landing on curved roads, and power-stall approaches over twenty-foot-high barriers for very short landings. It included tactics for evading enemy fighter attack, which involved turning toward the attacker, rapidly changing altitude and direction, flying "in the nap of the earth," and landing as soon as possible. Attention was given to selection and aerial recon of landing areas, and, of course, to target identification and conduct of fire by aerial observation methods.

I don't recall having had much trouble or any really exciting incidents while at DAT-FAS until the day of my final Stage B check ride. As always, I dreaded and feared it, although I had never in my life failed any kind of major examination. To make my anxiety worse, my check pilot was one Captain Baker, the bogeyman of the entire DAT-FAS, as far as students were concerned.

We took off from the Rabbit Hill stage field and he told me to head off in a certain direction. Just as I reached five hundred feet, he yelled, "Enemy aircraft!" That was the signal for evasive action. I cut the throttle, rolled upside down, and pulled the nose toward the ground. I leveled off at about ten or twenty feet and proceeded to contour fly at full throttle back toward Rabbit Hill, still the nearest landing place I knew. Along the side of the field nearest me was a line of tall trees. As I approached them, I again cut the power and pulled up to clear them, thus killing off speed so I could make a three-point landing just beyond them. After that, according to the procedure, I would shut off the engine, leave the plane, and head for the nearest cover.

However, just as I touched down he shoved the throttle open and said, "Go on off." I tried, but the plane would not pick up flying speed, and it wanted to turn to the right. It was quickly evident that the right tire was flat, having been punctured by a stub or something when we landed. Grumpily, Captain Baker told me to taxi up to the tiny shack that was the stage field office and get another plane. He got out and went into the building, growling, "Let me know when you're ready."

I was nervous when we took off for the second time, but my flying seemed to satisfy him reasonably well as he put me through my paces. Finally, he looked down at a little place in the Wichita Wildlife Refuge and asked whether I had ever been in there. I hadn't, so he said, "Let's land in there." Well, I was clever, so I very conspicuously made my high drag and my low drag before I landed on the little weed-grown track. He told me to pull off and we'd have a smoke. We sat under the wing and got out our cigarettes.

After a while, Captain Baker said, "Well, I'm ready to go if you are."

I got up and got the seat cushion and chocked the right front wheel with it, ready to prop the plane myself—since check pilots didn't assist during Stage B checks.

He very carefully ground out his cigarette butt and said, "Have you seen everything you want to see around here?"

I assured him that I had, and he got in. I propped the ship from behind the prop, put the cushion back in, and away we went. He told me to go back to Rabbit Hill.

Returning to Rabbit Hill at this point didn't seem right to me; there were still things he had not checked. I began to feel that something was wrong, but I couldn't figure out what.

Finally, he said, "Will you tell me why you didn't walk over that strip before we took off?"

I replied, "Oh, hell! I knew I forgot something!"

He waited a few seconds while I was lining up to land at Rabbit Hill, and then he said, "Take me over to Buzzard's Acre."

Every student at DAT-FAS, whether he had ever been into Buzzard's Acre or not, had nightmares about it. It was a kind of shallow wash that sloped up into the side of a boulder-strewn hill. There was but one way in and one way out. It was steep, full of winding gullies, and studded with rocks and weeds and scrubby bushes. Directly off the lower end was another hillside that the pilot had to contend with both on approach and on departure. Even under the best wind conditions, it was no place to land an airplane, and wind conditions never seemed right. Obviously, a good wind going in was a bad wind coming out, and vice versa. The student couldn't win.

Nevertheless, the circumstances made me glad to be told to go over there. Again I dragged the landing area quite thoroughly, looking for anything I could see that might help me avoid trouble during approach and landing. I got in with surprisingly little trouble and tailed the plane off among the bushes for concealment from any imaginary enemy straf-ers. Then I walked that strip from end to end and side to side—a truly necessary procedure in the case of Buzzard's Acre. By the time I said I was ready to go, I knew precisely where my wheels were to run during every foot of my takeoff roll. We got away with no sweat. I had plenty of speed to enable a safe turn away from the hillside ahead, and we started climbing away.

I had barely reached two hundred feet altitude when Captain Baker chopped the throttle and said, "Forced landing!"

As I began my glide, I took a hasty look around for a possible landing place. There was only one, and it was almost directly under me, the worst possible situation with so little altitude. It was a small pasture with a pond, and the only safe place to set down was along a fence to the right of the pond. I turned quickly to my left, and by the time I had completed a 360-degree turn and was again headed into the wind, I was touching down—at just the right point.

As the wheels touched, he opened the throttle and said, "Let's go home to Rabbit Hill."

Back at the stage field, Baker walked into the hut without a word or a sign to me. Not until next day when I got a slip in my mailbox did I know whether I'd passed or failed the check ride. I passed. Everett Kelley was one of several who got the pink slip that meant failure; however, he was not washed out, but washed back for further training. He eventually graduated and served as a pilot for many years, finishing his career as a civilian helicopter instructor at Fort Wolters.

Now we got our AGF orders and could wear our wings. They asked each of us which way we wanted to go: east or west? I said I wanted to go west.

★

I said goodbye to Dorie at the bus station in Lawton. Her bus was going to Ohio, mine to El Reno, where I would catch a train. There were floods farther east, trains were late, and I waited more than twelve hours at El Reno before the train came that would take me to Indio, California.

I checked into a hotel in Indio and found there two more pilots who, like me, were assigned to the 33d Infantry Division Artillery at Camp Roberts. Hal Davis and Bill Brisley had their wives with them, and I joined the group for dinner on a very romantic second floor balcony surrounded by palms. They had already contacted Camp Roberts, twenty-five miles distant, and had been told that trucks would be sent for us the next day, 15 May 1943, to take us to our division, which was some 250 miles away in the Mojave Desert.

Herb Eder, Charles "Speedy" Spendlove, and Dwight Mossman joined us in the trucks that morning and, dressed in our pinks and greens, we rode in the back of a six-by-six truck from Indio through Blythe to Needles and on another forty miles on U.S. Route 66 to where the 33d dwelt in its tent city called Camp Clipper.

It was evening when we arrived. After eating, we were ushered in a group to the tent quarters of the Div Arty commander, Brig. Gen. Alexander G. Paxton. Before us, he had only two pilots: 1st Lt. Fred Hoffman and a Staff Sergeant Anderson. Now, with Lt. Don Vineyard, who had driven his car to Camp Clipper and reported in with us, he suddenly had nine pilots and no aircraft. Anderson, however, had elected to return to the AAF rather than go for an artillery commission, so we were still two short of the full table of organization and equipment (TOE) authorization.

It was significant that Dwight Mossman, a young man of a substantial St. Louis family, was a University of Missouri graduate, as his fellow alumnus, General Paxton, was quick to note. The general assigned Mossman to Div Arty HQ, where Hoffman was already on the roster. Davis and Eder went to the 210th Field Artillery Battalion (FA Bn), Brisley and Spendlove to the 124th, and Vineyard and Kerns to the 122d. At that point, the 123d FA Bn, the 155 mm general support battalion of Div Arty, had no pilots of its own. Much later, it would get George Donaldson and Ellis Pickett.

Hoffman had oiled down a little sand strip near the camp and had a wind sock up. We finally managed to borrow a couple of aged L-3s from the AAF liaison unit at Desert Center, and we started getting a little flying time.

One of our favorite pastimes was made possible by proximity to the

Southern Pacific Railroad. As the trains raced along through the Mojave Desert at speeds roughly equal to our own normal cruise, we entertained ourselves and the train passengers by flying alongside. People would crowd to one side of a car to look at us, then we'd hop over to the other side and they'd come swarming over there, waving and smiling at us. Engineers and firemen would wave and blow the steam whistles for us. And we'd sometimes buzz cars moving on the long stretches of Route 66, until one day someone hit the radio antenna on a jeep that happened to be carrying the division commander, Maj. Gen. John Millikin.

But I guess our favorite of all entertainments was buzzing the nurses' showers late in the afternoon. A few miles from Clipper, near the rail-road water point, called Fenner, was a field hospital with a lot of nurses in residence. Regulation latrine screens, which have no tops, concealed their showers from ground observation. Just about sundown every day those showers would be crowded with nurses. As one of our little planes puttered overhead at about fifty miles per hour, there'd be quite a flurry of excitement among them. Some nurses would run and grab their clothes and hold them up in front of themselves; some would bend over or squat down, hugging themselves for concealment; but many would simply stand up and wave and smile and, probably, yell at us. And that was as close as any of us ever got to the Fenner nurses, although one pilot whose cap blew off as he leaned out of his plane to shout at them had it returned to him through the message center.

This reminds me of the reason I never had one of those fifty-mission caps that were so talked about among pilots and their fans in those days. Because they often wore earphones over their service caps while flying, AAF pilots were allowed to remove the metal ring that gave form and rigidity to the top of the cap, and it would soon become so broken down and crumpled that a pilot wearing one was easily distinguished from his nonflying fellow officers. Pilots liked that. It was swagger, macho stuff, you know, because pilots invariably believe that there is nothing on earth so valiant and manly as roaring off into the wild blue. Lots of other people used to think so, too. But when we were interviewed in General Paxton's tent that first night at the 33d, I went out and left my service cap in his quarters. Bold, brave, daring young aviator though

I was (in my own mind), I never had the nerve to go back for it. I got along until near the end of the war without one.

The 33d was the first division then in the Desert Training Center to receive its authorized pilots. For that reason, it was tasked to provide a demonstration of organic air observation's capabilities for the benefit of commanders and staffs of other commands in the training center. For reasons I never knew, the 122d FA Bn was chosen to do the job, which meant that Vineyard and I, with the two old L-3s, would be the key figures in the demonstration. A small hill in the desert served as bleachers for the spectators. Targets were to be selected on the flats and on slopes and in ravines of a small mountain some distance away, the 105 mm howitzers of the 122d firing from behind and a little to the flank of the spectators.

The demonstration went off in fine form, both Vin and I doing our jobs well, the fire direction people and the gunners responding with the speed and accuracy that was to be their norm throughout the war. An Illinois National Guard unit, the 122d FA Bn of World War II remains the best direct support battalion I have ever known. The spectators, most of whom had never before seen what a difference aerial observation can make, must have been favorably impressed.

The demonstration was to end with our landing in the desert just in front of the spectators, where a truck track wound through the creosote shrubs and sand and rocky hardpan. The place was totally unprepared—no one had ever landed there before, and it was just a fresh trail made by the trucks that brought the spectators to the hill. The idea was to show that the organic air sections could "live with the troops" and land "anywhere," with minimum fuss and bother.

I had the last fire mission, and when I approached the landing site I saw Vineyard's plane already on the ground, just past a sharp bend in the track. He radioed me that it was extremely tricky, with a gusty crosswind that was getting worse by the minute. In the approved manner, I touched down on the main wheels only, holding the tail up so I could see over the nose to follow the ups, downs, bends, and other irregularities of the road, such as bushes the trucks had run over and mashed down. The crosswind kept trying to push me off to the left, so I also held the right wing down as long as I could, keeping directional control with the rudder.

The bend and Vin's plane were coming up very quickly, and I wished the tail would go down so I could use the brakes, but every attempt to bring it down only lifted the wheels off. Finally, when I had about decided I'd have to go around and try again, the tail came down—a bit reluctantly. Just as the tail wheel touched and I came onto the brakes, a sudden hard gust from the right front lifted the plane back into the air and gently set it down just off the trail to the left, where it quickly came to a halt. I shut down, and then I could hear the applause from up on the hill where the assemblage of brass was starting to depart.

My L-3 had a nicked prop and a few small rips in the fabric on the fuselage. I flew it back to Camp Clipper before any repairs were made, so obviously the damage was very minor. Nevertheless, as I went to the officer's mess tent about an hour later, Warrant Officer Rudy Krevolt, our personnel officer, yelled, "Well, here comes old 'Crash' Kerns." Everyone laughed, and from that day forward I was known in that outfit as "Crash." I liked that.

It should not be supposed that we aviators did nothing but fly around and have fun. We got the dirty details usually assigned to second lieutenants, and we took part in the physical conditioning activities of the battalion. When General Paxton heard that the infantry units were doing some horrible thing, his usual response was, "If them infantry baws kin do it, mah baws kin do it, too!" And then this bandy-legged little Mississippi cotton broker would set out to prove it. Thus, we arose every morning at 0400 hours and marched five miles to a "dead man" across the sand road and back again to camp before we had breakfast and began the regular training scheduled for the day.

This daily routine finally ended with a grand promenade of the entire Div Arty from Camp Clipper to Clipper Mountain, up the mountain, and back to camp, forty-six miles in two days. We arose at 0400 as usual, had breakfast, filled one canteen each of water, and set out for the foot of Clipper Mountain, eighteen miles away, where we would be met by mess trucks with water trailers. Plodding across the desert by compass, following no road or trail, under the blazing sun of June, we eked out our precious water to make it last the distance. I had still a couple of swallows left in my quart canteen when we reached the rendezvous point. The trucks had not yet arrived, so we settled down to wait. Lt. Ray Rohr and I spread our shelter halves over a creosote bush to make shade, and we both went to sleep.

Someone awakened us with the word that the outfit was about to move out to climb the mountain. It was nearly dark, and we could see the troops already starting to trail off toward the rocky, treeless ridges.

"Have the trucks come yet?"

"Mess trucks? Sure, they came and have already gone back to camp. Didn't you two get any supper?"

Supper would have been nice, but water was uppermost in our minds. There was none. Except poor old Rohr and me, everyone in HQ Btry had eaten, revived their dehydrated systems with all the water they could drink, and filled their canteens. The two of us had only about half a cupful each of hot, stale water that had sloshed in our canteens all the way from Camp Clipper. But the water trailers were gone. There would be no more until the morrow. We trudged dejectedly off into the gathering gloom to climb Clipper Mountain.

We had gone about a mile on the way when we came upon a certain corporal of the headquarters personnel, a man who later would repeatedly prove himself unworthy of his chevrons. He lay beside the trail, begging everyone who came along to give him a drink of water. Everyone I saw as we approached refused him, saying he had refilled his canteen at the foot of the mountain and had no more need than they did. He didn't deny that, but said he was dying for water. Being a very softhearted fellow, I offered him a sip of my meager supply, cautioning him not to take it all. I had to pull it away from him to save a few drops.

And on we climbed. At the top of the mountain, Capt. Phil Ryan, the HQ Btry commander, was checking off his men as they arrived. I told him I didn't think the dying corporal would be up, so when everyone else had checked through and gone on the way back down, I went back down with Ryan. We found the corporal still lying beside the trail, still begging for water. He claimed he was unable to walk a step farther, so big Irish Ryan hoisted him to his shoulders and carried the whining varmint back down to the camp.

Breakfast, with coffee and water, was on hand at earliest light next morning, and Rohr and I were first in line, believe me. And then we began the last eighteen-mile stretch back to Camp Clipper. Trucks and ambulances following the troops were rapidly filled with those who really couldn't cut it or who simply quit trying. Only two things kept me going: my self-respect and my gold bars. I marveled at the stamina of a couple of our sergeants who marched side by side, chests out, singing lustily like French revolutionaries in some romantic movie. They never seemed to weaken, but for the last few miles every step I took required renewed determination and a maximum physical effort. The old mess tent never looked as good as when Rohr and I finally dragged ourselves into it late that afternoon.

Long freight trains pulled up on the Southern Pacific. We loaded the whole division on them and hauled it up to Camp Stoneman at Pittsburg, California, riding in the boxcars with our equipment, halting for mess prepared by our own cooks in the boxcar kitchens they rigged up. Although it was midsummer and the weather very hot, we traveled in our winter wool ODs, our commanders hoping that enemy spies would think we were being sent to some cold clime—but it wasn't so. After a few days of processing, we shipped down the bay on ferries and boarded ships at San Francisco, bound for Hawaii. The 122d went down on the ferry *City of Sacramento,* and our transport to Hawaii was the former Moore-McCormack liner SS *Brazil.* It was mid-July when she stood off Port Allen, Kauai, and we debarked. Div Arty HQ, the 123d Regimental Combat Team (RCT)—including the 122d FA Bn—and certain other elements would be on Kauai, the remainder of the division on Maui and Molokai.

– Three –

KAUAI TO FORTIFICATION POINT

The 33d Division's mission in the Territory of Hawaii was twofold: to provide defense of the western islands and to continue its preparation for service elsewhere in the Pacific theater. Kauai, "The Garden Isle," westernmost of the major islands of Hawaii, was a choice location.

On Kauai, the 122d FA Bn put HQ and HQ Btry, of which the air section was an element, in a patch of forest about four miles from Lihue on the road to Kalaheo. We lived in small wood and tar paper shacks scattered about among the trees and ate in a larger shack that had screens against flies. Our firing batteries, in tactical positions for defense of our sector of the island, had living accommodations similar to ours. Our primary mission, of course, was training for combat missions in the southwestern Pacific area.

Just a week after our arrival on Kauai, we lost my friend Lt. Ray Rohr. On the day before our debarkation, Captain Ryan had called a meeting of the HQ Btry officers, at which he gave instructions for duties in debarkation and occupation of our camp ashore. Rohr had been informed of the meeting but went to sleep and missed it. Captain Ryan spoke to him quite severely and restricted him to the unit area except for duty for two weeks, effective upon debarkation.

We had been on Kauai a week, and I was officer of the (OD) day for the battery. I was in my quarters, reading *The Book of Boners* and laughing like a fool when Capt. Oliver Miller, the battalion doctor, looked in at the door to see what was so funny. As I was telling him, someone came running and yelling for him. He took off on a run. I got up, put on my gunbelt, and followed him, thinking there might be trouble the OD should look into.

When I reached Doc Miller's side, he was kneeling beside a man who lay on a stretcher on the ground beside the access road at the edge of the camp. There was blood on his jacket, his face was gray, his eyes sunken—I didn't recognize the man, and I asked Doc who it was. He replied, "It's Lieutenant Rohr. He's dead."

We had just that day received reissue of our sidearms, which had been shipped overseas in custody of the supply element. Rohr had picked up his .45-caliber pistol and had gone into the dugout that sheltered our tactical switchboard, where, as the battery's communication officer, he spent much of his time. According to Private First Class Bales, the switchboard operator on duty, Rohr sat leaning against a table, reading a magazine that lay on the table, while toying idly with his pistol beneath the table. The discharged bullet passed completely through Rohr's body, piercing his heart, and lodged in a heavy wooden door behind him. I remembered how, only two weeks before, Rohr and I had stood on a deck of the *Brazil* and watched the Golden Gate fading in the distance. He had remarked, "Some of us are seeing that for the last time."

Ray Rohr's death was officially recorded as a suicide, but I've always believed it was just a tragic accident. Many times had I seen him reading in the same way Bales described, always with some object in his hands, turning it over and over without being conscious that he was doing so. I think he just forgot that he was playing carelessly with a deadly weapon. Although I had only known Rohr for a few months, I had come to like him very much. He was just a big farm boy from North Dakota, simple and honest. It was hard to hold back the tears as I helped carry him to his grave at Koloa.

For a few weeks, we pilots, being second lieutenants and having no planes to fly, got a generous share of undesirable details, like supervising construction of unit latrines and garbage pits. When the planes finally arrived, direct from the factory, we hauled them to Isenberg Athletic Field at Lihue. There we uncrated, unpacked, assembled, rigged, and checked them out. And then we undertook a program of refresher training for ourselves, sharpening up our flying skills and getting used to working with our battalions.

About this time, we received new instructions for marking our planes, and we repainted the wing to eliminate the red dot in the center of the star. Someone had decided that it could be confused with the Rising Sun insignia of the Japanese. We may also have added the white bars on either side of the star at that time; if not, it wasn't long afterward that we did.

Our training program, which also included a lot of just plain fun, went along without incident except for one night when Brisley, flying a night fire mission over the mountain foothills, got into a sudden rainstorm, lost his visual horizon and his orientation, and had a hair-raising time getting out of it. Night weather flying without attitude instruments is a very tricky business.

In our L-4H ships, the SCR-610 radio, with power pack, was mounted on the chart board aft of the rear seat, its whip antenna sticking up through a grommeted hole in the Plexiglas. We never used the wire antennas provided with the planes, which were supposed to be let out behind after takeoff, stabilized by a small drag sock. In fact, we removed them. The SCR-610s were in the first generation of frequency-modulated equipment, and they had only two channels, crystal controlled. We used one for our own battalion FDC and the other for the Div Arty liaison channel. Since we flew from the front seat and the radio was behind the rear seat, it was not easy to switch channels in flight. Even with my long arms, I had to unbelt, half stand, and stretch to my full reach to operate the channel selector.

Hal Davis was incredibly skillful in flying the L-4. For instance, when we were doing our night flying at Lihue we used one improvised pop-bottle flare pot at the approach end of the short field and two of the same a few yards apart at the far side. Our approach was across two cane fields, the one nearest the landing field being up to a height of

The author at Isenberg Field,
with Hal Davis's cane fields in
the background.

about two feet, and another just beyond that one up about six or eight
feet high. On dark nights when the ground could not be seen from a
plane—nor our unlighted plane seen from the ground—we'd hear Davis
line up on the flare pots, cut his engine, and start his whispering glide
toward Isenberg Field. After a bit we'd hear the taller cane start to slap
his wheels, and there'd be a murmur from his engine as he added a
bit of power to maintain that altitude. Then the cane-slapping would
stop as he reached the edge of the tall cane, and soon we'd hear the
two-foot cane start to slap, the engine murmuring again. Then the cane
would be heard no more, and the engine would cut back to idle as he
left the edge of the two-foot cane, touching down on Isenberg with his
tail wheel almost on the boundary road beside our approach flare. He
did that many times, disdaining the "feeling-for-the-ground" tail-high
approach the rest of us used.

One of Hal's greatest pleasures was rat racing. Of course, he was
usually the leading rat, the others trying to follow his lead. After a while,
however, it seemed that I was the only one left who was still foolish

enough to try to follow him. One of his favorite tricks was to make a tight 360 over a cane field with his wingtip plowing the cane blades. Only once did I try to follow him through that maneuver, and his prop wash just about threw me. Even when I did it alone, the wash from my own plane nearly pulled me in as I completed the circle. But Hal did it with apparent ease.

On one unusual occasion when I was leading and Hal was following, I threw my plane on its side and slid between two tall palms that were maybe less than the wingspan apart. As I did, I felt a jolt and realized that I had torn out a radio antenna for the occupants of a nearby house. Of course, Hal came through behind me with nothing to hinder him, but the broken wires had slashed the fabric on my wings and cut deep grooves in my tires.

During a Div Arty CP exercise, Vin and I were asked to make a surprise raid with flour-bag "bombs" on Div Arty HQ at Kalaheo. We did so with great joy, using small paper bags filled with a mixture of flour and the red volcanic dust that makes up much of the island soil. One of my bombs went through the roof of a tar paper shack belonging to the signal corps carrier pigeon section. Looking back, I saw the door burst open and two men run out, bounding like deer across the area and looking back at the cloud of dust and flour billowing out the door behind them.

That gave us the idea of bombing the little strip near Hanapepe where Brisley and Spendlove based their planes for the 124th. We hit them just after dawn one morning, plastering the place quite liberally. It was so much fun that we decided to do it again the next day. As we flew in the calm air of early morning, maintaining our two-plane formation with sober dignity, as if our mission were of grave consequence, we spotted two L-4s going just as soberly in the opposite direction. We knew it was Brisley and Spendlove heading for our field, so we wasted no time in completing our mission and hightailing it for home. They had splattered our area quite well but had done no damage, and we felt relieved and happy with our little game. But soon the phone rang. It was Brisley, and he proposed the restoration of peace. Our first raid had put a hole through a wing of one of their planes, and that was not fun. We agreed, and that ended that.

Vineyard and I had continued to fly from Isenberg after the others moved away, since our battalion headquarters was only about four miles up the road. Isenberg was a good field, and our tents were in the corner farthest from the road and from Isenberg Gym, which was used then as a USO canteen. Our men lived with the planes, but Vin and I lived with the battalion. It wasn't bad from the viewpoint of convenience and comfort, but it wasn't so good in case of trouble; and, after all, we were there to help defend the island in case of attack. So the battalion commander, Lt. Col. Roland P. "Bud" Carlson, directed us to establish an airstrip no more than a mile from the battalion CP.

Colonel Carlson usually gave his orders to Don Vineyard, although he and I were then of identical rank and time in grade. "Uncle Bud" had to put one of us in charge, and he selected Vineyard—undoubtedly because Vin was a little older, more impressive in appearance and manner, and much more self-assertive than I was. And so Vin selected a site only about two hundred yards from the CP. The place would have been fine but for the fact that it would require a sizeable fill across a small ravine and the fill would require a culvert for drainage. This raised two problems: first the Lihue Plantation Company, which owned the land, was hesitant to permit the construction; and, second, the division's supporting engineer unit could not immediately get to the job.

My opinion was that the convenience of the strip would not be worth the effort required. Vin (who much later in his career would transfer to the Engineer Corps) was fond of planning big projects and seeing them carried out, while I was more inclined to the proverbial operation on a shoestring. And so when Vin left for Oahu and a school for jungle-warfare instructors, I immediately asked our S-2 to get permission from Lihue Plantation Company for us to use a field on a ridge about a half mile from the CP. I said that we would do no damage whatsoever, land and take off on the existing truck trail through the field, and keep vehicular traffic on the existing ranch road into the area. We asked only that they graze no cattle in that field while we were there, since they might damage our ships. The company granted permission that same day, and on the next I moved the air section up there. There was nothing to do but fly in the two planes and tie them down under the trees at the edge of the field, haul our gear up in our weapons carrier, set up our tents under the trees, and dig a latrine. We remained there in happiness for the remainder of our time in Hawaii. We had done exactly as we were supposed to do: use existing facilities, be as inconspicuous as possible, cause no avoidable problems, and keep out of sight on the ground. If Vin was a bit unhappy, he quickly forgave me.

The TOE in those days authorized the air section only one enlisted man, an airplane mechanic, but we soon realized that we needed more men and a vehicle of our own. Uncle Bud Carlson came through for us with a three-quarter-ton weapons carrier with driver and a mechanic helper. Our mechanic was T/3 Kennis Allen (we always addressed him as "Sergeant" Allen), a steady, quiet, Kentuckian from Manchester. His helper was T/4 Wendell Young, a young married man from Chicago; and the driver was Ted Kinsch, who was also a Chicagoan, I believe. Young and Kinsch eventually became just about as good mechanics as Allen himself, as did Eddie Janes, a Pennsylvania fireman who joined us much later, in New Guinea. Allen trained them all. I can't say too much in praise of these men. They were the very salt of the earth.

Not long after we moved up to the hill strip, the S-3 called me late one afternoon and said that an exercise was in progress and I would have to displace the air section to some location in an area he defined for me, and I'd have to displace them that night. I immediately told him I'd have to leave Vineyard's plane behind, because there wouldn't be time to return for it and get it into an emergency landing place before dark. He accepted that. I left Young to guard Vin's plane, and away we went, me in the air, Allen and Kinsch in the truck.

I searched the entire area assigned to me, but there simply was no suitable place for landing an airplane. At last, in desperation as darkness closed in, I decided to set down on a stretch of narrow, rutted dirt road between a field of tall cane and a graded-up cane field railroad. I knew that my left wing would be riding in the top of the cane, and I feared that the ruts might throw my right wing down onto the railroad track. But with extreme difficulty I got the plane down without damage, and the boys soon joined me. We remained there until daylight, at which time the exercise ended and I managed barely to waddle out of the place and go home.

Seems as if I always come up with these anticlimaxes, doesn't it? Maybe it's because I was a very good pilot. Or maybe it was just because I always had a lot of outside help. Regardless, these are the kinds of things that cost a pilot a lot of anxious perspiration. That wasn't always understood by the nonflyers who were our associates in the battalion. They picked up the current joke aimed at us "fair-haired boys," which was to ask, "We know what you do for flying pay, but what do you do for base?" We took it in good humor—the flying pay, that is.

General Paxton suddenly came to the realization that he had ten aviators in his Div Arty, of whom eight were of the same grade and date of rank. Except for Fred Hoffman, still a first lieutenant, and our new Div Arty air officer, Maj. Dick Bortz, we were all second lieutenants commissioned on 24 December 1942. And so it was announced that there would be a flying and shooting contest among the pilots, and the second lieutenant with the highest overall score would be the first promoted to first lieutenant, the others following at weekly intervals.

The contest was pretty much a hasty review of our training at Fort Sill, with flying and shooting scored separately. Overall, I came out on top of the pile, having a high score in flying and much the best score in shooting. Vin came in second, outscoring me in flying but not being able to overcome the advantage of my luck in shooting.

I never insisted on pulling my seven days of seniority in rank to take over responsibility for the air section from Vin. I don't think either of us, in those days, was at all concerned about such matters as experience in positions of responsibility or any other factor bearing upon career advancement other than doing our duty well, whatever it might be. But Vin was naturally inclined to take charge, while I tended to be a solitary individual, doing my flying and shooting and not worrying much about other matters. However, Vin never took advantage of his position to order me around; in fact, when decisions were to be made, we usually talked them over and reached agreement. We had no serious troubles, although Vin used to say, "Crash, ten years after this war is over I'll be able to buy and sell you."

And I'd reply, "Vin, there's not enough money on earth for you to buy me." (Today I might offer him a bargain price.)

Lt. Gen. Robert C. Richardson then commanded the Hawaiian Department and, I believe, all Army forces in the Central Pacific area. When he came to Kauai on an inspection tour, the 122d was selected to demonstrate its fire support capabilities for him. Vin and I supposed that our having won the promotion contest had something to do with that, but that may be slighting the rest of the battalion, which, as I have said, was the best of its kind that I have ever known.

For the demonstration, we flew from the paved highway just at the eastern edge of a small town—Makaweli, I think—and fired on targets designated for us by map coordinates or transfers from previously fired concentrations in the nearby hills. We were timed from the start of our takeoff roll until we touched down again after each fire mission. Of course, times varied considerably by mission type, target location, and difficulty, and, to some extent, the pilot's luck. On my last mission, I copied the target data as I climbed out under an electric power line that crossed the road. As soon as I got high enough to see the target, I called my mission to the FDC. The first rounds were very close, and I turned for home even as I called in a correction. As soon as those rounds burst, I gave a sensing that split the bracket I had achieved, and, putting all my trust in the accuracy of my sensing, I ducked for the road without even waiting to see the fire for effect. I touched down four minutes and eleven seconds after takeoff. General Richardson may have been impressed, but it was not at all realistic, and I knew that even then. Maybe he did, too. Still—I got the fire on the target.

In the very early days of our flying on Kauai, I set out one afternoon to see how high my L-4 would go. The service ceiling was supposed to be 12,500 feet above sea level, but I had never been that high in my life. I started climbing and just kept going. I passed 12,500 and kept climbing, but the altimeter kept moving more and more slowly. Finally, it seemed as if I were picking up altitude only as my fuel supply was consumed and the aircraft thereby lightened. I was over 15,000 feet by then. The sun was getting low, and in the breaks between the towers of pinkish cumulus below, I could see only darkness. But I felt great. I laughed and sang and carried on like a happy drunk—a common effect of oxygen deprivation at high altitude.[1] But the plane hung at 15,300 feet and showed no inclination to go higher, so I finally pulled on the carburetor heat, reduced power, and started down, threading my way among the clouds, which had thickened somewhat since I came up. I was surprised at how long it took to get the kitelike plane down without exceeding the redline airspeed. It was just about totally dark when I landed.

About twenty miles south of Kauai is the little island of Niihau, which in 1943 was just one big cattle ranch owned by a family named Robinson, I think.[2] The only exception to the ranch was a small village that was the only community of pure-blooded ethnic Hawaiians left in the islands. The village was the home of Benjamin Kanahele, who had become a national hero shortly after the Pearl Harbor attack when, with his wife's help but without a gun, he killed a Japanese officer who had crash-landed his damaged plane on Niihau and, aided by a Japanese American ranch employee, had seized control of the island.[3] Although unauthorized visitors to Niihau were prohibited, Vineyard and I decided to go calling.

One Sunday, without a word to anyone, we flew to Niihau and landed our planes on a rocky little space near the village, far from the ranch landing strip. The Hawaiians came out of the village en masse and greeted us with bright, friendly smiles and handshakes, exemplifying traditional island hospitality. We spent about an hour with them but didn't get to see Benjamin Kanahele, who was away somewhere, although we did meet some of his relatives. We each bought twisted strands of tiny white shells as souvenirs. On the way home, flying low across the water, we passed over two whales swimming together, the first whales I ever saw.

Before the war, it had been a practice of the manager of the Lihue Plantation Company to make occasional aerial inspections of his domain, but private flying had been essentially at a halt on Kauai since the war began, and it had been quite a while since Burns had been able to make his flyovers. Uncle Bud Carlson had become good friends with Mr. and Mrs. Burns, who lived in an impressive white mansion on the slopes behind Lihue. They spent much time fishing together in Burns's boat, and Colonel Carlson caught a fish of some large variety that was of record size. Out of this relationship came an agreement by Uncle Bud to let Vin and me fly the Burnses on an aerial tour of their realm. And so it was done, without incident. I flew Mrs. Burns.

In gratitude, the Burnses invited Vineyard and me, with Colonel Carlson, to dinner at their home. Of course, there were hors d'oeuvres and cocktails for some time before dinner. Vin partook quite freely of the latter, and there was a bit of concern on his part as to whether he could successfully conceal the fact that he'd had a couple too many. I was my usual conservative self but was so afraid of doing something wrong that I could not fully enjoy the wonderful meal brought in by a Chinese servant. Never before or since have I had a steak to compare with the one I had there.

Our L-4s were not the only airplanes around Kauai, of course. The Navy had some Grumman F4F Wildcats stationed at Barking Sands, and Army Curtiss P-40 Warhawks showed up from somewhere. Some of the P-40 pilots got a kick out of diving from behind and passing at high speed just in front of an unsuspecting L-4, which would then fly into the turbulent wake and just about flip.

I suppose these were the same planes that flew the security checks we tracked in the filter center at Lihue, where I pulled a couple of weeks' duty as liaison for the 33d Division. My job was to sit up on a balcony that ran all around a pit where several girls, supervised by officers, shoved markers around on a big map table to show the movements of aircraft in the area. If something of importance came up, I was supposed to notice it and make the proper report to Division G-2 on my hotline. During my two weeks, I had no occasion to make anything but communications checks and negative reports.

One aspect of duty at the filter center was really much less appealing than it sounds, although not actually unpleasant. The civilian girls who worked there were very carefully screened, and their activities were controlled for security reasons. One security measure was that if a girl left the compound she had to be accompanied by at least two other girls and a male officer of those on duty in the compound. Volunteers for escort duty were not accepted—officers were detailed to the duty. I was once detailed to escort three girls to the local movie theater and return. Two of the girls were sisters, Linda and Peggy Christian, from

Samoa, descendants of Fletcher Christian, the leader of the storied mutiny on the British ship *Bounty* that resulted in the abandonment at sea of Capt. William Bligh and his loyal crewmen. They were, of course, of mixed Caucasian and Polynesian ancestry and were very attractive and intelligent young ladies.

One Sunday, having nothing better to do, I flew alone over to Barking Sands and was hanging around the operations building with a few others watching some P-40s going through a mock dogfight two or three miles offshore, when two of the planes collided in midair and went their separate ways down into the glare and shadows of the ocean. We saw one parachute open and drift toward the sea.

The Navy operations officer immediately called for pilots and planes to search for survivors. I could have gone in my L-4, but the only other pilot available was a Navy lieutenant junior grade whose airplane was a twin-engine C-45, which I think the Navy called an SNJ. He was not permitted to fly without a copilot, so the operations officer asked me to go with him.

Hastily, we climbed into his ship and took off. He was a bit irritated with me because every time he asked for something the copilot was supposed to do, he'd have to show me where it was or do it himself, with rare exceptions. I did manage to get the gear up by myself, and as he banked toward the site of the accident he looked at me and asked what I'd been flying. With a straight face, I replied, "L-4." After a few seconds delay, he said, "Oh."

We saw some wreckage floating and a patch of yellow water from a dye marker, but I don't think either of the P-40 pilots was ever seen again. If they were, I never heard of it.

★

South of Nawiliwili Harbor there are some steep cliffs along the shore, and on these cliffs—in 1943, at least—there were wild goats. Vin got the idea of trying to shoot one with a carbine from the plane while I flew the plane. After several tries, he brought one down—and then we both wished he hadn't. It would be almost impossible to recover the carcass, and what would we do with it if we had it? So we left the goats to themselves after that.

In the early days on Kauai, before we got our planes, I was detailed to Btry A of the 122d, and the BC, Captain Hurlbut, sent me out to his OP—just to get me out of the way, I suppose. The post itself was an artificial rock built in among some real ones on a bluff about midway between Nawiliwili and Koloa. It had just a narrow slit through which our BC-scope looked out southeastward over the sea. A hundred yards behind us, hidden from the ocean side, we had a cook shack.

We had a dog there, and one night he growled and then ran off in the direction of the cook shack, as if he were going to tear something to bits. But then he came backing up, running to and fro across the path but always losing ground, and barking frantically. At least three possibilities ran through my mind. One was guerrillas, but I doubted that there really were any in the islands then, if ever. Another was wild hogs or goats. The third was a sneak thief over at our cook shack. I decided we'd better investigate.

Leaving three men at the OP and taking the sergeant with me, I set out to cut around to the left of the path and down a little gully until we were near the shack. Then I sent the sergeant farther down to where he could watch the path below the shack for anyone leaving that way. When he was in position, he whistled to me and I moved in on the shack, pistol ready. If someone had hollered "Boo!" I'd have disappeared for several days. But my luck held. If anyone had been there, he was either gone or well concealed somewhere by the time I arrived. We never did find out what the dog was barking at. Possibly it was menehunis, the Hawaiian version of leprechauns. But it gave me a chance to show how brave I was, and how great a tactician.

★

Flying down Waimea Canyon one day, Dwight Mossman suddenly became aware that he was about to fly into three power cables strung across the canyon some four hundred feet above its floor. He pushed the nose down to go under them, and his landing gear caught an unseen fourth cable that was swinging lower than the rest. The cable didn't break. It flipped the airplane over itself and left it plunging steeply toward the ground at low speed. As Mossman regained partial control, he tried to pull up, but the plane passed between two trees, tearing off both wings, and then the fuselage slid into a heavy clump of light undergrowth and came to a halt. He and his passenger suffered only minor injuries.

Shortly after our arrival in Hawaii, Maj. Gen. Percy W. Clarkson took command of the division. Flying General Clarkson into the 210th Bn's strip one day, Fred Hoffman failed to see some field wire the communications people had thoughtfully strung across the approach. The resultant difficulty didn't hurt Fred or the plane very much, but it did wrench the general's back rather severely.

Div Arty's airstrip at Kalaheo was a small baseball field on top of a hill barely large enough to hold it. Trees and a high hedge blocked two adjacent sides. Another side had the chicken-wire backstop as an obstacle. It wasn't too bad if you had a pretty good wind from a handy direction; otherwise, it was slightly difficult.

Early one morning I flew into Kalaheo. There was not a breath of wind, and the grass was still wet with morning dew. I set the plane down at the very edge of the longest axis of the field and began trying to stop, but the big slick tires just slid on the wet grass as if it were ice, and my brakes were useless. With the hedge rapidly coming up ahead, I had to ground-loop to get stopped and avoid it. The only damage was that the little solid-rubber tire was knocked off of the tail wheel. The Div Arty mechanics put it back on within five minutes and it was as good as new.

But Fred Hoffman deemed it necessary to chew me out and lecture me in a very unpleasant way—from the vantage point of his silver bar over my gold one—as if I had committed an unpardonable offense. I resented that, so if I tell a funny story about Fred later on, you'll understand that I'm just getting even. Actually, he wasn't a bad sort; it was just a bad morning for him.

We didn't get to do a lot of shooting while on Kauai, but when we did shoot, the pilots had the task of clearing cattle out of the range area. That was fun—low altitude, close quarters, up and down the draws and around the thickets, driving the dogies just like old cowhands.

I helped Mel Harker, our battalion assistant S-2, experiment with a method of extending survey to points in the target area that could not be seen by the surveyor on the ground. He set up his aiming circle and marked it with a white panel, then he tracked my plane with the aiming circle while I flew a course that placed his position directly in line between me and a point he wanted to locate. When I had them in line, I called on the radio, "Mark," and he stopped tracking and recorded the azimuth reading on his aiming circle. We took three readings on each of several points, and then he moved to a new location along his selected survey baseline and we repeated the procedure with the same points. Averaging the readings at each point and plotting the reciprocals of the azimuths, he was able to locate the points accurately enough for artillery-fire control. However, I don't think we ever had occasion to use such a procedure in combat.

Among the nonflight details I was given while on Kauai was to make the annual inventory of all PX (post exchange) facilities on the island, which had stock worth something like $250,000. I was given a sizable force of civilian clerical personnel and more authority than I had ever enjoyed before. I guess I did a satisfactory job, since I heard no word to the contrary.

Flying in those days, there on Kauai with our simple little airplanes, usually with no radio, no flight plans, and no direct supervision by anyone, was a great pleasure and relaxation. I made a practice of going up for thirty minutes or so every morning as soon as I got to the airstrip, whether there was a need to or not. It woke me up, cleared my head, and made me feel good for the rest of the day.

One morning I came down from such a flight, during which I had flown loops and spins and other maneuvers, and discovered that my safety belt had been unfastened during the entire flight. A serious unco-ordinated movement—such as stalling on top of one of my loops—might have had catastrophic results, since we never carried chutes on routine flights. On one occasion (not this same one) I accidentally performed a whip stall, in which the plane is flown straight up until it stops dead in the air, then slides backward for a short distance and quickly swaps ends (because of the engine's weight) and falls nose first toward the ground until it regains control speed. Every bit of dust and dirt and trash that had accumulated inside the plane was thrown into the air and floated around me. I felt very much as if I were up there without an airplane, and it was a most unpleasant sensation. If I had not had a safety belt then, I might have come down alone.

Returning from one of my wakeup flights one morning, I was met by T/4 Wendell Young, who looked very worried. As I started to get out of the plane, Wendy came up to the door and said, "Sir, let me show you something." He pointed to the two bolts that hold the main spars of the wings to the frame of the airplane. Both were in place but there were no nuts on them, not to mention the normal cotter-pin safety. If one of those bolts had worked out, a wing would have immediately separated from the airplane, no question about that. It was another case in which I had just jumped into my plane and taken off without checking the aircraft status symbol in the Form 1. In this case, it was a red X, meaning non-flyable. Sergeant Allen had removed the bolts for inspection and had replaced them but had left for breakfast before replacing the nuts.

Despite little oversights like that, I managed to survive to fly about five thousand hours as an alleged pilot. I sometimes wonder how.

Pvt. Joe Dzyb had more than an unusual name, he also had a talent for painting in oil. He also had a desire for an airplane ride, and he offered to paint a picture on my plane if I'd take him up. We made the deal quickly, and Dzyb carried out his part of the bargain, then he came down to Isenberg for his ride.

"Now, sir, I've never been up before and I'm not sure I'm going to like it, so please don't do anything fancy."

I promised I wouldn't, and we took off. I had little more than cleared the edge of the short field and had not so much as started a gentle turn when he tapped me on the shoulder and asked me to take him down. As gently as I could, I circled the field and landed. Dzyb got out and lay on the ground, his face on his arms. Thinking he was just feeling a little nauseous, I went inside the tent and left him there. But it must have been thirty minutes later that one of the men told me that Dzyb was still lying there. He would not respond to anything we said, and even shaking him would not rouse him, although he appeared to be conscious. The medics came and took him away, and it was about a week before he was released from the hospital.

On Sundays the beach at Nawiliwili was always crowded. One such day, when many people were well out into the bay, I spotted from the air two very large manta rays, great devilfish, headed in toward the beach, getting very near the swimmers. Having no radio, I hurriedly landed at our strip and called our CP by phone. They, in turn, called the Lihue police. A few minutes later, I was back in the air and watching when the word about the rays reached the beach. The water appeared to boil with people heading for shore, and very shortly the rays had the bay all to themselves. Considering that the largest devilfish are about twenty feet wide and weigh up to 3,000 pounds, I wouldn't have cared to tangle with one, either. The ones I saw at Nawililwili must have been among the largest.

Mount Waialeale is 5,080 feet high, just 90 feet lower than Kauai's highest peak, Mt. Kawaikini. Waialeale has one of the world's greatest recorded annual rainfalls, averaging 456 inches. That's mighty wet, and it's not easy to find a time when the mountain is not clouded, but on a day when ceiling and visibility permitted, I flew low across the broad, flat top of it. You may have trouble envisioning a swamp on a mountaintop, but that's what it looked like to me. The vegetation was quite dense but low, and I don't recall seeing any large trees up there.

While I can recall many details of my time in Kauai, strangely, I don't remember much about our leaving it. We did not take our airplanes with us, but I don't recall what we did with them. I do know that when we moved out of our airstrip we left no sign of our passing—except for a few tent stake holes in the ground and a small wooden sign that read: "OLD LATRINE 4/44."

At some time in my life I rode a small, gray ship that seemed to be constructed of nothing but steel, and it was called *Shanks*. I believe that was a ride from Kauai to Oahu to board the prewar Pacific cruise liner *Matsonia*, which I had often seen docked at Honolulu. It had been gleaming white then, with the Matson Line's big "M" on its stacks, but now the ship was in wartime gray and her upper decks were all but hidden by dozens of gray life rafts on their skids. Gun tubs had been built for her five-inch deck guns. But I don't remember boarding the *Matsonia*. It's a blank spot in my memory. I only recall heading out over that hazardous ocean aboard her, having no idea where she was bound.

Inside her big gray hull, the *Matsonia* carried the officers and men of the 123d Infantry Regiment and the 122d FA Bn. There may have been men from other units; I'm not sure. It was an administrative move, as distinct from a combat movement, so our equipment was stowed as cargo, not ready for immediate use upon debarking.

Being an officer, I was assigned a stateroom on an upper deck—with seven other officers; it was so crowded we could hardly move when we were all in there. I took my meals at a designated table in the former grand dining salon, as scheduled, always with the same two officers sharing the table with me. One was Lt. Melvin Harker of my unit, and the other was a Navy lieutenant commander who was the ship's senior navigator. Harker and I cultivated the navigator's friendship, in hopes of getting some advance info as to our destination. He told us that we were on a course that would take us near Palmyra and the Christmas Islands. When we reached that point, he would be permitted to open another sealed envelope and learn the next destination.

We were without escort in an ocean where Japanese submarines roamed in search of big juicy troopships like the *Matsonia,* so she was constantly zigzagging along her effective course in hopes of spoiling the aim of any enemy torpedo man and fooling anyone who might try to guess her real course after only brief observation. Strict blackout was observed, and a dire fate was planned for anyone caught throwing anything, even a cigarette butt, overboard. Only designated members of the ship's crew were permitted to dump trash, and only shortly after dark each evening.

We crossed the equator at a point I have forgotten, but which must have been somewhere between Baker and Jarvis Islands. Shellback ceremonies were conducted, but since there were so many Polliwogs, only representatives elected by their unit personnel got the full treatment by

King Neptune's Court. Those representatives then had the privilege—in fact, the duty—of initiating the other members of their respective units. Phil Ryan represented HQ Btry. I received a secondary treatment: I had my hair clipped right through the middle from front to back, then I was slung with my head down over the side of the ship while a bucketful of seawater was poured over me. It was brief but impressive. I've lost the Shellback Certificate I was issued that day.

We were going into a region where tropical fevers were as great a hazard to the unprepared as the enemy himself. Worst of all was malaria, and the new medical miracle against malaria was Atabrine, a little yellow pill with an abominably bitter taste. We had to take five a day for five days to get an initial concentration of the stuff built up in our systems. It was quite common for the pills to come back up, and when they did, we immediately took five more. After the five days, the dosage was reduced to only one pill—one a day as long as you remained in the South Pacific. Fingernails, toenails, and whites of eyes turned yellow, but malaria, which had almost defeated the early divisions in New Guinea, was no longer a major problem.

The first land I saw after leaving Oahu was a blue bulk, low on the horizon off our port beam. Our navigator friend said it was Espiritu Santo, an island in the New Hebrides. Passing there, we were entering the Coral Sea, and one morning, after passing near a number of very small green-forested islands, we anchored in Milne Bay at the extreme southeastern tip of the huge island of New Guinea. The day was not over, as I recall, before we set sail again, and a couple of days later we landed at Base F, the big staging area at Finschhafen.[4] It was May 1944, and the war was definitely going our way.

Our advance party had set up a tent camp for us at Finschhafen. Being rushed and shorthanded, they had pegged only the four corners of each tent, leaving the rest to be done by the main body upon its arrival. But it was late and we were tired when we got there, so we just sacked out for the night. I was not much surprised or disturbed when, during the night, the fell and its rough canvas lay directly on top of me. I just went back to sleep, lulled by rain beating on the slack cloth.

Morning came, announced by much cursing and splashing about as

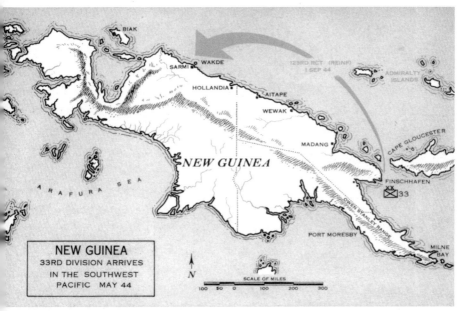

The 33d Infantry Division with attached 33d Division Artillery Battalion landed at the big staging base at Finschhafen, May 1944, and then the division artillery moved farther up the coast to Fortification Point (Map from Sanford Winston, *The Golden Cross*).

others around me made their way out from under their fallen tents. I swung my feet over the side of my field cot and was shocked to find that muddy water was only two inches from my back. Shoes and assorted items of clothing floated together with other debris in a camp that had become a muddy lake. It was an appropriate introduction to New Guinea.

Without planes for the moment, Vin and I once again got more than our share of the dirty details as the 33d began demonstrating the basis of one of its nicknames, "The Camp-Building Division." Ditches were dug to drain the camp area, and many tons of caliche were hauled in to pave roads and paths through the mud, while wooden duckboards floored our tents. Before long, we were quite comfortable. And training started once more.

But for the Div Arty commander, Base F was totally unsuitable as a training area. Chanting, in his Mississippi accent, "Gotta git mah boys some trainin'," he talked General Clarkson into letting him move Div

Arty some forty miles up the coast to a modest cape called Fortification Point. Up there was open, hilly country with patches of woods and large areas of tall, brown kunai grass; we could do some shooting at targets we could see, and there was no one to bother us except one small Australian outfit—which was no bother at all. The serious problem would be logistics, because the only land route to the point was passable only by jeep, and when the monsoon rains came it would be utterly impassable. Beaches did not exist there, only steep banks of loose small boulders along the shore, not good for landing craft.

Div Arty built its new camp at Fortification Point, and the air section of the 122d was sent up to prepare an airstrip for the entire Div Arty. Vin and I selected a level shelf between the camp and the Massewang River, half a mile away. To ensure its usability during heavy rains, it was necessary to ditch the sides and ends of the runway and surface it with PSP, that marvelous pierced steel planking that surfaced so many airfields during the war. The engineers had us so low on their priority list, however, that the chance of having them do it for us was hopeless; but they agreed to loan us a small bulldozer and supply us with PSP. Because we had to clear an approach lane through a grove of trees, they also agreed to let us have some dynamite, primer cord, blasting caps, and fuse. Vin and I had both been trained in Hawaii to use explosives, and we figured we could learn to handle the bulldozer.

We constructed ditches along the strip, carefully sloping the shoulders so they offered no big problem for a plane taxiing across them, although they were about eighteen inches deep. Vin was the chief engineer, but we took turns driving the bulldozer. An LCV (Landing Craft, Vehicle) from Base F brought up our PSP, and we piled it beside the strip, ready to be laid over the mud—for the rains had already hit us. And that's the way things stood one rainy afternoon when Bortz and Mossman flew up from Finschhafen to see how we were coming along and to bring us a case of dynamite and some other explosives. The plane they came in was an old L-4A that Bortz, with his gold leaf and Princeton brass, had scrounged from I Corps. It was an unflyable heap at first, but he had cannibalized other wrecks for parts, and the Div Arty crew had finally got it flying. It had the tail number 1167. When 1167 came over that afternoon, we tried to wave them off, since the freshly graded strip was nothing but deep mud and puddles of water. We knew that even if he got down safely he'd not be able to fly out that night. But Bortz came in anyway. On landing, he lost control, ran off the runway, and bounded over the pile of PSP, fortunately doing no more damage than tearing some fabric. The plane was still flyable.

They unloaded the explosives, commented on our progress, and started to leave for Base F. It was almost completely dark by that time, but nothing daunted our fearless Dick Bortz. Despite the best arguments of Vin and me, away they went. Lined up as far back as he could get, Bortz held the brakes until the engine was at full speed, then started rolling. The plane slewed from side to side in the mud, but slowly gained speed and soon disappeared from our view down the dark runway. Over the sound of the engine we could hear mud splattering up against the wings and tail surfaces, and there was an occasional big splash as she hit a puddle of water. And then, suddenly, the engine sound died and we saw the silhouette of the tail appear above the dark horizon and disappear again.

We found 1167 upside-down in a large pool of muddy water just off the end of our runway, but Bortz and Mossman were unhurt. Our men worked all night on the plane. The prop was broken and cracked, but they trimmed it down to rebalance it and reinforced it with doped fabric. They patched some holes and cleaned the mud out of the engine. They beat out the cowling to approximately its original shape. By daylight, they had checked the rigging and the controls and pronounced the ship flyable. Sergeant Allen did admit that, since we had not yet received all of our supplies, he'd had to use pocket handkerchiefs instead of regular airplane fabric for some of the patches. After an early breakfast, Bortz and Mossman were up and away.

Well, we got the PSP laid and we cleared our approach through the patch of jungle, making fullest use of the explosives to knock down trees too big for our little bulldozer to push over. This led to two memorable incidents. In the first, Vin drove the bulldozer over a large log, and as the nose dropped on the other side it threw him out of the seat and spread-eagled him over the engine hood. The bulldozer kept grinding on across the landscape while Vin frantically scrambled back into the seat and in control of the situation.

The 122d Field Artillery Battalion Air Section planes and ground crew on its new "airbase" at Maffin Bay, 1944. Note the PSP surface. From left: Wendell Young, Kennis Allen, Ted Kinsch, and Eddie Janes.

In the second incident, we came upon a large tree that was the beloved home of a colony of the largest and fiercest ants I have ever encountered. Several times they drove us away when we tried to place explosives on the tree. Finally, Allen tied string around his trouser legs and collar, put on gloves and tied the wristlets over his sleeves, and generally made himself as antproof as reasonably possible. We strung several blocks of dynamite on a length of primer cord and capped and fused the whole thing, and then Allen dashed in and tried to fasten it around the tree before the ants could get to him. On the first try, he dropped it and ran back out. All of us fell on him like maniacs, beating the ants off him. Then he ran back in, and this time he got the belt fastened before he had to dash back out to take another beating from the rest of us. On the third trip he lit the fuse, and we beat him again as we all ran to get safely away from the blast. That was the last big tree on the approach. Our airstrip was finished.

★

Our planes finally came, and were assembled by the boys at Base F. Everyone got a new plane—except me. The plane that would have been mine was diverted to some outfit with higher priority, and I was issued good old #1167. I was somewhat upset about that at first, but it turned out to be the best L-4 I ever flew. It was beautifully rigged and trimmed, had a good engine, felt easy, smooth, and lively on the controls, and, with its slicker finish, cruised a couple of knots faster than the newer ships. I claimed it was a better plane because it was experienced.

But one night after dark we got orders to bring a plane to Finschhafen immediately. It was to be dismantled and flown by C-47 to Hollandia to replace a combat loss in the 24th Division. Since #1167 was the oldest ship we had, she was elected, so Wendy Young went along to help tear it down, and we felt our way down the dark coast to Base F and loaded the plane in the dark. Not long after that, I was issued a new plane. Its tail number was 79608, and I named it *Booby Trap II*. Vin, although a Missourian by birth, had lived in Arizona, and he named his plane the *Arizona Keed*.

There was a period—I don't recall how long or why—when Vin and I with our planes were staying at Base F and flying out of a little corner of the big airfield there. I think the Japanese air in that area was quite weak by then, but the P-38 pilots seemed to be finding something to hit on occasion, because now and then we'd see one come low and fast across the field, then pull up and do his victory roll, his wingtip contrails drawing spirals in the air. I think they were patrolling over New Britain at that time. The cocky little pilots with their crushed hats could easily get on one's nerves, you know. They were the glamour boys, and no one knew it better than they. In one such case, I was talking with a second lieutenant of the Quartermaster Corps. He said he'd had enough braggadocio to last him a while, and he invited me to come aboard his ship and we'd have a drink.

At first, I thought he was kidding, but I found that he did have command of a ship, all his own, that he had skippered all the way from New Orleans, through Panama, and across the Pacific to New Guinea. It was seventy-five feet long and twenty-five feet in beam, had a high forecastle and a high bridge, and between them it was quite low where a single hatch gave access to the hold. It looked something like Christopher Columbus's *Santa Maria* without sails. On the bridge, which was typically nautical with lots of varnished wood and polished brass, he mixed us some grape Kool-Aid and spiked it with medical alcohol. Best of all for me, he cooled it with real ice cubes, something I had not seen since Hawaii. He told me that his crew for the little ship was fourteen men. He loved the job, and I sort of envied him.

At one time I was asked to land on a baby aircraft carrier much different from the second lieutenant's ship—that was anchored in the harbor at Finschhafen. It was the kind that Navy aircraft took off from but did not ordinarily land on, their main purpose being to replace airplane losses from the larger carriers. I went out and made a couple of flybys. Then I asked if it was really important for me to land there. They said no, they just wanted to see how it looked to an L-4 pilot. I told them I could probably land OK if I had to, but the damned thing looked much too small for comfort, just sitting out there with no wind.

The Div Arty camp at Fortification Point was right up to the camp builders' standard, but Vin and I and our air section men lived at the airstrip nearby. Vin and I shared one tent, while the four enlisted men—Eddie Janes had now joined us—shared another about fifty yards away.

One night I walked down to the men's tent to speak to Sergeant Allen about something. The walls of the tent were rolled up, and as I approached I could see Allen and Young sitting on their cots on opposite sides of the tent. Each had a clipboard on his knee and was intent on writing a personal letter. There was not a sound except the hissing of a Coleman gasoline lantern hanging on the tent pole and the light scratching of their pens. They didn't notice me come up to the tent entrance. At the entrance I stopped, because on the canvas cot at Allen's right elbow was a grayish-brown snake about five feet long. It was coiled, but about half of its length was raised, placing its head nearly level with Allen's shoulder. It slowly swayed to and fro, apparently watching Allen's hand move as he wrote.

It occurred to me that if I spoke, or if one of the men should see me there, both would immediately stand up, and that would surely cause the snake to strike Allen. Glancing around for a weapon, I saw an extended entrenching tool leaning against the tent rope at my right side. I grabbed it, then, as fast as I could, I leaped across the tent, swept the snake's reared-up body off the cot, and killed it. It was over before Allen knew what was happening, I think, although Young saw the snake as I knocked it off, and I believe he helped me kill it.

In accordance with the medics' standing request, we called for them to identify the snake. It was a cobra, they said, a common cobra.

On another dark night, I heard something down near our planes, and I was a bit intimidated when I made out several tall figures that did not show the familiar lines of American soldiers. When I approached them, one spoke up.

"Good ev'nin', mate! We're your neighbors from across the river. We thought per'aps you chaps might like to come over for a spot of tea."

They were officers from the Australian unit camped on the other side of the Massewang, and I'm afraid none of our people had had the grace to call on them or invite them over. I guess they came to the airstrip because we were nearest to them. But thereafter, some of us did go over and visit with them on several occasions. Among my loot from those visits was one of their famous bush hats, which had one side pinned up by a bronze insignia of the Royal Australian Engineers on a background of red felt. I lost the hat somewhere, but I think I still have that insignia. And another visit ended with my wading back across the Massewang carrying a submachine gun and a waterproof bag containing about six hundred rounds of ammunition. If the friendly Aussies got anything in return for their generosity, I doubt that it was anything more than my undying goodwill toward their country.

Our airstrip was barely finished and the other air sections moved in before the rains hit us in full force. Rain was heavy and almost constant. Additionally, the change in winds made our beach landing area extremely difficult for the boats that had been supplying Div Arty. One of the boats rolled over in the surf, and the Quartermaster Corps, which operated the boats, refused to come in anymore until conditions improved. And so it was that for two whole weeks nothing came into or went out from Div Arty except by L-4 airplane.

Now bear in mind that the legal payload of an L-4 was 370 pounds, including the pilot's weight. You can see that we had to do a lot of flying. We had ten planes and eleven pilots, so each day one pilot was detailed as dispatcher, and we had an officer from Div Arty to determine load priorities. Our planes flew to and from Base F from dawn till dark, halting only long enough for fueling and for the pilot to grab a drink of water or a bite to eat. We were loaded both going and coming, hauling up to 500 pounds, regardless of the 370-pound limit. We hauled about everything from food rations to jungle rot patients, from routine personal mail to classified official papers and ranking officers. Despite the rain and low visibility along the forty-mile route, we had no accidents.

But in the worst of the conditions, navigation did pose a real problem. We worked out a system for finding and getting lined up on our inconspicuous little strip. Always we were coming up the coast from Base F, very low, following the white line of the surf pounding the shore at the foot of often invisible green hills. Watching closely, we could recognize the mouth of the Massewang, then we'd watch the land side until we could make out the row of officers' tents that lined the shore just below the main camp. At that point, we'd make a ninety-degree left turn and watch the camp flow by a hundred or so feet beneath our wings. When the tents ran out, we'd execute another ninety to the left, count three seconds, then make another—and in a few more seconds we'd spot the strip, just about under the nose. Set down, taxi over, unload, reload, and go again.

Come to think of it, it's rather surprising that we didn't have at least one head-on collision somewhere along the coast. We must have had some rule to preclude that, but I don't remember what it was.

Lt. Lorne Stanley, Don Vineyard, and I had all graduated from the "kill or be killed" school for jungle warfare instructors on Oahu. In fact, Stanley had remained there for a while as an instructor in bayonet and knife fighting. The three of us considered ourselves pretty hot stuff when it came to fast hip-shooting with a rifle or carbine, among many other things, and we missed the opportunity for practicing our art—and showing off before the other boys. One day, accompanied by Lt. Voris "Okie" Taylor, we went up the coast a few miles to a coconut grove to have a little fun with our carbines. There was a silly rule prohibiting officers from driving vehicles (because they didn't have to do the first echelon maintenance on them), so we got a Technical Sergeant Anderson, of the battalion communications section, to drive for us.

While we four lieutenants amused ourselves and shot up lots of ammunition for an hour or so, Sergeant Anderson sat quietly in the truck, his cap down over his eyes as if he were dozing. When one of us finally asked him if he'd like to try his hand at the carbine, he allowed himself to be coaxed into giving it a whirl. He unwound his tall, lanky frame and came over and took the weapon someone offered him. He looked around rather uncertainly.

"What should I shoot at?" he asked.

"Oh, just pick out anything—like that palm tree over there."

No sooner were the words out than Anderson's carbine was spitting bullets—ba-ba-bam!—three shots so close together they sounded almost like one. And right in the middle of the palm tree, about waist high and spaced vertically about six inches apart, appeared three holes. He proceeded then to show us what a carbine could do if one really could shoot. It was finally made known to us that even before he got into the Army, Anderson was an NRA champion, and he had continued his superior shooting since joining the service, adapting it to combat fire techniques. He made us feel silly.

Lt. Col. Thomas Truxtun was our Div Arty G-2 (intelligence officer), a tall, slim, handsome, and distinguished fellow who looked exactly as an officer and a gentleman should look. At Fortification Point he was not very busy. Needing something to brighten his days, he asked me to fly him in to examine a Japanese bomber that had been reported down in the hills some forty-five miles northwest of us.

The wreck was on a grassy hillside maybe five miles from the coast. Half a mile from it was an extreme rarity in that part of New Guinea: a house. The hillside where the bomber lay offered no prospect for a safe landing, so I picked a spot not far from the house and looked it over carefully. A crackup in that isolated spot would be a problem for sure. The grass was tall, about shoulder high, but I figured I could land in it OK, then trample down a takeoff lane. I did land without difficulty, except that near the end of my short rollout the plane dropped over a bank about four feet high that the grass had concealed from me. She nearly went over on her nose, but I gunned the engine and brought the tail back down.

We walked over to the bomber. It had been down for at least several weeks, and it had about it an unpleasant atmosphere of deteriorated rubber and mildew. Under the tail lay the skeletons of two crew members. While the colonel began examining various items of equipment, I asked if I might investigate the old house.

It looked very much like a poor farmhouse somewhere in the southeastern United States—a small frame building with tin roof and weathered, unpainted wooden siding. The windows were long ago broken out and everything inside had seen many rain soakings. It had that musty smell like the airplane. I found an old pedal-pumped organ still in fair condition, and quite a few items like tubs and chairs and a clothes wringer. And there were some books. One, which I took with me, was a German-language biography of Bismarck. Another was a ledger in which was a list of words in some New Guinean native language with German translation beside it. There were scraps of religious songbooks in German, and the whole thing led me to conclude that the house had been home to German missionaries now displaced by the war.[5]

When I saw Colonel Truxtun heading back for the plane, I did likewise. With just a few yards of grass mashed back in front of the plane, and with the takeoff run carefully walked over to be sure there was no hidden obstacle, we got off with no problem. Once in the air, he asked me if we could land on an old Japanese fighter strip we had seen just where we turned in from the coast. About a mile from it, at the foot of the hills, was a village that he wanted to visit. We flew over the village without seeing a solitary human being and then landed on the equally deserted old strip. We walked along a well-beaten path through the kunai grass until we came to the village.

There were perhaps fifteen or twenty huts of bamboo, grass, and poles, standing seven or eight feet above the ground on posts. Each hut's only opening was in its floor. The central area around which the huts stood in a ragged oval was damp, black earth, patted flat by hundreds of bare feet, and the whole place had a dank, sour smell that made me lose all interest in hanging around.

But out in the middle of that central plaza we stood, and Colonel Truxtun yelled, "Hello!" several times without getting any response. At last, a pole with projections on it to make a crude ladder poked down from the floor door of the largest building, and down it climbed a most interesting individual who proved to be the headman of the village. He was about five feet four, I guessed, barrel-chested and bandy-legged, and black as human beings ever get to be. He looked to be an extremely hale and hardy sixty years; the whites of his eyes were yellow, his teeth black, and his tongue and gums bright red from chewing betel nut. His only garment was a rawhide thong tied tightly around his hips and supporting a wicked-looking knife as well as a little doohickey to cover his otherwise utter nakedness. His chest, upper arms, shoulders, and face were marked with patterns of welts formed by inserting clay under the skin, and his earlobes were long loops of skin that hung down to his shoulders. His hair was short and kinky and black with liberal signs of gray.

He clambered agilely down the pole ladder and walked toward us like a man with a purpose. He greeted Colonel Truxtun in a manner cautious but not unfriendly, and they began to converse in the pidgin English Truxtun had learned from a book and was using for the first time. He wasted no time in giving the chief a little gift of a tropical chocolate bar and offering to trade more of such stuff for some fresh papaya and some seashells of a certain kind that he wanted.

Very soon other men appeared, one or two at a time, until a large group stood around us. Most of them were younger, and all were armed, most of them having spears or bows and arrows. I saw no guns. They dressed the same as the headman, but few were so ugly as he and very few had the welts and the stretched earlobes, which Truxtun later told me identified a man who had distinguished himself by killing an enemy in battle, then cooking and eating his flesh. Only the old men had such markings.

These men stood by and watched and listened, having very little to say, and saying that in undertones so as not to disturb the two big men who were negotiating a trade. But there appeared an old woman, the first female we'd seen. We guessed that she must be the headman's head woman, for she would dart in through the crowd to his side and talk loudly and harshly to him, gesturing vehemently. He'd stand and listen patiently until she finished and left again, then he'd resume talking.

As the trading session proceeded, other women and children began to appear, all coming from a brushy area at the mouth of a ravine just outside the village, where I suppose they had concealed themselves until their menfolk had discovered the intentions of the visiting white men. The children were stark naked, the women nearly so, with spindly limbs and distended stomachs. Like the men, most of them had plentiful scabs of sores on their legs. They assembled soundlessly on the outskirts of the group of men.

As the crowd thickened, so did the atmosphere, and I was eager to depart long before Truxtun was. As we finally headed back across the path toward the airstrip, I led the way. The colonel followed me, and the chief was right behind him, followed by all the other men and then the women and children, everyone strung out in single file.

At the strip, the colonel continued to engage the chief in conversation, and they got onto the subject of big snakes. Truxtun asked whether the people ever hunted python, and the chief eagerly assured him that they did. When asked how they went about it, he turned to one of the young men and spoke a few words to him. The fellow was one of the best looking of the men, relatively tall, his slender dark-brown body strong and supple, looking cleaner and healthier than most, and intelligence was evident in his dark face. He walked away from the group a few paces to the expanse of tall kunai grass at the edge of the airstrip, and then, suddenly, he went into character, like an actor on a stage.

The young hunter tensed, crouched slightly, and with his bow in one hand and an arrow in the other, carefully parting the chest-high grass ahead of him, he began stalking his prey, moving very deliberately, step by step, alert and intent upon the ground ahead of him.

Suddenly he stopped, crouched lower, his gaze fixed on an imaginary big snake hidden from us in the grass. Quick as a flash, he fixed the arrow to the bow and let fly. Instantly he whipped another arrow from the rawhide quiver hanging from his waist cord, and with quick aim, fired it at the supposedly wounded python. He hastily fitted a third arrow to the bow; this one he did not fire but held ready as he very cautiously circled and examined the phantom serpent until certain that it was, indeed, slain. Then he slung his bow, drew his knife, and went through the motions of skinning the python. That done, he returned to our group, smiling broadly and obviously proud of his achievement.

Colonel Truxtun made a deal with the chief by which, on the following Sunday, one week hence, the natives would take the colonel and me on a python hunt. And then we boarded our L-4 and flew back to Fortification Point. All the way, Truxtun sat in the rear seat holding in his lap a steel helmet half full of his precious seashells, with the putrid remains of their former residents still inside. I flew with my head out the window.[6]

★

In spite of abhorring all snakes, I was truly looking forward to that python hunt. But it was not to be. There were plans for a change of scenery for the 33d Division, and Colonel Truxtun's G-2 duties prevented his going, so that let me out, too. But I did go up to the fighter strip the following Sunday for reasons of my own. I had devised a way of fastening my Australian submachine gun on the wing struts of my L-4 and firing it by wire from the cabin. Of course, I couldn't do that at Fortification Point, so I flew up to the old Japanese strip, mounted my weapon, and proceeded to fire up some ammo on rocks out in the surf. For a short-range gun hastily rigged up like that, it did pretty well. At least I didn't shoot myself down.

As I landed again to dismount my armament, I saw our friend, the chief, followed by his entire band, coming across the long path toward the strip. By the time I had my gun put away, they were standing around the plane. The chief looked about with a puzzled expression and then spoke to me.

"Whah numbah one white mahstah?"

I knew he was wondering why Colonel Truxtun wasn't there for the python hunt, but I didn't know how to explain to him. The best I could do, trying to imitate the colonel's pidgin talk, was to say, "Numbah one white mahstah, 'e no come."

I don't know whether he understood me or not, but he looked most displeased, and he spoke harshly this time.

"Whah numbah one white mahstah?"

The friendliness that had characterized our earlier contacts with these people was obviously deteriorating rapidly, and I was acutely conscious of the fact that I was forty miles from any white man and nobody knew where I'd gone. I had my submachine gun but it was stowed in the plane. I had a .45 on my hip, but common sense told me that if they were so minded the men could have me drawn and quartered before I could even get it out of its holster. While I knew that missionaries had influenced these people in years past, I could not help remembering Colonel Truxtun's explanation of the patterns of welts on the faces and bodies of the older men, and thinking of the long abandoned mission-ary residence up in the hills. But I could think of no words with which to explain and apologize to the chief, who quite evidently was highly offended by Truxtun's failure to show up as agreed. And here was I, a lonely, bedraggled, and insignificant little lieutenant who couldn't even communicate.

"Numbah one white master, 'e no come."

No doubt about it now, the chief was highly teed off. Glowering in a very unpleasant way, he growled a few words to the men crowding around us, and they responded in kind, shuffling restlessly. Every man was armed with a bow or a spear, and each also had a knife of some variety, and I had a feeling that they would not hesitate to use them on me under present conditions. In short, I was scared, but I don't think I showed it. I tried not to show undue concern, but the situation called for some decisive action on my part.

I was standing beside the open door of my plane, the native men crowding close around me, the women and children pressing in all around even the tail of the L-4. Ignoring whatever more the chief might have had to say, I pulled the propeller through a couple of times and got it ready to start. I reached inside, cracked the throttle, and turned on the magneto switch. Then I waved my hand in a gesture that told them to stand back, and bracing my foot against the right wheel, pulled the prop through from the rear. The engine caught immediately, and I crawled inside.

All this activity on my part had momentarily taken their minds off the colonel, I guess, for they had just stood and watched. Now I revved the engine and they began to move back. I swung the tail around and they scattered out of the way. As soon as there was a path open, I was off—and I never returned.

The Massewang was a fine stream for bathing. It was swift and clear and cool as it hurried down out of the hills, and just below our airstrip was a rocky rapids in which we air section people had lots of fun while most of the other personnel of Div Arty seemed to prefer the salt water down where the supply boats came in. But one sad event is related in my mind to the Massewang. One day as several of us were swimming there, someone noticed that Hal Davis was floating off down the swift current, evidently unconscious. He was pulled out and taken to the medics, and his flying days were over. As I recall, they diagnosed his trouble as epilepsy. He returned stateside and became a maintenance officer at Post Field, Fort Sill. Dorie and I visited him and his wife when we got back to the States.

Coming back from the river one day, one of the boys found a human skull, stuck up on a stake in a corner of our tent, and we had many jokes at the expense of "George," as we called him. While we played cards and talked and laughed, George gazed solemnly and sadly at the ground from his place in the shadowy corner and never spoke a word. Eventually, one of the less sensitive souls in the outfit got the idea that an appropriate fate for George, as one of our enemies, would be placing him in our urinal as a target of sorts, and so there he went. That became George's salvation, for a visiting doctor recognized that George was not Japanese but Caucasian and, therefore, undoubtedly one of the Australian soldiers who had died in a fight with the Japanese there beside the Massewang.

Well, some of us had felt ashamed at treating the remains of any human being the way we had George, and now, knowing that he was one of our allies, we were horrified in retrospect at our own callousness. How could we make amends? We should have turned him over to the Australian officers across the river and let them handle it, but I guess we didn't think of that. Bill Brisley, as he often did, came up with what we all thought was an excellent idea, in this case a very romantic end for poor George.

On nights when the moon was bright, we sometimes went out over the ocean off Fortification Point and practiced our limited aerobatic routines. Brisley's idea was to clean George up and take him out there and bury him at sea. And so he did it, sending the pitiful remains of some Australian mother's lost son plunging from an American L-4, far down into the shimmering silver of a moonlit tropical sea.

The incident of George made me recall a lecture we'd had while attending the jungle warfare instructors' school on Oahu. The lecturer was an infantry battalion commander of another division that had recently participated in the conquest of one of the Japanese-occupied atolls in the Pacific. In the battle, he had won particular notice, and he related several bloody tales of the fight, but his principal theme was "HATE THE ENEMY!" The idea was that men would be motivated to fight better if they fiercely hated the enemy, and this officer's aim was to instill some of that hatred. To help do that, he brought along a skeleton, which he suspended from a wooden rack beside his lectern. He informed us that this was the remains of a Japanese soldier killed in the recent battle, and from time to time during his lecture he cursed and reviled the bones and viciously spat on them.

We listened, and maybe there were some in our large group who responded to the lecture as the officer desired—but I was not one of those. In fact, I was repelled by the brutality of his words and actions, especially by his desecration of the bones of this Japanese soldier who had honorably fought and died under the flag of his country, who was probably a beloved son, perhaps a husband and father, in any case a human being who in death deserved at least the dignity of a decent disposal of his remains. After the lecture, I talked about it with a number of men, and every one of them felt the same as I did. In the rest of that war and two other wars following it, I still could not find it in myself to actually hate individual enemy soldiers, who merely tried to do their duty as it was given to them. But I know quite well that there are veterans of that war who not only hated the Japanese then but continued to hate them—as if each Japanese soldier were not just as helplessly caught up in the war as we were ourselves.

I happened to be at Finschhafen one day when an LST arrived with a load of Japanese POWs from Hollandia, where the 24th Division had taken control. There were about 250 of them seated in a natural depression in the ground, surrounded by guards. I was told that these were the survivors of a much greater number that had started the trip. En route, some had died of sickness or wounds, and many had committed suicide, most by jumping overboard. This was their escape from what they considered the disgrace of surrender—or perhaps they feared the terrible death they had been told awaited them if captured by the Americans.

The prisoners seemed completely beaten and dejected, many looked sick, and all sat looking at the ground—all except one, who was right in the middle of the group, sitting on a log. He gazed around defiantly at the guards and the curious bystanders like me, and his eyes burned like fire with hate. Maybe if I had experienced what that man had, I could have learned to hate, too.

– Four –

TORNADO

TASK FORCE

There is nothing at all in my memory about our leaving Fortification Point, but we did, sometime along about the end of August 1944. I recall being aboard an LST, one of several that were shoving through sunny blue seas toward the northwest along New Guinea's long coast, while off to port was a bank of clouds beneath which I could see wet, forested hills. One of those people who always knows told me that we were in the vicinity of Wewak and Aitape.

The decks of the LST were crowded with the various vehicles of the 122d, each carefully laden in accordance with loading plans long before worked out by the brains of the battalion to be certain there was a proper place for everything, ready to be found and put into use with the least delay upon our arrival at our destination. Among the vehicles were the men, and somewhere aboard were two wooden crates containing two Piper L-4 airplanes.

On a fair afternoon the little convoy hove to a few hundred yards from shore at the eastern end of a long and shallow indentation of the coast called Maffin Bay. About ten or twelve miles farther up, the bay terminated at a blunt little peninsula on which lay the remnants of the town of Sarmi. The locale lay in that half of New Guinea that then belonged to the Netherlands but is today a part of Indonesia. It was to be here that elements of the Golden Cross Division, the 33d, would meet the enemy for the first time.

But not the entire division. The 123d Infantry and the 122d FA Bn formed the nucleus of a task force. There were small reinforcing elements from Engineer, Quartermaster, Signal, Ordnance, and Medical Reconnaissance Troop, among other groups, to enable the task force to operate independently of the division, and Btry B, 123d FA Bn, was attached to provide the longer range and harder punch of its 155 mm howitzers under control of the 122d. The whole thing was commanded by the 33d's assistant division commander, Brig. Gen. Donald Myers.

Other divisions—the 41st, 6th, and 31st—had already fought the hardest part of the war at Maffin Bay. The 41st and the 6th had been relieved to go on to other tasks. Now we were to relieve the 31st Division so it could prepare itself for the invasion of Morotai. The Japanese forces remaining in the area, however, could not be left to themselves, since they were quite capable of delivering artillery fire, if nothing more, against Wakde Air Base, which lay on a small island just off Maffin Bay. Therefore our mission was, first, to cover and assist the withdrawal of the 31st and, second, then to maintain the security of the Wakde air base to ensure its continued operation.

On 1 September, the enemy at Maffin Bay was well aware that a relief operation was in progress, so he took advantage of the excellent opportunity to pull off the best attack he could against the 31st. Anticipating that event, the 31st had strong patrols out, and as we arrived off the perimeter that afternoon we could see the fighting in progress up the beach beyond the Woske River. We could see a tank burning, and, nearer at hand, smoke was rising from a burning supply dump.

I don't remember going ashore, but a few hours later there was HQ Btry sitting on a big sandbar on the east side of the mouth of the sluggish Tor River. It was late in the day by then, and it had been decided that we would bivouac there for the night rather than try to set up in the darkness of the jungle that crowded the beach. We began to gather driftwood and improvise supports for our jungle hammocks in anticipation of a night of rest.

The jungle hammock incorporated in one item not only a hammock but also a roof and a mosquito bar into which one entered through a zippered opening. It offered reasonably comfortable repose, secure from mosquitoes, other insects, and rain. This was our first experience with them—and I don't think I ever used mine again.

I was fortunate to find some good pieces of drift and soon had my hammock securely slung above the loose, dry sand. With the lulling sound of the rolling surf nearby, it seemed to promise a night of pleasant repose. But for me this was not to be.

There was some sort of a general plan, as I understood, to furnish one case of beer per month to each soldier in our division and, I suppose, other divisions in this hot, humid, and utterly uncivilized part of the world—assuming, of course, that the soldier wanted it. But the 33d had been down there now for several months without having received the first bottle of brew. It just so happened that two or three months' ration for our troops had arrived at Base F just in time to join our convoy for Maffin Bay, and now the small freighter was given priority at the solitary small dock to unload the beer and then to reload with cargo of the outgoing 31st Division. My job, whether or not I might choose to accept it, was to supervise the unloading and proper distribution of that shipload of beer.

For the task, I was given a six-by-six truck and a platoon of infantry. Besides a driver and assistant driver, I put four armed guards on each truck as it was loaded and proceeded along the dark, rutted, muddy roads through the thinned-out jungle inside the perimeter to find the unit for which the load was destined. Some of the detail worked in the hold, filling the cargo net, while others were on the dock, loading the trucks. I moved about the ship and the dock, doing what I could to prevent the theft of the entire cargo. Members of the ship's crew would sneak cases into remote areas of their vessel; our own men would hide cases on the wooden bracing under the dock; men on the trucks, including the guards, would divert cases of beer to their own personal or their units' interests; and other cases simply vanished into thin air. This went on all night, and when all accounts were considered, it was estimated that the equivalent of one truckload of beer had failed to reach any known destination in the task force.

122d Field Artillery Battalion Air Section at beach strip near Tor River, Maffin Bay, Dutch New Guinea, 1944. From left, standing: Don Vineyard and Raymond Kerns; kneeling: Wendell Young, Kennis Allen, and Eddie Janes holding the section's K-20 camera (Photograph by Ted Kinsch).

It was dawn when the beer job was done and I returned to our bivouac on the sandbar, to a scene of utter disaster. For reasons known only to those who understand the ways of the sea, the combination of tide and surf during the night had swept suddenly through the camp. Men sleeping snugly inside their zipped-up hammocks were rudely awakened by being plunged into chilly saltwater as their improvised driftwood supports collapsed. In the darkness and confusion, many hammocks were severely ripped as soldiers struggled to get out of them. Shoes and clothing, web equipment and weapons left outside the hammocks were scattered, buried, soaked; and in the gray morning light, bedraggled and disconsolate soldiers wandered about, trying to collect their belongings. My unoccupied hammock had come down, too, and I joined the dismal search.

But before the day was over, HQ Btry was properly encamped in its pyramidal tents among the huge trees just off the beach a short distance east of the Tor. Right in front of the camp, Vin and I selected a stretch of beach to be our airstrip, and the boys uncrated and assembled our planes. Initially, they slept in the crates, but before long they, too, had a tent, and we used the crates as a workshop and for storing air section gear and supplies. To keep off the surf, we built a low sandbag dike along the seaward side of our strip. And we took to the air.

There was no such thing as a briefing or an orientation by 31st Division pilots who had been flying in the area. Vin and I simply began feeling our way. We did know that the Woske River, a winding, muddy, sullen stream a quarter mile west of our nearest perimeter positions, was essentially the boundary between "us" and "them." Crossing the Woske, we—each on his own—flew on up the shoreline another three miles or so to the Sawar Airdrome, occupied by the enemy but no longer used for flying. Its runway and dispersal areas were overgrown with tall grass. At the far end of the airdrome was a swampy little creek for which it was named, and another mile brought us to the nose of a low plateau called Mount Haako—which marked about the limit of the seven-mile range of our 105s. Beyond Mount Haako, some ten miles from our airstrip, was a seven-hundred acre clearing split down the middle by a dirt road that intersected the beach road perhaps two miles from the ruins of Sarmi. That was the Foe Maoe Plantation.

We explored up the Tor and the Woske, with their mud bars and their numerous crocodiles, their overhanging jungle, and occasional black natives in dugout canoes. Away from the shore, the deep jungle was unbroken except by rare small clearings and, in one area, a cluster of small black-mud knolls kept barren by the feet of natives who lived there and who scattered like flushed quail into the jungle as we flew over. A few miles up that way was a jungle-covered eminence called Mount Aftawadona, a position the Japanese stubbornly defended in an effort to keep open an escape route for their survivors of the battle for Hollandia.

In the relatively open coastal areas, I saw many shell holes and bomb craters, many destroyed trucks, a few wrecked tanks and airplanes, and various areas where trenches and foxholes had been dug and bunkers constructed. In many of the places where shells or bombs had thrown up fresh earth, the Japanese troops were raising little vegetable gardens. But I flew for a week without seeing a single man of the two thousand troops the enemy was thought to have left in the area. If Vin spotted one during that time, he said nothing to me about it. Meanwhile, our expanding explorations had taken us well beyond the range of our guns, not because we were asked to go but simply because we were curious.

I was flying over the Foe Maoe Plantation about a week after we arrived on the scene. It was late afternoon and the sun was shining, casting long shadows from the few posts still standing along the line of an old fence on one side of the plantation road. And then I suddenly realized that the shadow of one of those posts seemed to indicate that the post was split at the bottom and set into two holes, although it was just one post farther up. The truth finally bored its way through my skull: I was looking at a Japanese soldier!

He was the first one I'd ever seen in the wild. I had made a breakthrough, of a kind, in my career as an observer, and I was really excited about it. But there was no way I could attack him, out there even beyond range of the attached 155s. Nevertheless, I felt a compulsion to let him know that I had discovered him, so I dove right down at him as if I intended to scoop him up with my landing gear. As soon as it became evident to him that I had seen him, the Japanese—and two other nearby fence posts—dived for the roadside ditch. I passed low over them and then headed for home, exulting as if I'd won a great victory.

After that, Vin and I both began to spot Nips all over the place, but usually out of cannon range.

★

My first fire mission on a live target came nearly two weeks after our arrival at Maffin. Company B of the 123d had crossed the Woske and moved up to the Sawar drome in one of the first of many patrols the task force conducted for experience and for keeping up with what the enemy might be doing. Vin and I alternated in keeping contact with Company B and a smaller patrol that had gone up toward Aftawadona. I happened to be overhead when the company reached the limit of its planned penetration and halted at Sawar Creek. Before starting their return toward the Woske, they needed to replenish their water supply, so several men took canteens and crawled toward the bank of the little creek. At that point, a hidden machine gun opened on them and killed Lt. Walter Roper, a platoon leader—the first man of the 33d Division to be killed in action in World War II.

I searched from the air, and those on the ground did their best to spot the location of the lethal enemy gun, but for several minutes we did not succeed. The company dropped mortar shells blindly into the area across the creek. Then S.Sgt. Winfield Green volunteered to crawl forward and recover Lieutenant Roper's body. This drew more fire, and someone on the ground spotted the creek-bank bunker near the mouth of the stream. Its firing slit covered both the stream and the beach.

The location was described to me, and when I identified it I called our FDC with my first combat-fire mission, giving them map coordinates and the nature of the target. Since it was a point-destruction type of target, the mission was assigned to the 155 mm howitzer battery attached to us. The first round from that extremely accurate weapon burst a few yards beyond the creek, so I sent a sensing that would cause the range to be shortened with no change in deflection. The second round burst in the creek directly in front of the bunker, and I split the bracket and called for fire for effect—which, in a point-destruction type mission such as this, would be a series of single rounds fired by the same piece. But there was no need for a series: the first round, in effect, was a target hit. It laid open the top of the bunker, and Japanese soldiers came pouring out, running for predug foxholes in the flats beyond the creek. I counted eleven of them, and as they ran I noted a couple of secondary explosions—of their ammunition, I suppose—that completed destruction of the bunker and, I imagine, finished off a few wounded who had not gotten out.

Its mission had been completed, so Company B broke contact and withdrew rapidly down the beach, carrying the body of its unfortunate officer. It reached Maffin without further incident, and Staff Sergeant Green became first in the division to be decorated with the Silver Star for gallantry in action. I'm not certain, but I think I had become the first pilot, if not the first observer, in the division to adjust fire on the enemy. It was rather late in the war, 13 September 1944, nearly three years since my only earlier shot at the enemy, the strafing dive-bomber over Schofield.

Vin and I saw and recognized the enemy and his installations and equipment more and more as days passed—but it was seldom easy. Japanese camouflage and concealment measures were excellent, and their discipline was seldom breached. In most situations, the Japanese soldier would freeze and not move a muscle if he thought he might be under observation but not yet detected. One ruse the enemy used successfully for a while against Vin and me at Maffin was to pretend that their good trucks were wrecks. They would carefully cover their tracks, park the vehicles in the same spots all the time, and do whatever they reasonably could to hide the fact that they had been moved. And they did most of their hauling at night.

Once, however, I wandered up to Foe Maoe when they either didn't expect company or had such an urgent task that they had to risk daylight operations. I spotted several of their trucks in a ragged convoy on the plantation road, and I looked at them carefully as I approached. But they were far out of our range—we had no responsive air support for such minor targets—so I just looked and then turned to leave. Looking back, I saw the trucks begin to move. I turned back toward them, and they immediately halted. I turned away and they started again. For about thirty minutes I tormented them that way. I guess they never caught on.

Although we often found worthwhile targets within our range, they seldom were as good as those we couldn't hit. This led us to consider alternative means of clobbering our neighbors across the Woske. We began to carry fragmentation hand grenades to throw at patrols we caught in the open, and sometimes we got a little effect with them.

Returning from a special long-range reconnaissance some thirty miles beyond Sarmi up toward Cap d'Urville, I was flying downwind, very low over the beach and looking into the shaded trails under the jungle, trying to see evidence of enemy movement of troops from the west into our area, which our intelligence staff suspected. In all that long and rather nervous trip, I saw but one Japanese. He was all alone, strolling along the firm sand in the same direction I was going, fully equipped with field gear, his rifle slung. As I came along behind him, I suppose the noise of my L-4 was covered by the roar of the surf, and he didn't hear me until I was within a hundred yards of him. By then, I had the pin out of a grenade.

He stopped, turned, started to unsling his rifle, decided it was too late, and started running toward the jungle. From an altitude of about six feet, I rolled the grenade along the sand. He saw it coming and fell flat on his face. The grenade exploded just as it struck his side, and he was lifted a foot or two into the air. I had pulled up and into a steep left turn over the water, and I saw him immediately get up onto his feet. Clasping his arms around his stomach, he staggered about for a few steps, then collapsed and lay still.

Up to that point, I had thought only of attacking an enemy, but now I felt very sorry for the poor guy lying down there, a simple soldier who only a minute earlier had been walking peacefully along the pleasant beach, perhaps daydreaming of his home and family, and who now was a bloody hulk breathing his last. What bothered me was that it didn't have to be that way. I could just as easily have gone on my way and let him live, and I immediately wished that I had done so.

Sergeant Allen went out with me one day, and he took several frag grenades along, just in case. Sure enough, we caught a patrol of about a dozen men in a relatively open area, and he wanted to hit them. It was his first experience at dropping things from the air, but his first grenade hit right in the middle of the patrol, which had flattened on the ground. But the grenade bounced well away from them before it exploded.

"Go around again, sir. I'll get 'em this time!"

"OK. You get your grenade ready and I'll tell you when to drop it."

Just as I was turning toward the Japs for the second try, I heard the flat pop that I knew meant a grenade had been armed. At the same time, I heard Allen curse loudly and emphatically. I looked back to see him reach under his seat for the deadly little bomb that had slipped out of his hand, and then he flung the hissing grenade out the door. It burst only a few feet from the plane, and Allen and the boys had lots of small fabric holes to patch later.

Until now, it had never occurred to me to wonder whether any of those Nip soldiers died from laughing at us.

Just at the west end of our beach strip was a corps battery of 155 mm guns—not howitzers, but guns, which have longer tubes and longer range. And they have a tremendous muzzle blast. I know, because they fired all four of them together one day when I was about a hundred feet above the muzzles on final approach to our landing strip. The corps battery also had a couple of pilots, and those lads seemed only too glad to leave the enemy-occupied parts of the region to Vin and me while they waited for movement to somewhere else. They did most of their flying eastward, and I don't blame them.

Late one afternoon I had completed registering our batteries on the base point and various checkpoints—a daily routine—and was about to land when FDC asked me to fly on eastward down the beach as far as my fuel supply would permit and see if I could find the two corps pilots. Both in one plane, they had flown off that way earlier in the afternoon. They had to be down somewhere by this time.

I flew a long way down the coast. I don't know how far. My fuel got dangerously low, but I hated to give up when just one more minute might discover them and perhaps save them from some horrible fate. And, sure enough, just at dusk, as I was actually starting to turn back, I saw the plane, sitting at an odd angle on the sand. As I flew toward it, I saw one of the pilots run from a native village nearby and climb into the plane. His radio was weak from earlier calls for help, but he managed to make me understand that they had intentionally landed to visit the village, had hit a log in the sand, and had washed out the gear and prop. The friendly villagers had assured them that there were no Japanese around anywhere and that they would be OK until help could be sent tomorrow, he said.

Before his message was finished, I was heading back toward Maffin, and in the last fading light I saw the fuel gauge hanging by its nose on the filler cap, indicating empty. The minutes from there on were long, indeed, and it was with exceeding great joy that I finally sighted the lights from HQ Btry tents among the trees. I called FDC as I approached and asked them to get some light on the strip for me. They replied that Lieutenant Vineyard was getting some vehicles together and would have the strip lighted in just a few minutes.

"Hell, I can't wait! This thing is likely to quit any second. I've got to land now!"

I flew past where I knew the strip was, but I couldn't make it out at all. All I could see was the few dim lights in the tents back among the trees, but I knew the strip was right in front of them and six or eight feet lower. I also knew that the strip was not as wide as the wingspan of the L-4, and if the left wing didn't project over our sandbag dike, the right wing would hit either our crates or the trees.

I lined up and started in. I was on very short final when Vin came bouncing up in a jeep, shining its headlights across the approach end of the strip. That helped me some, but once I passed the jeep and flared for landing I could see absolutely nothing. I fully expected to wash out my ship, but she rolled right down the sand just as nicely as if I could see and guide her. As I came to a halt, Sergeant Allen came running with a flashlight to lead me in.

I wondered where in the hell that flashlight had been when I needed it. But Kennis Allen was much too conscientious and dignified a man for a whippersnapper like me to take to task. I knew there was some good reason for its not being seen before.

I blasted the tail around to follow Allen to our tie-down—and the engine quit, out of fuel. I swear it's true!

In our quest for longer range strike capability, the AAF maintenance people on Wakde were very helpful. Of course, it was Vin who made the contacts over there, and the first weapon he got for us was a supply of twenty-five-pound antipersonnel bombs. They were a type the AAF used in clusters, I suppose, for they referred to them as cluster bombs. These were too heavy for a pilot to handle safely alone, so we carried a bombardier when we used them, either one of the air section enlisted men or Vin and me riding double. Each of these bombs on its nose had a little spinner that required an eight-hundred-foot fall to release a safety ring and arm the fuse, and this handicapped us quite severely. Dropping from that high an altitude, we were not sufficiently accurate. So we held

TORNADO TASK FORCE 151

the bomb out the door in the slipstream until it armed, and then we could drop it from whatever altitude we wished. We usually dropped them from four hundred feet, getting more accuracy and not too many fragments. We did a bit of damage with them but nothing real serious, as far as we knew. But the supply dried up after a few weeks.

And then Vin flew the *Arizona Keed* back from Wakde one day with a light .30-caliber machine gun mounted between the landing wheels. The armorers over there had taken this well-worn gun off of an AAF plane of some kind. They made a special bracket to sling it from the cabane "V" of the landing gear and ran tubular braces from the breech to the lower longerons of the L-4. On top of the gun they mounted a steel box that held 250 rounds of ammo. They put a storage battery on the floor between the pilot's feet and wired up a solenoid firing mechanism. It worked like a charm. The line of fire passed about two inches below the low point of the propeller arc, and it converged at two hundred yards with a line of sight across the top of the fuel filler cap. The gauge wire served admirably as a vertical reticule for the sight.

I can't give you full details of Vineyard's career with his Piper fighter, but I recall that he shot up at least one Japanese patrol and strafed some spots he considered worth the ammo. And he lit into a large building we had discovered in the jungle near the Foe Maoe Plantation. His tracers set the thatched roof on fire and the whole place burned to the ground. Only as it burned were we able to see indications that it might have been a hospital.

And then it was my turn to try the gun. I had two definite targets in mind before I took off from the beach strip, and I headed directly to Foe Maoe. The *Arizona Keed* felt strange to me, since I wasn't used to flying it, but it clearly was very nose-heavy with the gun, the ammo, the battery, and me, all in the front. The balance provided by the SCR-610 radio and its power-pack back on the chart board behind the rear seat was barely adequate to make the plane flyable.

I passed over the jungle inland from Mount Haako and came over Foe Maoe Plantation from the rear. At about a thousand feet, I flew down the plantation road until I saw the first element of my target: two "destroyed" trucks off to the left of the road near a creek, close together. I dove on them, building up speed to about the redline, and when I thought it was time I pressed the firing switch.

As the tracers raced out in front of the plane, I could very distinctly feel deceleration from the recoil. The nose wanted to tuck under. But I could see the bullets kicking up dust around the nearest truck and out of the trash that camouflaged it. A man leaped from the cab and flopped into a nearby hole. I shifted my fire to the second truck and tried to put the bullets into the engine. And then, very quickly, I was past the trucks and heading for the second and bigger of my targets.

Across the beach road from the junction of the plantation road, a large dump of fuel in drums occupied the space between the beach road and the beach itself. There were scattered coco palms in the dump and palm fronds had been laid over the drums, but the nature of the installation had long been evident to us. And so, as I passed the trucks, now down to about two hundred feet and skimming along at about 120 at full throttle, I headed for that fuel dump. I watched the bullets knocking dust out of the palm fronds, I saw the tracers disappearing into the drums, and I watched for something to happen. It began to look futile, but just as my last rounds went out, I saw a small explosion and a couple of drums rolling around. Then I passed over just above the palms and kept going on out to sea for about a half mile before turning down the coast for home.

It was noon when I landed, so I immediately went to the officers' mess tent, where most of the HQ and HQ Btry officers were having lunch. But as I walked up there, I heard someone at the EM mess tent yell, "Three cheers for Lieutenant Kerns! Hip-hip—" And then all the men yelled "Hooray!"—and repeated it three times.

It's a fact that I had no idea why the men were cheering me and all the officers smiling.

"What's that all about?" I asked.

"Haven't you looked up toward Sarmi?" someone replied.

I stepped outside the tent and looked. A column of oily black smoke was rising high into the clear noon sky. Occasionally a balloon of red flame would rise like an elevator from the base of the column until it dulled and was lost in the billows of smoke. Even from ten miles away, it was an impressive sight. A squadron of A-20 attack bombers had recently hit the area without any such dramatic display—although the squadron lost two planes and four men in the attack. I felt a little bit like Frank Luke, back from another successful balloon busting. An aerial photo later showed that the fire went far past where I had hit the fuel dump and advanced through other supplies of some kind as it moved toward Sarmi and out of the picture.

But General Myers, too, had been impressed by the big smoke far up the coast, and he wanted to know how it came to be. Since the gun was on his plane, Vin was elected to explain. He later told us that General Myers, with tongue in cheek, chewed him out for several minutes, lecturing him about compliance with directives prohibiting weapons on artillery airplanes (the AAF didn't like competition, I guess); and then, taking his tongue out of his cheek, told him, "Get that damned gun off of that plane!"

Soon after that, we were forbidden to drop any object from our planes except message bags and smoke grenades. It put a bad crimp in the private war of Vineyard and Kerns.

There came a day when the situation at the beach strip became unmanageable. For several days we had been fighting a losing battle against the surf, and on this day we were overwhelmed. The dike vanished in rolling waves and shifting sand, and it was getting worse by the minute. Vin was in the air, we had significant combat action going on, and I would soon have to relieve him. I had FDC tell Vin to plan on returning to Wakde at the end of his mission, and I got the men busy loading our truck, ready to be taken to Wakde on the ferry as soon as possible. With Sergeant Allen and his toolbox in my L-4, I began my takeoff run down what used to be our private airstrip.

I started my run just as a wave broke, hoping I could get airborne before the next wave came in. I almost did but not quite. I went roaring down the beach, the wave came roaring onto the beach, and when we met, the L-4 disappeared in a cloud of spray. Out of that it came waddling like a duck, barely rolling but its engine still roaring. Maybe I could beat

FOE MAOE PLANTATION
ENTRANCE. The straight
road running inland
from the coast passes the
northwest end of Mount
Haako and runs into and
through the middle of the
seven-hundred-acre plantation (not cultivated during
the war). The fuel dump I
burned on that same flight
was just left of the road
intersection, between the
coast road and the beach.
This road junction was
about ten miles northwest
of our nearest positions.

the next wave. Well, I almost did, but not quite. Again the heavy spray drenched us and brought us nearly to a standstill, but we came out with the throttle wide open as we went on down the beach, already far past the end of what we had considered our strip.

Unknown to Allen and me, most of HQ Btry was watching us, and they were having the biggest laugh of all their time in New Guinea. Some were literally rolling on the ground as they watched the stubborn little airplane trying so hard to fly but being repeatedly defeated by the surf at the critical instant and momentarily vanishing in the white spray.

I don't know just how many times we hit the surf, but it was many. We did not completely circle the island of New Guinea on this takeoff run, but we were far from the old airstrip before I finally managed to stagger off in a three-point attitude and coax the L-4 to remain just above the water until it slowly picked up enough speed to climb. And then we headed across the eight miles or so of water to Wakde—with Allen and me soaked to the skin and water running out of every drain hole the plane had.

At Wakde, we made ourselves at home in the wingless fuselage of a wrecked C-47 and tied our L-4s down nearby. We soon made a telephone connection with our S-2, and we were doing business as usual.

Flying from Wakde was fine, except for the fact that we were across several miles of ocean from our battalion. General Myers got the engineers busy building us a strip at Maffin, but it took time. Meanwhile, we hobnobbed to some degree with the AAF people who, permanently or as transients, inhabited the aircraft maintenance base there.

Air traffic was light, so our lack of radio communication with the tower was not a serious handicap. The long runway enabled us to take off in whatever direction suited us, regardless of wind, and the tower usually let us go as we wished. We'd taxi out to the runway near our C-47 home and swing around to face the tower. They'd give us a green light and away we'd fly. But on one occasion, this informality led to a near tragedy.

It was to be our last patrol of the day. I taxied out, faced the tower, and—most unusual—got a red light. However, this was followed almost immediately by a green light, so I swung my tail toward the tower and accelerated out onto the runway, heading west into the low-hanging sun. I was hardly more than airborne, no more than a hundred feet above the surface, when I had just a feeling, not a real sighting, of something between me and the sun. I rolled hard to my left, and as I did so a P-40 slid by on my right so close that his right wing almost hit my landing gear. But it didn't hit, so I continued on my mission and soon forgot all about the incident.

When I returned at dusk, there was a P-40 lying on its back in the middle of the runway, and when I went into our abode Vin told me that I was to call the base operations officer immediately. As soon as I had reported to our S-2 by phone, I called the officer. He lit into me without a preamble, saying that I had disregarded a red light and taken off in the face of traffic, causing the crash of the P-40 and injury to its pilot. I insisted that the red light had been followed by a green—but it began to dawn on me that the green light must have been intended for the landing P-40, which had been right in line beyond me as seen from the tower.

I was beginning to visualize myself as a nonflying type when someone interrupted the base operations officer and he told me to hold on. Soon he came back on the phone with an entirely different tone and said that the P-40 pilot had regained consciousness and had said my L-4 had nothing at all to do with his crash—in fact, he hadn't even seen me at all, which made me very glad indeed that I had sensed his coming. He was making an emergency landing because of trouble with the fighter's hydraulic system, and his brakes had locked up on touchdown, causing the nose-over. So I was off the hook.

My best pre-Army friend was C. C. "Buzz" Perkins, a good old West Virginia boy living in Ohio, now a radio operator and gunner on a 5th Air Force B-25 based at Sansapor, far up at the west end of New Guinea on the Vogelkopf. When three pilots from his outfit showed up at Wakde to take home three of their ships, I got a three-day leave of absence from Captain Ryan and flew as copilot with a Lieutenant Hull in one of the Mitchell bombers. That was a big deal for me, although it was nerve-racking to hold position on the right side of our "V" formation. From the right-hand seat, I could see absolutely nothing of the lead ship except the top of the arc of its port propeller, and it made me most uncomfortable. I would ease out and down a bit so I could see more, but Hull would impatiently order me to close back in. Of course, from his seat he could see the entire plane, and I think he got a kick out of harassing me.

We refueled at Biak Island, where I saw the only Red Cross doughnut girls I ever saw during the whole war, so far as I can recall. To receive such services, you must be at the right echelon of the right outfit and in the right place at the right time, and I guess I never was. And then we were off to Sansapor.

In order to associate freely with Buzz and his enlisted friends, I removed my insignia of rank and passed as a private. That was easy for me. I looked like a yardbird to start with. I had a good visit with my old buddy and greatly enjoyed the navy beans served at their mess. They were sick of them, but I hadn't seen my favorite kind of bean in ages. My appetite took no notice at all when a machine-gun opened fire on the nearby defense perimeter and all my gun-shy companions in the serving line hit the deck. They had been running low-level missions to Celebes (now Sulawesi), where machine guns gave them hallelujah every day. And, in fact, they were celebrating the rescue a day or two earlier of their colonel, who had been downed on Celebes.

The story current among these wild-blue boys had to do with the fact that the rescued colonel was known to be the well-to-do owner of a large ranch in Texas. In expressing his gratitude to the young soldier who had sighted him and brought about his rescue, the colonel told him that whatever he wanted he could have. "Just name it," he invited.

"Well, sir," said the lad, "if you will just get me a discharge I'll go on home and take care of our ranch."

I heard there another tale in which the hero was a former member of my old outfit, the 89th FA Bn, in Hawaii. I had been acquainted with him but, unfortunately, I can't recall his name. He had transferred to the AAF in the early months of the war and had become a B-25 crew member; I believe they called him a flight engineer. On a bombing mission, his plane had been set upon by a number of Japanese fighters and riddled with bullets. Miraculously, the plane continued to fly, but every member of the crew was killed except the engineer, who got the dead pilot out of his seat and took over the controls. By some quirk of fate, he managed to get away from the fighters and flew the ship back to Sansapor. When he contacted the tower, he was ordered to bail out rather than try to land the plane, but he refused, thinking someone aboard might still be alive. Anyway, he said, the only parachutes he could reach had been damaged by the gunfire and were not reliable. So he brought the plane down. And he was successful in the landing until near the end of his rollout, when he veered off to one side and nosed into a dirt revetment. He was not seriously hurt.

It happened that Buzz was due to leave with his crew and their plane on a trip to Darwin, Australia, where the boys would get some well-deserved R & R while the plane was in maintenance. In preparation, Buzz had saved an entire Val-Pac full of cartons of cigarettes, because they cost him $1 a carton and were worth $5 a carton in Darwin. But his farewell to me was quite an emotional one. He climbed up into the belly of the B-25, then stuck his head back down to say goodbye once more, and I saw tears running up his forehead.

I caught a ride a few minutes later on a C-47 bound for Hollandia. En route, we flew right over Maffin Bay but they could not stop to let me off. At Hollandia, however, I quickly found another C-47 going to Wakde, and again I got a little multiengine copilot time.

It was dark when we landed at Wakde, and I barely had time to catch the last scheduled ferry run to Maffin. The ferry was an LCVP (Landing Craft, Vehicle and Personnel) operated by a sergeant of the Quartermaster Corps. The only other passenger was Lt. Steve Allured of my battery. Steve and I stretched out on the cool steel deck and talked as the small craft wallowed along through the dark waves. It was an overcast night, pitch black, and there was nothing to see, so we just talked and smoked. But after more than an hour, I raised up and looked ahead, expecting to see the beacon light at Maffin Beach close at hand. There was a light not far ahead but it didn't look quite like the Maffin beacon. Far back down the beach to our left rear was a light that I could not identify, and beginning to fade over the horizon astern were the lights of Wakde.

Steve and I discussed the lights for a couple of minutes before I called the sergeant's attention to the light on the port quarter.

"Sergeant, what's that light back here to our left rear?"

"I don't know, sir. I've been wondering about that. There's not sup-posed to be anything down that way."

"It looks just like the beacon at Maffin, doesn't it?"

"Yes, sir, but it's not. The Maffin beacon is right ahead of us here."

"The trip seems to be taking longer tonight than usual."

"Yes, it is. I guess there must be some unusual current along here, or something. But we'll be there very shortly, sir."

I had a feeling that something was wrong, and I began trying to make out the horizon over the land to our left. It was very dark, but I could faintly see a long, low, flat-topped shape that could only be Mount Haako. With that as a reference point, I determined that the light toward which the ferry was heading was approximately at the point where I had burned the fuel dump at the entrance to Foe Maoe Plantation. We were within minutes of landing in the midst of the enemy, at least eight miles from the nearest point of our own lines, ten miles from Maffin Beach.

"Hey, Sergeant, we're heading for the wrong place. This light back here is Maffin. That one ahead is at Foe Maoe Plantation, in the enemy area."

Standing at the wheel on his tiny armor-plate bridge, the sergeant chuckled.

"No, sir, this is Maffin ahead of us. I don't know what that is back there, but I'll report it when we get in and they'll probably investigate it."

"Sergeant, I'm telling you, I can see the west end of Mount Haako right over there. If you land us up there at that light we'll all be dead within five minutes. Let's head back down the coast to the other light."

"Sir, believe me, I make this run every day and lots of nights. I know what I'm doing. This is Maffin Beach right ahead of us. We'll be there in a few minutes and you'll see that I'm right."

"If you take us in there, Sergeant, we'll never get out alive. Turn back to this other light. I'm Lieutenant Kerns of the 122d Field Artillery, and I'm telling you to turn right now. That's an order."

"Well, OK, sir—but I'm going to be in a lot of trouble."

"You won't be in any trouble, Sergeant. I'll take responsibility."

The sergeant was not convinced of his error until we were close enough for him to recognize the familiar scene at the little Maffin dock. He was astonished. He did not understand how he could have made such a mistake. Neither did I.

★

An AAF transport outfit equipped with C-47s spent a few days at Wakde while we were there. The pilots were amazed to learn that we regularly flew over Japanese territory in our vulnerable little planes, and they asked if we ever saw any enemy troops. Upon being assured that we saw them every day, they were still more incredulous, since they had been in the theater for months and had never seen an enemy. One of their number, a Lieutenant Scarr, asked Vin if he could go along on a flight and get a chance to see his first enemy soldier.

To be reasonably sure of getting Scarr a close-up look at a Nip, Vin took him far up beyond Sarmi and flew low along the beach, looking back under the trees. As they passed the mouth of a small creek, they saw a soldier sitting on a rock, washing his feet in the stream. Scarr had his pistol in hand, and he snapped a quick shot at the unfortunate bather as they passed. The man slumped over into the water and lay still. It was one of those one-in-a-million shots—which seem to happen with remarkable frequency.

It didn't take long for the engineers to get our new strip completed at Maffin, and as soon as they did we moved back to the main island. The strip was diagonal to the shoreline, and our takeoff lane was right over the Maffin dock. We always took off that way, because tall trees and 122d headquarters and firing battery positions near the other end made climbing out a bit difficult, but we landed in either direction. Along the inland side of the strip was jungle, with the perimeter a hundred yards or so out. On the other side was the camp of Company G, 123d Infantry. The strip was surfaced maybe thirty feet wide with PSP, and at two spots it had tracks of PSP where we could pull off the runway to our tie-downs. We felt as if we had our own AAF base.

You understand, I think, that the enemy could have made life much more interesting for us than he usually did. He didn't like our artillery, he didn't like the occasional air strikes, he just didn't like to be seen; therefore, until he knew he had been discovered, he kept a very low profile, and even then, except for rifles, he was usually careful not to invest ammo unless there was a good chance of worthwhile returns. But when he did cut loose, he could be rather discouraging.

According to our S-2, headquarters of the bypassed Japanese forces in the area were in the seaward cliffs of Mount Haako. From those low bluffs, a slope with scattered coco palms ran down a few hundred yards to the beach road. The location was a hot spot, well beyond range of our cannon, so Vin and I had not been pressing our luck too much in there. However, on one particular day I decided to have a good close look.

I roared out over Maffin Dock that morning and headed northwest at treetop level behind Mount Haako. When I reached an area near the northwest end of the mountain, where it was still about four hundred or five hundred feet high, I suddenly cut right and climbed over the mountain, still near the treetops, bearing hard right to stay out of the antiaircraft fire I knew would be waiting for me if I got too close to the old fuel fire area. Descending on the ocean side, I was down to no more than a hundred feet above the trees as I passed over a rocky point where the beach cut in almost to the road. (The spot can be seen at the right end of the aerial photo of the Mount Haako area.) It was at that point, still more than two miles from the enemy headquarters, that a Japanese soldier appeared a short distance ahead, running hard down the middle of the road as if trying to outrun me.

Thinking about it later, it seemed to me that he may have been a decoy, sent out for the express purpose of leading me all the way into the trap. Or maybe he was running to man a gun in the local air defense setup. At the time, however, I thought only of striking at him, so I grabbed a rifle grenade, hastily pulled the safety pin, and dropped it like a tiny bomb as I came up behind the fleeing soldier. I really didn't expect to harm him, only let him know that I'd seen him and possibly scare him a little. Employed in this manner, the grenade ordinarily would have had little effect against personnel on the ground, but it was the great misfortune of that brave young man that the grenade detonated on some obstruction just above him, possibly a tree limb, and it appeared to me

MOUNT HAAKO AREA. These two overlapping aerial photos show the Mount Haako area. The cove at left is the site of the Japanese headquarters in the Maffin Bay area. At right, where the beach cuts in almost to the road, I hit a solitary Japanese soldier with a rifle grenade and received forty-seven holes in my L-4, including one that locked my right wheel and blew out the tire. Note the Japanese barge grounded on a reef near the right of the picture. The right edge of this picture almost touches the one on page 154, showing the entrance to the Foe Maoe Plantation. The left edge of the photograph is about half a mile from the south end of Mount Haako and the maximum range of our 105 mm howitzers. At that limit, the enemy placed a big red warning sign by the road.

that the armor-piercing slug struck him squarely between the shoulders. He fell sprawling in the middle of the road.

As if the explosion had been a signal, three machine guns opened fire at the same instant. There was a light gun behind me, a light gun ahead of me, and a single heavy machine gun that seemed to be just under my right wing. The air crackled and popped all around me as I put the L-4 over on its left wingtip and shoved down toward the water, scooting away from the beach at about a forty-five-degree angle and wishing the airplane were a submarine. The two light guns soon stopped firing, but the heavy machine gun just kept hammering away, and I felt as if every bullet and tracer was coming straight into my spine. I could see the tracers going by and hear the bullets striking the plane. Skinny as I was in those days, I involuntarily tried to make myself narrower, already feeling the bullet that I fully expected would find me at any instant. They were hitting the plane—how could they miss me?

But they did. The last burst died away and I ventured to turn parallel to the shoreline and make for home as I looked around to see what damage had been done.

I could see that the right wheel was damaged, the tire blown out, but the engine was running smoothly, the controls were all functioning, and there was no real problem—except, possibly, upon landing. I reported the facts to FDC and told them I might have some trouble getting the plane down safely, so would they please have a medic stand by at the airstrip, just in case I should nose over? They would. I didn't really expect serious trouble, but I've always believed in being careful.

I set the L-4 down on the right side of the PSP-surfaced strip, with the right wheel held off as long as airspeed would allow. When the damaged wheel had to come down, I jammed my heel hard on the left brake as I opened the throttle and hauled back on the stick to hold the tail down. The plane veered off the PSP to the right into the black mud, with the tail so high the prop should also have hit the mud, but it didn't. As the tail started back down, I let off the back pressure and she settled gently into a normal attitude—except for the flat tire.

One of the slugs from the heavy gun had gone through the wheel and brake drum, locking them together. Sergeant Allen reported that he and the crew patched forty-seven bullet holes in the fuselage and wings but found no other serious damage. There were quite a few vital parts inside L-4 #79608, but there was also a lot of empty space in there.

★

A military force facing an opponent of overwhelming strength often comes up with clever ideas to try to reduce the odds against itself, and the Japanese were very good at that. When the Japs stopped flying from the Sawar Drome, they left there a number of hundred-pound aerial bombs, and the ground troops occupying the strip concealed some of them at strategic points, wired for detonation from a remote position, as part of their defenses. One of our patrols had suffered a number of casualties from one of these at the east end of the airstrip.

One day I was asked to take a close look at the numerous bunkers along the beach at Sawar Drome to determine whether any of them were occupied. Vineyard and I often flew along that stretch right down on the sand, so it was no big deal to me. But as I buzzed along at ten feet, alternately glancing at the bunkers and at the beach ahead of me, I spotted the noses of two of those hundred-pound bombs protruding about a foot above the surf-washed sand no more than seventy-five yards ahead of me. It was very close to where the patrol had been blasted, and I instantly knew what they were. In the same instant, I realized that they might well be intended for remote detonation as one of our planes passed over them, and still in that same instant I pulled up, up, and away as violently as the plane would respond. I warned Vin, and we avoided that beach thereafter.

Since the rest of the 33d Division still was not into combat, some of the junior infantry officers were sent up to visit with our task force—which, by the way, had inherited from previous forces at Maffin the dramatic title "Tornado Task Force"—to get the feel of enemy contact. One lieutenant, not a flying officer, went out with me one day to see a Jap soldier, and he had his M-1 rifle along.

Flying over a long, narrow clearing along a jungle trail that I think ran between Aftawadona and Foe Maoe, we saw several Nips hurry to conceal themselves in some huts. Of course, my passenger wanted to shoot at them, so I wheeled around, let down into one end of the clearing, and barreled through as he fired out the left window with his Garand. Arisakas winked back at us from the openings of the thatched huts. I held down in there as long as I could, then I pulled up to clear the towering trees at the end of the clearing, the throttle wide open.

We were still a little below the treetops when I felt the throttle come back forcefully against my hand, and the engine died to an idle. The plane began rapidly to slow, of course, and I was momentarily puzzled, trying to understand what had happened. It was evident that if we didn't get power back within a very few seconds, we'd be crashing into the jungle canopy. Fortunately, the truth hit me very quickly. I whirled around to see the lieutenant with his rifle swung far to the rear on the window ledge, still firing back at the Japs, and the rifle was jamming the rear throttle. I yelled at him, grabbed the rifle with my left hand, and then shoved the throttle hard forward, so hard that it's a miracle the engine didn't choke on it. But it roared to full power without a whimper, and we went staggering across the jungle, barely clearing the top, for a few more anxious seconds before I could get speed to climb.

One of my infantry friends—in fact, about the only one I had—was Lt. Raymond Utke. Utke was a blocky, blond-mustached fellow, very quiet, but with a fearsome reputation as one of the I Corps Alamo Scouts, officer and NCO volunteers who were specially trained for solo infiltration of enemy-held areas for intelligence gathering. He was said to be one of the best, and it was alleged that on at least one occasion he returned from a mission bearing the ears of Japanese he had dispatched along the way. But he was quite modest and gentlemanly, and he used to spend hours sitting in our tent at the airstrip, talking with me and the other boys.

Utke was one of three lieutenants sent out with several enlisted men to set up an ambush west of the Woske and try to take at least one prisoner—something not easy to do with the Japanese of that war. But the task force intelligence officer needed a prisoner. In charge of the expedition was Lt. John Durant, and the third officer was Lt. Francis Peebles, both outstanding young leaders. On the day before they started, I flew Durant over the area so he could better appreciate the terrain before finalizing his plan.

To make the story shorter, suffice it to say that the plan didn't work. The enemy turned the tables, and the ambushers got ambushed. Mortar and machine-gun and rifle fire lashed at them from hidden positions, and Durant ordered a retreat. It became a rout, actually, as the Americans broke out onto the beach and literally ran toward the Woske, trying desperately to get out of the fire. Utke picked up a wounded sergeant and was carrying him on his back when a shell burst close behind him on the beach. The sergeant was killed, but his body shielded Utke from the fragments. Nevertheless, Utke was stunned, his eyes were filled with sand so that he was temporarily blinded and, as he told me later, crazy for awhile. He found himself off the beach, running sightless through brush, colliding with trees, not knowing which way he was going. Fortunately, he eventually made it to the river and was assisted back to the perimeter.

When the cost was counted, five men were missing, among them John Durant. Vin and I could see their five bodies lying up there on the sand, but officialdom demanded more proof that those were, indeed, the bodies of our missing men before they could change their legal status from "missing" to "killed in action." The commander refused to try to recover the bodies, since it would mean the almost certain loss of more lives, so I was sent out to get a detailed description of everything that could be seen.

For about fifteen minutes I practically taxied on the beach up there beyond the Woske, making note of everything I saw. Everything was there that should have been with the exception of weapons. Five bloody bodies dressed in HBTs and canvas jungle boots, with ammunition belts, canteens, first-aid kits, helmets, and so on. Farthest up the beach, about fifty yards from the others, lay the sergeant that Utke had carried. The bodies of the other three enlisted men—whose names I never knew—lay in a group near a large stump of driftwood over which was sprawled the giant figure of Lieutenant Durant, a gaping bloody hole between his shoulder blades. It was painful to remember the young officer's boyish grin of only two days before.

I filed an official written report of my observations, and the five were then reported as killed in action. As we flew up and down the area daily, Vineyard and I watched the five bodies swell, turn orange, then black and greasy, the clothing darkly stained. Something, probably crabs, ate their flesh, the waves washed sand over the bones, and finally we could see no sign that John Durant and his four soldiers had ever existed.

Historians sometimes get things all twisted out of shape. I know that it is difficult to get a straight story from skimpy official reports and that reports written by officers preoccupied with the more pressing affairs of combat may very well be skimpy indeed, and even inaccurate. An example—in a history of the 33d Division in World War II—is an account of a five-day reconnaissance of the Sawar Drome area by Company C, 123d Infantry. I won't relate the whole story nor point out errors in the official version, but here's a rough idea of how I saw it.

Company C, commanded by Capt. Martin Marchant Jr., crossed the Woske and proceeded to the east end of the airdrome, made a recon about halfway up the seaward side, then went through the dispersal areas in the edge of the jungle on the landward side. On each of their three nights and at various times during the days they had to fight.

The third night, spent in the dispersal area, was a nightmare of repeated enemy assaults on their position, exhaustion of their potable water supply (they had to drink from bloody shell craters), and near exhaustion of many of the men after three days and nights of movement and fighting with little chance to rest. On the morning of the fourth day, they began to move back toward the Woske.

Vineyard and I had been relieving each other in the air to keep constant surveillance over the company during daylight hours, and I was up when, near noon, the leading elements were clearing the dispersal areas

From left: Lieutenants Francis E. Peebles, John L. Durant, and Raymond R. Utke prepare to set out on their ill-fated patrol. Durant would not return (Photograph from Sanford Winston, *The Golden Cross*).

on the inland side of Sawar Drome and proceeding through the tall grass toward the bridge over the small stream at the east end of the airstrip. Vin had just taken off to relieve me and I had started edging toward home when I spotted a Japanese light tank on the beach, camouflaged with palm fronds. I immediately informed Captain Marchant even as I carefully searched the vicinity for other elements of what might be an enemy effort to cut off the company from withdrawal back to the Woske. I immediately discovered a second tank in a position between the road and the beach, its gun covering the road, several riflemen dug in around it. Closer to the company, just east of the creek and on the seaward side of the road I saw numerous infantry in foxholes where

Company C had fought off an attack on the first night out. They were in perfect position to ambush and split the company as it crossed the small bridge. I gave all the information to Marchant, and then, my fuel about gone, Vin relieved me and I went home.

Vin, in cooperation with our forward observers (FOs) with Company C, Lieutenants Paul Giudice and Keith Setterington, both of HQ Btry, adjusted the howitzers of the 122d and the company's mortars on the main ambush position at the bridge. He adjusted artillery fire that knocked out the tank on the beach and, meanwhile, discovered a third tank hidden under overhanging trees right on the beach road, and he also clobbered it with artillery. Strangely, Vin apparently overlooked the second tank I had located, although it was relatively easy to see.

When I came back up to relieve Vin, the company was within a few hundred yards of the bridge, and I was forcibly struck with the realization that if they tried to cross there the result would be a slaughter of company troops. The only way around the Japanese trap led through a deep swamp that extended far into the jungle and would be extremely difficult and time-consuming to pass through. But from my aerial viewpoint, I could see the situation much more clearly than Marchant could from the ground, and I suggested a plan, which he accepted and carried out. He crossed through the swamp about a hundred yards above the bridge, then turned toward the shore road while we placed a heavy, sustained concentration of artillery fire on the Japanese position near the bridge. The position rumbled and boiled with scores of explosions as the Americans came out of the swamp and hit the road running toward the Woske. Once clear of the now stunned enemy at the bridge, they slowed, reformed, and began a deliberate movement along the road in the normal way.

At that point, I turned my attention to the remaining tank and its infantry, which was still between Company C and the Woske, waiting patiently. Although the history says the company "could not account for the one remaining tank observed earlier in the afternoon," it appeared to me that Marchant had forgotten all about it. The company was swinging nonchalantly down the road with its radio turned off, so I could not tell it anything. If we brought artillery fire on the tank now, the company would be directly on an extension of the gun-target line and a long round might hit the head of the company, so I didn't ask for fire. But as the point men got close to where they would come under fire from the tank, I dove on the company, revving the engine and motioning for the troops to hit the ground. They did so, and soon Marchant came on the air to ask what the trouble was. I explained that within another ten paces his point would come under fire from the tank and surrounding infantry. I told him that there was a small knoll in the bushes near the beach from which he would be able to get a shot at the tank with a bazooka (a two-and-a-half-inch rocket launcher), and I recommended that he send someone to do that. Despite my description of its location, he still had trouble understanding just where the tank was, so I circled it at low altitude, then repeatedly dived low above it on a path perpendicular to the road. On one of these dives, I met Vin heading in from the ocean side. He came on the radio to say that he had brought up some smoke grenades and would use one to mark the tank. Being thus relieved, I headed toward our airstrip.

Immediately after I went down, Marchant sent his 3d Platoon forward in a frontal attack on the Japanese block while he personally led a small group to the knoll I had told him about. From there he hit the tank with two of three bazooka rounds. Meanwhile, Lieutenant Blake's 3d Platoon knocked out three Nambu machine guns around the tank and killed several riflemen. The road to the Woske was clear, and Company C proceeded in good order—although a day earlier than planned. Although the company had suffered a number of casualties in earlier fighting during the patrol, its casualties suffered in getting through the double ambush while destroying three tanks and killing a number of Nips amounted to eleven walking wounded.[1]

Of course, the 122d helped, and Marchant, who seemed to think that all the air observation had been done by Vin alone, wrote Vin—alone—a glowing letter of recommendation. However, Col. Paul Serff, commanding the 123d Infantry, knew the facts, so in his forwarding endorsement he added the names of Giudice, Setterington, and Kerns, saying that if regulations permitted he would award us each the Combat Infantry Badge, because, in his opinion and that of his officers and men, we were, indeed, combat infantrymen. Uncle Bud Carlson's endorsement concurred with Colonel Serff's opinion and added that we also were "combat field artillerymen of the highest order." I think I can safely say that the others felt as I did about that: good.

★

Capt. Tom Healy was a fine example of a Boston Irish gentleman, highly respected by everyone who knew him. He commanded Btry B of the 122d, but that did not prevent his going as FO with a unit reconning the vicinity of Mount Aftawadona. The infantry got into a fight at very close range in the heavy jungle, and Healy, unable to communicate directly with our FDC, contacted me to help him get fire on the Japanese positions with which they were engaged.

Circling above, I could see nothing at all of either our own or the enemy troops or positions, and landmarks in the immediate area were nonexistent—with the exception of a patch of deadened trees where a concentration had been fired weeks earlier. However, Healy seemed to know exactly where he was. He gave me coordinates of his position and asked me to get a couple of rounds of high-explosive (HE) shell within two hundred yards of him and he would complete the adjustment by sound sensing, since he could see no more than twenty yards in any direction.

I sent the fire mission request to FDC, giving a cautious shift from the old concentration toward where I figured the infantry was, according to Healy's coordinates.

FDC came back with, "Baker, center, one round Willie Peter. Wait . . ." And a few seconds later, "On the way. Over."

"Roger. Wait . . ."

It was the center platoon (two pieces) of Healy's own battery, and the first fire would be white phosphorous shell, which produced thick white smoke easily seen in the deep forest. And I saw these two bursts, right where I had expected them to be.

"One hundred left, two hundred long. Over."

"Roger. Wait. . . . On the way. Over."

"Roger, wait . . ."

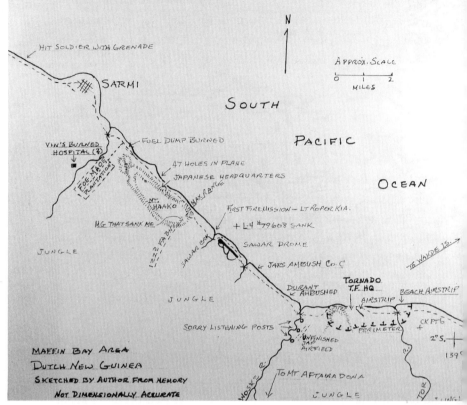

Author's sketch of Maffin Bay area of operations, showing locations of events described in text.

The second pair of Willie Peter (WP, white phosphorous) bursts were still at least two hundred yards from where I thought Captain Healy would be able to take over. However, it was time to switch to HE, which was far easier to sense by sound than the WP shell and which would be fired for effect on the target. Since the ballistic characteristics of shell HE were different from those of shell WP, I made a still more cautious correction this time, but I made it very quickly. A split second after the WP burst, I was calling FDC again.

"Five zero long, request shell HE. Over."

As soon as I let off my microphone button, Healy was yelling, "Cease fire! Cease fire!" And I immediately repeated, "Cease fire! Cease fire!"

But I don't think there was a faster 105 mm howitzer battery in the Army than Tom Healy's Btry B, and the reply came back, "Sorry! Center, one round HE, on the way!"

"Sorry, Tom. HE, already on the way!"

"Oh, my God! Those last rounds were right on the target. These will be in the middle of us!"

Two seconds after he spoke, I saw the HE bursts, right about where I had expected them to be, and far from where Tom had thought he was. It could have been worse, but it was bad enough. Two infantrymen were hit, both seriously, one of them very nearly losing an arm. When the patrol got home, I wanted to go with Captain Healy to visit the men in the hospital, but he would not permit it. He insisted that it was his responsibility alone.

Down along the lazy loops of the Woske, from a quarter to half a mile from the main perimeter, Colonel Serff had established three bunkered positions called the "Sorry Listening Posts." Vin and I thought they were well named. Flying over the area during daytime, we usually saw men out along the river near their bunkers. They might be washing their clothing or themselves or sometimes just sunbathing or reading, showing not the least concern with the possibility of danger. But on numerous occasions we saw Japanese soldiers squatting amid the weeds and brush on the opposite bank, watching very closely. Any sniper over there could have picked off one or more of our men with ease, and a machine gunner could have found opportunity to wipe out most of a squad with one long burst. Probably the reason they did not attack in that manner was their knowledge of the defensive barrages registered in at those very points by the 122d FA, to be fired on call. Further, they probably considered the Sorry bunkers little or no hindrance to anything they planned to do, so why ask for trouble?

At dusk, our men would close up the gap in the booby-trapped wire entanglement around each bunker and batten the hatches for the night. They could see nothing then except the river and the far banks as viewed through a narrow firing slit. Vineyard and I often talked of how helpless they were, and how careless. We repeatedly recommended—through our own battalion commander, of course—that the listening posts be taken out of the bunkers and placed in open foxholes and that their positions be changed each night. Colonel Carlson passed these recommendations to Colonel Serff's headquarters, but nothing changed.

I was the duty officer in the battalion CP one night, and at about 2230 hours, I had just dozed off on a cot when the duty NCO woke me. Capt. Garth Rowls, our liaison officer with one of the infantry battalions, was on the phone. As I got up, I could hear from the direction of the river the distinctive sound of incoming mortar shells. Rowls said that the Sorry Listening Posts were asking for their defensive barrages.

I told the duty NCO to alert the batteries to stand by to fire the Sorry defensive barrages at my command, and I sent another man to wake Colonel Carlson and Maj. Bill Hadfield, our S-3. They were on the scene within two minutes, and Major Hadfield started the batteries firing. Within a few more minutes, Captain Rowls reported that communication with the Sorry Listening Posts had been lost, and no one knew what had happened.

That was still the situation when, in the first dim light of dawn, I took off in my L-4. I found the three bunkers blown open, the holes showing the yellow stains left by picric acid. Around the bunkers I could see a number of dead or wounded men. One man lay on his back, a stream of blood from his head running down the mud bank into the river. Another sat in the debris and tangled wire beside his bunker, holding a rifle, his face white—and he didn't move. I realized that he was dead. Another man lay stark naked in the grass, his body bruised and scraped and seared, but he waved weakly as I passed over him. I was able to count about half of the more than thirty men who had been in the three widely separated bunkers.

Having reported that much of the picture, I was told that a relief party was preparing to move out to the Sorry posts. I was quite upset by that information, and I asked—without expecting an answer—why in hell they were still "preparing" some seven hours after the posts were lost? And then I began to examine the area for signs of how the attack had been made. My observation of fresh trails and trampled areas in the grass, together with my knowledge of the mortar fire, the signs of picric acid, and my long acquaintance with the blind situation of the Sorry posts soon led me to a conclusion that became generally accepted.

Up the river above Sorry 3, the enemy had emplaced three mortars, one for each of the bunkers. They had sent three demolition teams of two men each across the river to move down behind the bunkers and take cover in existing foxholes that were all over the area. On schedule, the demolition teams in place, the mortars fired several rounds at the three bunkers to be sure all the Americans were inside and buttoned up, and probably also hoping to detonate some booby traps outside. As soon as the mortars ceased fire, the demolition teams moved up and thrust the picric acid charges through the wire on long bamboo poles, then moved back into their foxholes and waited until their demolitions had blown up the bunkers and the 122d had finished firing the defensive barrages. Then they swam the river and walked away, unscathed. It was very easy for them.

Nearly half of the Sorry Listening Post men were killed, and many of the survivors were wounded. After that, the posts were moved out into foxholes and their positions frequently changed, as Vineyard and I had long recommended. The Sorry Listening Posts are not mentioned in the 33d Division history, *The Golden Cross*.

A 105 mm howitzer shell, HE, is a deadly thing. It weighs thirty-five pounds and is composed of a steel casing filled with dynamite and equipped with a fuse that may detonate it on impact, or at a certain time after firing, or when in proximity to a sensed target. The steel casing—the shell—breaks up into a large number of fragments of varying size and shape, which are propelled through the air with the velocity of bullets. The fragments can make terrible wounds, and they travel far and wide. Flying at eight hundred feet above a 105 mm shell burst, I have had a fragment of it strike and cut halfway through a metal structural tube just behind the windshield of my L-4. On another occasion, a jagged fragment the size of my middle finger penetrated and lodged in the wooden main wing spar of my L-4, less than a foot from the fuselage and not much farther from my honorable head. Vin had a hot fragment come through the floor of his plane, through his handkerchief and his hip pocket, and sear a sizable spot on his bottom. Fred Hoffman had his aileron cable cut by one—all these being fragments from our own shells. For people on the ground close to the burst, there is the added shock of concussion and heat and the dirt, dust, rock, and other debris turned into missiles by the blast. A friend of mine died in awful pain when a ricocheting enemy shell struck a nearby tree and filled his body with wood splinters. When an entire battalion of 105s, consisting as it did in World War II of twelve pieces, fires "battalion three rounds," a total of thirty-six shells burst in the target area within about eight or ten seconds from first to last. When it is not preceded by adjusting rounds, and therefore comes without warning, such a concentration is a terrible thing, especially for people caught in the open, unprotected. Try to imagine such a thing—if you haven't seen it yourself—and keep it in mind while I tell my next story.

To develop a correction factor to be applied in computing firing data for artillery, a unit establishes a base point and a number of check points within its sector of fire, each of these at a known location. By firing a registration on one of these points and stripping out known standard data from the adjusted data for the point, a correction factor is determined that then is applied to standard data for any target within transfer limits of the point. This enables delivery of reasonably accurate fires without necessity of observation and adjustment of fire. In combat, these registrations normally are conducted daily, shortly before dark, and in the jungle environment of New Guinea, where ground observers could see little, the registration job usually fell to Vineyard or me.

One afternoon I had registered on the base point and all the check points except the last one, Check Point #6, far around to the east end of our perimeter. The check point was a large dead tree at one end of a small jungle clearing, and as I got into position to observe the registration, I noted that a band of about eighty natives, whole families of men, women, and children, had set up one of their temporary brush camps in the clearing. I reported this to FDC.

"Huron 8, this is Huron 3—Roger—Wait. . . . Huron 8, prepare to observe battalion three rounds. Over."

I could hardly believe the response. I had thought that I'd be told to skip the registration until a patrol could be sent tomorrow to clear out the natives, but now they were going to place a devastating concentration of fire on the people. Why? And then I remembered: the ignorant natives seemed to have little understanding of the war or of where their proper position in it might be. Some of them had made a practice of giving any information they had to either Americans or Japanese whenever asked. Further, they had occasionally picked off a soldier—American as well as Japanese—bringing up the rear or otherwise relatively exposed along the jungle trails. Their arrows and spears were deadly and silent. And so orders had been issued that our patrols would avoid being seen by natives if possible; if seen, they should kill every one involved. And none at all were to be permitted to remain within three miles of our perimeter. Check Point #6 was only about two miles out.

With a heavy heart, I replied, "Ready to observe."

For a few seconds, the clearing and the nearby trees boiled with explosions as the people fled in all directions. When it was over and the smoke cleared away, I could see freshly turned earth, freshly fallen limbs and green leaves, motionless black bodies, and splotches of red. Obviously, we had the Check Point #6 data right to a T, so we skipped the registration.

Whenever I have nightmares about that war, they're about Check Point #6.

★

Uncle Bud Carlson was as fine an artillery technician and tactical planner as you will ever find. In fact, I could say he was an artist among redleg practitioners of warfare. But his position as our battalion commander afforded him little opportunity to do any shooting himself, to get out and call the shots and watch them hit the target. He missed that sorely. So one afternoon he came out to the airstrip and announced that today he was going to conduct the registrations. Away we went.

He registered the base point and five check points without a hitch, and we proceeded out to the last check point—Check Point #6. He reported ready to observe. FDC reported "on the way," and we saw the WP round burst well short and left of the target. For some reason I have never understood, Uncle Bud sensed it as right and over, so as soon as he let up on his mike button I said, "Cease fire!"

"Cease fire? Why cease fire? What's wrong?" asked Uncle Bud.

"Sir, your sensing is in the wrong direction. It'll put your next round back here in the perimeter."

He scoffed at the idea. "Oh, no, no, no! You'll see." He pushed his mike button. "Disregard cease fire. Fire on my original sensing. Over."

I positioned the plane so Uncle Bud could see the check point out the right front, but I watched the left rear, where the line of our defense perimeter ran nearly parallel to our course. And I saw his round of WP burst—inside the perimeter. It burst high up on the trunk of a giant tree that had been left standing when the surrounding area was cleared. Chunks of the burning chemical, trailing thick, white smoke, showered down into a dump of 155 mm artillery shells standing on their bases on dunnage, and upon a pyramidal tent belonging to the ordnance ammo unit.

"There's your round, sir."

"Where? Where?" Uncle Bud craned his neck, looking every direction except the right one.

"Back here, sir. Inside the perimeter."

"Oh, my God! Take me down! Take me down!"

As soon as we got down, he hit his jeep on the run and was gone for about two hours. He returned somewhat calmed, since the only damage had been the burned tent, but he announced that henceforth he would leave the aerial shooting to those who were accustomed to it.

For some reason I never quite understood, the Navy wanted to shell the remains of Sarmi, the town that had once been the only settled place within a hundred miles or more in any direction. Two destroyers came up the coast, and Uncle Bud took me with him for a conference with the senior naval gunnery officer. We left one of our radio operators onboard to link me with that individual, and I set out to adjust naval gunfire for the only time in my life.

It was a notably unsuccessful venture. With the low, flat trajectories of the destroyers' guns, at least nine shells out of ten would either burst in the palms along the beach short of the town or would pass over and burst in the low hills back at the base of the peninsula on which the town was situated. I was soon disgusted with the effort and asked whether they could raise the trajectories by moving farther out to fire at greater range. They said they couldn't, but they kept firing. When I finally was able to report a hit on one of the few reasonably intact buildings left in Sarmi, they seemed satisfied.

On another occasion, I was heading out along Sawar Drome when I saw a vessel rounding the Sarmi peninsula and bearing rapidly down the coast toward Maffin. I reported it as an unidentified warship and was then asked to go out and see whether it was friend or foe. I took a diagonal course out to intercept the ship, flying at about five hundred feet. The farther I got from shore and the closer to the ship, the more I thought about pictures I'd seen of the antiaircraft fire naval vessels can put up. The L-4, too, was very sensitive to such things, and it was difficult, indeed, to keep it on the intercept course. I strained my eyes to make out a flag, a number, any marking that might clue me in, but I could not tell whose ship it was, and I just kept getting closer and closer. . . . And then FDC said never mind. Task Force Headquarters had gotten communication with the ship, an American destroyer.

On the morning of 2 December, Vin and I both went out to mark targets on air photos to be used for an air strike by an A-20 squadron. At their request, Sergeant Allen rode along with Vin, and T/4 Wendell Young went with me. When Young came out to the plane, he was carrying Mae West life vests for himself and me. Although Vin and I seldom used them, I humored Young by putting mine on without comment.

We had finished our task and were starting home. Coming eastward along the back side of Mount Haako, we heard Vin call for a fire mission against a Jap machine gun that had fired on him from the eastern end of Haako, just at the maximum range of our 105s. Young tapped me on the shoulder and asked whether we could watch the fire, since he had never seen a mission fired. We watched until Vin had clobbered the place, clearing out a considerable amount of overhead cover in the process. I had often wondered what was there, and now was a chance to see, so I pulled on the carburetor heat and dived a little, passing over the site at about eight hundred feet and descending, using power to increase our speed to probably a hundred miles per hour. We had barely passed over the position, heading southeast, when either the same gun or another opened fire on us. Almost immediately, the engine sputtered badly, then surged, then died completely. The wooden prop stood motionless out in front.

I was on a perfect final approach to Sawar Drome, where I knew a company of Nips would welcome us warmly. To the right was the forest primeval, the deep jungle, where our landing would be in a treetop about 150 feet above ground and from which escape, if any, would take weeks. To our left was Maffin Bay, in whose blue waters we often saw sharks cruising. Behind us, of course, was Mount Haako and the handy machine gunner.

Vin and I had often discussed what might be best to do in such a case, and we had never really reached a conclusion. But at that moment, faced with the situation for real, I made up my mind in less than two seconds.

"Huron 3, this is Huron 8. My engine is dead over Sawar Creek. Am going to land in the ocean. Can you send a boat?"

I had already turned toward the water. Whether boat or sharks, it would all be over in short order. No treetop crash; no struggle to survive, evade the enemy, and get out of the jungle; no long imprisonment or tortured death at the enemy's hands.

"Roger, Huron 8. Wait. . . . We're calling the Beach. . . . The speedboat is over at Wakde but they're sending an LCVP. Over."

"Huron 8. Roger. Thanks."

"Crash, this is Vin. I'll keep an eye on you. Good luck."

"Thanks, Vin."

It occurred to me that Young, unaccustomed to flying, might be badly upset. I turned around and said, "I'll do the best I can for you, Wendy."

He calmly replied, "I know you will, sir."

The beach was behind us by then, and I was thinking about how best to ditch the plane, something we'd never been told about. While I was thinking about it, Young asked whether he should loosen his safety belt or leave it fastened. I didn't know what to tell him, so I didn't answer. I did decide that I didn't want to get tangled in my headset and its wiring, so, when we were down to about fifty feet I called FDC again.

"Huron 3, this is Huron 8. Taking off my headset now. Checking out of the net. Over."

That business about checking out of the net was my old radio operator training coming out, but the report and the calm way I said it impressed the people in FDC who were listening. They thought I was pretty cool.

"Uh—uh—Roger, Huron 8 . . . Lieutenant! Lieutenant!"

That was the last I heard. I don't know what else the operator wanted to say. Maybe he thought I was done for—and just wanted to say goodbye.

I flung off the headset and began holding off about ten feet above the tops of the waves, which were probably about six feet high. At the last minute, I flipped loose my safety belt, took the stick in my left hand, and braced myself with my right hand on the diagonal tube at the right of the windshield. The door and windows were open. The plane stalled and dropped into the side of a wave. It looked as if someone had jerked a white sheet up over the windshield. Vin said later that the plane momentarily disappeared into the water, then recoiled back to float with the wings on top of the water.

I was thrown forward rather violently but was not seriously hurt or stunned; however, about a quart of seawater was rammed down my throat, and in a very few seconds I had pulled myself to the surface in front of the right wing and spewed it out. Then I looked for Young. I ducked back under to see him kicking out behind the wing. He came up, gasping, "I can't swim!" I told him to pull the cords on his life vest. He did, and it instantly inflated. I pulled the cords on my jacket and nothing happened, so I was relieved when Vin flew by with Allen holding up our only inflatable rubber raft, indicating that they were going to drop it for us.

The raft hit the water about forty yards away, and I swam out to get it while Young scrambled up onto the plane. But the carbon dioxide bottle on the raft was empty, so I swam back empty-handed and feeling rather exhausted. I joined Young on the floating plane, sick from the sea water and wishing we'd been more careful in maintaining our emergency gear. But on examining my Mae West carefully, I discovered that the inflation capsules were upside down. I pulled up on the cords, the vest inflated, and I was much happier.

The plane was settling farther and farther into the water, and I figured it wouldn't be long before the wings would be full of water coming in through the drain holes, and then the plane would go down. It was evident, too, that we were drifting nearer to the beach—to those bunkers along Sawar Drome—and I wondered whether I should try to get my carbine out of the plane. It was inside a waterproof plastic bag, and I could see it floating up against the Plexiglas in the top of the plane. I could kick out a panel and get it. However, there was also a large air bubble there, and I knew the plane would sink sooner if I let that escape, so I let the carbine go. We watched the horizon for the promised LCVP.

The plane floated for about thirty or forty minutes, and in the meantime Vin had to go down for refueling. While he was down, the enemy dropped one or two rounds of either artillery or mortar fire that missed us a long way. Before they had a chance to adjust the fire, Vin came back up and the Japanese put their gun away.

We decided we'd better not be on the plane when it sank, so we slid off into the water and floated nearby and waited a very short time before my faithful #79608 slowly dropped below the surface, then shoved up a wing to show the white star and bars, and slowly went down forever. We bobbed up and down in the empty waves and watched the horizon for a boat.

At first, the bow of the LCVP was just a square dot on the horizon, but to one who is floating in the water the horizon is very near, so it wasn't long before the boat was swinging around near us while a sergeant kept a .50-caliber machine gun covering the shore. The crew tossed ropes to us and pulled us aboard. They pulled me up first, and this has bothered me ever since. It made me feel like a captain being first to desert his sinking ship. But it was a great relief not to be anticipating the slashing jaws of a hungry shark. We took off our wet clothing and, wrapped in blankets, sat on the deck and smoked and answered the crew's questions about what had happened.

During the hour-long ride back to Maffin Beach, we met a "water buffalo," an amphibious truck. It was wallowing through the waves between us and the shore, loaded to the gunwales with men, rifles sticking out in all directions. It was Phil Ryan and a dozen men from HQ Btry, including Young's brother, Carl. When Ryan had heard that we were down and drifting toward the beach at Sawar, he had the water buffalo cranked up and asked for volunteers to land at Sawar Drome, if necessary, and bring us out! Everyone in the battery volunteered.

See what I mean when I say there's nothing finer than a good soldier?

When we landed back at Maffin, Uncle Bud and Doc Miller were waiting for us, Uncle Bud smiling happily. Doc questioned us about how we felt, gave us a very cursory examination, and administered a shot of medicinal bourbon and a sedative. We both were still shivering a little, although it was hot weather, so he told us to sack out, wrap up in our blankets, and take a nap. He was about to dismiss us, but Colonel Carlson wasn't satisfied.

"Don't either of you have any cuts or anything?" he asked.

"No, sir. Well, I did kind of cut my leg a little."

I pulled up my trouser leg and showed him a small cut from which blood had trickled down and dried.

"And I guess I've got a few bruises—a knot on my head—but nothing serious."

Young had the same sort of very minor injuries, but Uncle Bud wasn't going to miss his first chance to award a decoration.

"You boys are wounded! Fix 'em up, Doc. I'm going to award them the Purple Heart."

I sacked out for a couple of hours, awoke feeling fine, and joined in the officers' late afternoon volleyball game. But Doc Miller wouldn't let me fly for about three days. He was afraid there might be some adverse psychological effect, I guess, and he questioned me at great length about it.

While I'm talking about Doc—whose home was Bloomsburg, Pennsylvania—I'd like to relate a couple of little stories about him.

Although he was a fine fellow in every way and was quite well liked by everyone, as far as I know, it seemed to me that the long months in the dreary atmosphere of the primitive equatorial island sort of got to him. One thing that bothered him was what he considered the inequity of his receiving only the regular pay of a captain while Vin and I, with our flying pay, made more.

"I spent sixteen years getting my basic education, thousands of dollars and eight more years of hard work in medical school and internship, I was on the surgical staff of a large hospital; yet you young lieutenants with no more than a high school education and six months of military training make more money than I do in this war."

Vineyard and I argued that our extra pay was given not for our level of education but for what we could do for the war effort, and for the unusual risks we were daily required to take. That didn't satisfy Doc at all. Then I posed him a hypothetical situation that, however unfair it might have been, did suffice to stop his arguing with us.

"Doc," I said, "let's suppose that you and I trade places. I'll be the doctor and you be the pilot. What would you want me to do—something that is a common, routine task for a surgeon?"

After thinking for a few seconds, he replied, "An appendectomy. That's a very common surgical procedure. Every surgeon must be able to do it."

"OK. Now obviously, I know little or nothing about surgery, and you are equally ignorant about flying a plane, so we would both need advice, right?"

"Right."

"All right now. You give me a qualified surgeon to stand by and tell me what to do while I perform an appendectomy. I'll give you a competent pilot to ride with you and tell you everything to do while you simply take off, come around the field, and land an airplane—something every pilot needs to do on every flight. Which of us do you think would be more likely to succeed?"

"I must admit, you'd probably win the contest," he said.

But he was wrong. Even if I had his eight years of training, I don't think I could perform a surgical operation. I'd be in dreamland after the first incision. I think doctors deserve the extra military pay that later was authorized for them.

★

One of the busiest and most resourceful men in the 122d FA Bn was a private first class named John Paul Jones. Whatever you wanted, Jones could get it for you—which is how I came by my first pair of combat boots. If you managed to have a camera and a few rolls of film with you and took some pictures, Jones was the man who had the means of developing and printing them for you. He served informally as orderly for a number of officers. And in New Guinea he was detailed as our malaria control specialist. In that capacity, it was his function to make sure everyone had a serviceable mosquito bar, that bug bombs were issued as needed, and that all mosquito breeding places in the area were periodically sprayed with kerosene to kill the larvae. One of those potential breeding places was the three-holer latrine used by the officers.

One afternoon, minutes after Jones had sprayed kerosene quite liberally into the dark hole beneath the latrine box, Doc Miller strolled casually into the latrine, seated himself on the center hole, and lit a cigarette. Just as casually, his mind probably ten thousand miles away in Bloomsburg, he raised up one haunch and dropped the lighted match into the hole.

Need I say more on that subject? Fortunately, Doc wasn't seriously hurt.

★

Our mail deliveries probably averaged one a week, but they were quite irregular, for the ships that brought mail from the States were subject to the many uncertain winds of war. Camped there on the rim of the huge, untamed island of New Guinea, we were in what some newsmen called "the backwash" of the war in the Southwest Pacific. We were in contact with the enemy, but nothing big was happening there anymore. MacArthur's island-hopping war had moved on ahead of us. MacArthur himself was well down on Washington's priority list, and our small task force was probably near the bottom of MacArthur's list. Bigger things were happening elsewhere.

The folks back home knew that their letters normally took one to two months to reach us there on the other side of the world, so they did their Christmas mailing early. And so, sometime in October of 1944, a ship dropped anchor off Hollandia (later Sukarnapura, and still later, Jayapura) that had onboard a large amount of Christmas mail for men in units all up and down the New Guinea coast. Hollandia, where MacArthur then had his headquarters, was a very busy place, and there was no dock space to accommodate the mail ship. Unfortunately, the ship was scheduled to join a convoy to support the invasion of Leyte in the Philippines. When she had waited as long as she could, her captain used his small boats to put the cargo on the Hollandia beach, and away he went.

There on the beach lay the ordinary canvas mail sacks filled with all the love and tender concern that thousands of mothers, wives, sisters, and sweethearts could wrap up in packages of cake and candy and favorite sausages and cheeses, and whatever they could find and mail that they thought would please their loved ones overseas. They lay there for two months, exposed to the hot, humid tropical climate, before someone finally got them picked up and sent on their way.

Our mail clerk was a Sergeant Perkins of Louisville, Kentucky. He was probably the oldest man in the outfit, a good and sensitive man who was almost like a father to many of the men, so when they pestered him about when they were going to get some mail he good-naturedly assured them that there was no need to worry, the mail would be in before Christmas. And it was. Only a day or two before Christmas, Perkins returned from our one crude little dock with his truck piled high with mailbags. Smiling happily, he began tossing them off in front of the mail tent, and then the men—and officers too—gathered from all directions.

It was obvious that no one was in a mood to wait for the usual sorting, so Sergeant Perkins just started opening bags and emptying the contents out on the ground. Bag after bag he opened and emptied, and it was all the same. When he finished, he stood facing a huge pile of greasy, moldy, stinking garbage. Tears streamed down his kindly face as he stood, unable to speak, and motioned with his hands as if to say, "Go ahead, men. See if you can find your name." Then he turned and stumbled into the tent.

The men began slowly and carefully sorting through the mess, each looking for a piece of paper with his name on it, anything he could identify as being intended for him. Some were lucky enough to find some soiled scrap bearing a familiar name or address, perhaps a package more or less intact, but inside would be only garbage where loving hands had placed some good food three months ago. A few men were, like Sergeant Perkins, in tears as they searched, but most were merely sad and disappointed. It was touching to see some soldier's pleasure at finding just his name and knowing that someone had sent him something.

There were a few nonperishable items, of course, although many could not be identified as to addressee. The only major item in this category was canned fruit juice—orange, pineapple, apricot, and others. Since so little could be claimed by any individual, we pooled the juice so everyone could have some.

As for me, I had asked my mother to send me one of the two-pound blocks of American processed cheese, which then came packed in a wooden box. I searched hopefully for the cheese—and I found it. The wooden box was intact. Inside I found a shriveled, heavily molded, very stinking chunk of what had once been cheese.

That was my Christmas gift—and like the other men I was very grateful, just knowing that it came from home, from someone who loved me.

★

The American offensive along the coast of New Guinea broke up the Japanese forces into fairly well isolated groups, and communications among these various pockets of resistance was usually poor, often nonexistent. Thus it was that a Japanese construction unit consisting of about five hundred Okinawans under the command of a civilian engineer hit the trail from the Aitape-Wewak vicinity with the intention of evading the American forces and joining the stronger friendly elements at Hollandia. It was hard going as they made their way on foot over rough jungle trails with scanty supplies of food and medicine. There were deaths, even early in the trek, but they kept on.

They reached the Hollandia vicinity only to find that it had been taken by the Americans, and the remnants of the once powerful Japanese force there were hiding in the forested hills several miles inland. Never mind, said the Japanese leader, they would go on to Sarmi. Surely the Americans were not there, too. But as they struggled through the jungle to bypass the Americans at Hollandia, they found that the Japanese soldiers hiding in the hills were not always friendly to these laborers, these Okinawans. In fact, it seems that there were instances of starving Japanese soldiers killing Okinawans for food. Whatever the truth of that, the strength of the labor unit dwindled quite rapidly, and less than two hundred completed the circuit of Hollandia and began the 120-mile march toward Sarmi. By this time, the men were quite weak and morale had disintegrated. They were desperate for food and nearly all were ill, tormented day and night by the myriad mosquitoes and other insects, threatened by snakes and crocodiles—and the locals.

A mere handful of them finally, in desperation, approached a village—the same one, I believe, where I had found the two errant corps pilots down on the beach. But to the starving, practically helpless Okinawans, the people were anything but friendly. Apparently, only two managed to escape death at their hands.

After a further tortured march of some thirty miles, those two reached Maffin Bay, and there they found more Americans: Tornado Task Force. For two days they lay out in the jungle among the roots of huge trees and debated whether to continue searching for friendly Japanese or come in and surrender to the Americans. On their second day out there, Company G of the 123d Infantry, camped right beside our airstrip, test-fired its mortars. The rounds happened to burst very close to the two miserable Okinawans, and one of them made up his mind to come in and surrender. The other was determined to continue on up the coast. And so they parted.

It was still dark next morning as the men of Company G filed sleepily through their chow line. One scrawny little guy with his fatigue hat pulled down over his face held up a canteen cup to the server, who withheld the ladle of powdered eggs and asked if the soldier didn't have a mess kit. There was no reply, just the lowered head and the thin hand holding the canteen cup out for food. The mess server leaned over and looked under the brim of the old hat—into the frightened eyes of an Asian.

"Hey! This here guy is a Jap!"

The people we had relieved at Maffin Bay left us no maps to show the dense antipersonnel minefields they had emplaced in front of the defense perimeter. One of our officers had lost his legs to one of those mines. Manned log bunkers and pillboxes were only thirty feet apart all along the perimeter, and in front of them were entanglements of barbed wire, which concealed trip wires for explosives and noisemakers of various kinds. Yet this poor, weak, sick, and exhausted little man, in the blackness of night, had made his way into the enemy camp, equipped himself with parts of an enemy uniform and mess gear, and had the courage to try to enjoy a meal with the enemy troops.

I had spent some time with our battalion interpreter and had learned a few words of Japanese, so he invited me to go with him when he interrogated this prisoner. He was the only prisoner the task force had, so the "POW compound" was quite small. In fact, it was about the size and style of a hog pen. A wire fence enclosed a mud hole about the size of the average American living room. Across one corner a few planks were loosely placed, but they provided no real protection from the elements or the mosquitoes. In the middle of the pen was a narrow plank, and on that, the center of which was sunk into the mud, lay the Okinawan, his head resting on an empty C-ration can.

When we walked up to the fence, he got up, faced us, and bowed gracefully in the Japanese way, smiling politely. The interpreter told him that we wanted to ask him some questions, and he nodded agreeably. I offered him a cigarette, which he accepted with evident pleasure. Of course, the interpreter did nearly all the questioning and he translated all the replies for me, but he did allow me to ask a few questions that

I had prepared in advance. I was gratified to note that the prisoner understood me without difficulty.

He answered all our questions honestly, I believe, and out of his answers came the story I have related. Along with the other Okinawans, he had been drafted to serve in the labor battalion and had worked on Palau before coming to New Guinea. But he denied all knowledge of matters involving the Japanese forces other than his own unit. Of course, he was soon evacuated from our area. I hope he eventually got home and is still enjoying life. He was a nice guy, with sustained courage such as most of us don't possess, I'm afraid. And I hope that his buddy, too, survived the war and has lived a happy life since. I mean that most sincerely. What tales they could tell!

There were a couple of other Japanese that I know of who got inside our perimeter there at Maffin Bay. One night I was sitting in my tent, reading by the light of a Coleman lantern, when Mel Harker, another occupant, ran in and hastily turned out the light.

"Get your gun!" he said. "There are Japs in the perimeter!" And then he dashed away toward the CP.

I took my carbine out of its plastic cover, thanking myself for having traded Rudy Krevolt my pistol for it. For a moment, I stood listening outside the tent. A short distance away, over near the dirt road that wound past our camp, I could hear men running, a few shouted words, intermittent small arms fire. Not knowing what the situation might be, I crouched down beside a large log and watched for a silhouette against the slightly lighter background of the sky, but nothing appeared. I was all alone. The shooting soon ceased, the shouting stopped, and I heard the quieter voices of men coming back from the road into our area.

This was at a time when the equipment and supplies of Task Force Tornado troops were being loaded on vessels standing offshore in preparation for our movement to other climes. Two of our men who had been working at the beach were driving back to the Headquarters Battery area when the lights of their truck picked up two men walking beside the road. The men held their arms over their faces as if to shield their eyes from the lights, but one of our men recognized them as Japanese. They drove on into our nearby CP area and told Major Hadfield about it. He called one of the infantry companies near the scene, and a squad was dispatched to investigate. Meanwhile, Major Hadfield went alone to try to locate the intruders. The affair ended in a brief gunfight in the darkness, in which Hadfield and the infantry squad killed a Japanese lieutenant and a sergeant.

Investigation determined that these two individuals had been in our midst for probably two weeks, living in a hole under the roots of a large tree in a clump of grass and weeds just across the road from the 122d FA Bn CP. The hole was still stocked with American rations and Pall Mall cigarettes—which we Americans had not seen since arriving in the Southwest Pacific. When our men spotted them, the daring Japs were going toward the task force CP, where General Myers was holding a premovement conference and briefing with all the senior commanders. The two Japanese were well armed with pistols and grenades, and it was suspected that they may have intended a suicidal attack on the officers there.

To protect our withdrawal from Maffin Bay and, thereafter, to evacuate the cemetery and close out American occupancy of the locale, elements of the 93d, a black division, had been brought in. They were totally lacking in combat experience, so our boys had made the most of the opportunity to kid them a bit. There were awful stories told of such things as Japanese infiltrators slitting the throats of Americans while they slept. It just happened that the very first night those troops spent at Maffin Bay, the incident of the two Japanese took place right beside their camp. It seemed to erase any doubts they may have had as to the veracity of the throat-cutting tales, and loud challenges were frequently heard in their area for the rest of the night.

★

My lost plane was not replaced while we remained at Maffin Bay, the *Arizona Keed* did double duty, with both Vin and me flying her. Then came the day when the boys dismantled and packed the *Keed* in her crate, and filled *Booby Trap*'s crate with section supplies and tools. We were all set to go. Only one air section task remained to be done.

There had been very little visiting between Maffin Bay and Hollandia. I had made one trip down there, during which I visited the 24th Division and saw my flying school classmates and friends Bud Kelly, Lee Guild, and John Brady, the division air officer. They were under trees on a hillside, while out on the flats in front of them fighters, bombers, and transports raised huge, blinding clouds of dust everywhere they went.

But one of those bombers was piloted by an adventurous fellow who decided to get off the beaten path. Without really asking, he took somebody's Stinson L-5 one day and flew it up to Maffin Bay. It might not have been too bad a trip, except that just as he arrived in the vicinity of our little strip, the old Lycoming quit on him. He came in dead-stick, clipped the top of a pyramidal tent, smashed into a quarter-ton trailer, and rolled the L-5 up into a little ball on the approach end of our runway.

The hero was taken back to Hollandia nursing minor injuries. The AAF sent out a representative to strip the L-5 of usable parts, and the engine block was left lying there on the ground.

As we prepared to ship out, Task Force HQ told us that we must leave nothing behind that could possibly be used by the enemy and said that the engine block must be destroyed. OK, we said, we'll bust it up with a sledgehammer. No, no, no! We'll send the engineers over to destroy it. Fine!

An engineer sergeant came over, measured the diameter of the engine, did some computations, pulled off a cylinder head, and stuffed in several quarter-pound blocks of dynamite. Then he set it off.

The Japanese could hardly have done more damage with a hundred-pound bomb. There was an explosion that blew the engine to smithereens, and fragments flew in all directions. Nearby Company G tents were ripped. A man sitting on his canvas cot while cleaning his rifle was slightly disturbed when a piston descended through the top of the tent, passed through his bunk no more than a foot from his side, and buried itself in the ground. We had to uncrate the *Arizona Keed* and repair damage done by fragments that went through the crate and plane. But soon we were on our way.

– Five –

LUZON:

LINGAYEN TO THE HILLS

Our Liberty ship lay at anchor off Wakde all through the dark night after we boarded her. Among several officers of battalion headquarters there was a big game of Black Lady Hearts that night. I was the scorekeeper, and, just for the hell of it, I kept the score in Japanese numerals. When anyone wanted to know the score, I told him.

Capt. Norman Olsen, our assistant S-3, consistently lost, and although there was no money involved, losing the game troubled him sorely. After a few lost games, when he asked the score, I told him, and he asked to see the pad. I'm sure he didn't suspect me of falsifying the score, but when the saw the Japanese numerals, which he couldn't read, he became quite angry and left the table. The rest of us gave up the game and followed him outside to stand at the rail on the blacked-out, pitch-dark deck. Out there, Olsen recognized my voice and, in an unpleasant way that was unusual for him, he challenged me.

"Kerns," he said, "you're so damned smart, I'll just make you a bet. I'll bet you a hundred guilders I can come closer than you can to guessing the depth of the water here."

"Well, I only have fifty guilders, but I'll bet that. How are we going to determine how deep it is?"

"We'll ask one of the ship's officers. Whatever he says will be it."

"All right, sir, that's good enough for me."

"OK, I say it's two hundred fathoms. What's your guess?" said Captain Olsen.

I was astonished. "Did you say *two hundred fathoms,* Captain? Are you sure you know what a fathom is?"

"Hell yes, I know what a fathom is. That's my guess. What's your guess?"

His guess was so obviously far beyond reason that I really felt ashamed to go through with the bet.

"Captain Olsen, have you considered the fact that this ship is at anchor here within a few hundred yards of an island?"

"What's your guess, Kerns?"

"Well—I'll say ten fathoms."

We found one of the ship's officers on deck, and he answered our question: "Oh, about six or seven fathoms."

I hated to take Captain Olsen's money—fifty guilders was about $28 at the existing exchange rate—but he had asked for the bet, and I think it's the only bet I ever won. It took a while for him to start being friendly with me again, but he finally got over it.

Next morning it was anchors aweigh, and our small convoy bore northwest toward the Philippines. En route, we joined a much larger number of ships carrying the rest of the 33d Division from the Halmahera Islands, where they had helped to tame the enemy on Morotai, and we made quite a respectable and very warlike flotilla on the bounding main.

For the first few days aboard, it was hard to get a drink of water at one of the scuttlebutts. After months of drinking warm, heavily chlorinated water in New Guinea, our people formed perpetual lines for the good, sweet, cool water aboard ship, and many a soldier would move directly from the fountain to the end of the line. In New Guinea, we'd had essentially nothing cold to drink. The only way to cool a can of beer—if you had one—was to sacrifice a "bug bomb" by spraying its pressurized contents on the can, and that wasteful practice still left the beer a long way from Stateside cold. Once during our stay at Maffin Bay, some morale-building team visited us with a machine that dispensed cold Coca-Cola, and even Uncle Bud Carlson stood in line to get his half-a-canteen-cupful. That's all anyone got, but it was a red-letter day.

There were lots of card games and crap games aboard our ship, much conversation on a wide range of topics but with emphasis on favorite restaurants, it seemed to me. In fact, eating establishments were a favorite subject throughout the war, and one on which I could never talk, because I'd never been anywhere or visited any fine restaurants. Well, there was the time Bill Gibson and Paul Arnold and I sat down at a table at Lau Yee Chai's in Waikiki and spent our entire month's pay for dinner, but I couldn't say that was my favorite place. Heiress Barbara Hutton could afford to party there, but we common soldiers certainly couldn't. But most of the fellows from the big cities, especially, considered restaurant quality the criterion by which to measure every place they ever visited, and it seemed to me to be the only thing they remembered about a city. I got tired of hearing about them.

Of course, there was the occasional gum-chewing Dane Clark type with his endless discussion of women he claimed to have known.

There was a lot of socializing among the infantry, artillery, and other branch personnel, and many new acquaintances were made with people who heretofore had been, at most, voices identified by radio call signs. That was good. For some reason, though, the two new acquaintances I recall best from that trip were both unpleasant personalities that would play interesting and contrasting roles in future events of my war experience.

Lt. Edward Schuster was a tall, slender, young infantry platoon leader with short blond hair and a disposition that seemed to dare anyone to try to be friendly with him. He would go out of his way to be nasty in response to just about any approach, and no one understood why. The other fellow—nameless, for the purposes of our story—was a burly, loud-mouthed captain with curly black hair and a red face. He was constantly sounding off about his personal prowess and bravery, and he bragged ceaselessly about what his company was going to do when they turned it loose in the Philippines.

Our ship stopped for a few hours off the shore of Leyte, where Douglas MacArthur had made good his promise, "I shall return," less than three months before. All we could see from the ship was a long stretch of sandy beach backed by blasted trunks of coco palms and hazy distant mountains. We talked of the great naval battle that had so recently been fought here in Leyte Gulf, and I thought of my brother-in-law Fay Lane, fighting somewhere on Leyte with the 7th Infantry Division. And then we were underway again, sailing through Surigao Strait and the narrow Mindanao Sea.

Despite the successes of our sea and air forces, we knew that these were still dangerous waters, and many of us spent most of our time on deck, scanning the sea and the sky, trying to identify the land masses that we could occasionally see on one side or the other. Colonel Carlson, who spent most of the day on the bridge, told us later that the ship's captain paced the bridge anxiously, marveling that there were no enemy airplanes to contest our passage. Late in the afternoon, we saw on the starboard side a distant coast that we knew was the island of Negros, and far to port was a bluish headland that someone told us was Tagolo Point on Mindanao. Our ship plowed on to the west into the Sulu Sea and toward the most beautiful sunset I have ever had the pleasure of witnessing.

I don't know what our route was from there on, but eventually our convoy slid into Lingayen Gulf and came to anchor amid scores of other assorted vessels. We climbed down cargo nets hanging over the side and dropped into an LCT (Landing Craft, Tank), I believe, which ran us in to shallow water about a hundred yards from the beach. From there, just like General MacArthur, we waded ashore.

Where the 122d FA went ashore, the beach was crowded and busy with logistical activities in support of the divisions that had made the assault landing a month earlier, and I think it was about the same all around the several miles of Lingayen beaches. Nevertheless, the first man I spoke to when I reached the beach was one I knew well, PFC Gilbert Higgins of Vermont, a member of my old unit, HQ Btry, 89th FA Bn. Big Higgins was there with a detail expediting supplies for the 25th Division.

The contingent from Morotai had brought a replacement for my lost L-4. This one was transferred from the 31st Division. It may not have been the worst plane the Dixie Division had, but it certainly wasn't the best. Just the same, I was happy to have my own ship once more, and as soon as we got our tents up on the old 43d Division strip at San Fabian, the boys got busy assembling and checking it and Vineyard's *Arizona Keed.*

The strip was a good one, sandy but firm, lined on one side with coco palms that provided some shade and concealment. The fire-blackened frame of an L-4 lay at one side.

As we worked to get our planes ready, local citizens began informally to visit us. Many of them had something to sell—a homemade candy wrapped in banana leaves, hand-rolled cigars in bundles of fifty tied with twine. Coming from a family of Kentucky tobacco farmers, I was pleasantly surprised to note that this was a tobacco-growing region. The men were clean and intelligent looking, most of them wearing beautiful pure white shirts. Old women squatted, grinning, in the background, smoking roll-your-own cigarettes with the lighted end inside their mouths—not just to show off, but by preference, we learned. Younger women were more shy around the soldiers and therefore less in evidence. Children were everywhere.

Some of the men told infuriating stories of atrocious or degenerate conduct on the part of Japanese soldiers during the occupation, and some claimed—maybe truthfully, maybe not—to have been guerrilla fighters against the Japanese. Some of these people impressed me as sincere and honest, but others, I'm sure, were merely seeking favor for whatever benefit it might bring them.

One young fellow made a deal with Vin: if we could get him some lard, he would bring us a fried chicken. Fried chicken! It was music to our South Pacific ears, and our boys went all out to scrounge some shortening from a mess sergeant. I guess we gave him about three or four pounds of it, and then we waited. But nothing happened. Finally, Vin saw fit to press the matter. The result was a few small pieces of (presumably) chicken, dry, tough, hard, cooked without breading of any kind, and really almost inedible. War is hell!

★

Lingayen Gulf, with its many fat ships and crowded beaches, was a prime target for Japanese air. Apparently unable to mount a massive and sustained campaign against it, which could have seriously hindered logistic support of the American offensive, they limited their effort to nightly harassing missions. Flying from fields on Taiwan, four hundred miles to the north, they kept at least one dive-bomber over Lingayen all night long every night for about the first two weeks we were there. The planes would come in high. As soon as one flew over the area, American searchlights would stab their beams into the dark sky and begin swinging to and fro as they tried to find it. When one got on it, the others would converge at that point, and the Japanese plane, twisting and turning in its frantic efforts to escape them, would shine like a star with the reflected light. Every gun on every ship and every gun ashore that could be brought to bear would open fire, and the whole gulf would be alight with tracers, flashes, and shell bursts, all aimed at that one enemy plane. The universe would roar and shake with the sound of guns. Sometimes the Japanese pilot would manage to escape the searchlights, and then the uproar would cease, but he would never back down from his mission, and soon he'd be in there again to face the music.

When he had just enough fuel remaining to make it home, the brave Nip would roll into a dive toward his selected target, and down he'd come, into a regular maelstrom of fire. Sometimes he'd be destroyed in midair, but surprisingly often he would come through apparently untouched, release his bomb, and vanish into the darkness over the sea or up the coast to the north, hugging the surface for security. I admired those enemy pilots.

One night when two or three of these guys were giving us a hard time and lots of ammo was being wasted on them, a bomb struck a pile of some kind of torpedoes on the beach near our San Fabian strip. The explosion was tremendous. We were lying in a shallow ditch, and it seemed to me as if the ground dropped away about a foot, then came up hard and hit me. At the same time, there was the warm impact of overpressure in the air. We heard that eleven men of a black supply unit that had been working on the beach were killed.

We didn't stay long at San Fabian. Under I Corps, the 33d "Golden Cross" Division was to relieve the exhausted 43d, which had been holding the north flank of the American forces while the 37th "Buckeye" Division and the gung-ho 1st Cavalry Division drove hard toward Manila, and the 25th "Tropic Lightning" fought its way straight eastward across Luzon.

Three days after our landing, the 33d's 123d Regimental Combat Team (RCT) was first to go into the line, relieving the 158th RCT on high ground just north of the road between the coastal village of Damortis and the town of Rosario. To support the 123d Infantry, Uncle Bud Carlson put his batteries into positions near the village of Rabon, and a Div Arty airstrip was established not far behind them. Our strip was bounded by the beach on one side and a railroad on the other. Paralleling the railroad was a highway. Beyond the highway was a flat area where the division ammunition company set up its tents, and right behind that was a long, low knoll that contained the 33d's ammo reserve. In the midst of the ammo dump were several light antiaircraft guns.

Our ten L-4s were lined up facing the strip, their tails to the railroad, and most of our tents were on the ocean side, on top of a ten-foot bank that sloped steeply to a narrow sand beach. Along there, behind the tents, we dug foxholes for protection in case the night raiders strayed from their usual targets. There were no trees nearby, and we used no camouflage for tents, planes, or vehicles.

As the other regiments went into line east and southeast of Rosario to the vicinity of Pozzarubio, the other battalion pilots established forward airstrips in their respective zones, occupying them during the day but returning to the Rabon strip at night. With the Div Arty pilots, Vin and I used only the Rabon strip for a while, since it was ideally located in our own zone of operations. Being old hands at the business now, we immediately began getting acquainted with our new battlefield and the local enemy forces.

While the other regiments—the 130th and 136th Infantry—had more immediate hot action, the 123d had the most critical task to perform. Anchoring the west end of the whole Sixth Army line and with the coastal highway providing the enemy an assault axis pointed directly at Colonel Serff's men and into the logistic base at Lingayen, the 123d had to hold at all costs; therefore, its initial actions were cautious, feeling out the enemy, and trying, of course, to determine his probable capabilities and intentions, while remaining at all times prepared to deal with a major attack. In making minor adjustments in its defensive dispositions, the 123d experienced some of its first fights on Luzon.

One of these early fights that I remember very clearly involved Lieutenant Schuster, the unfriendly young man I had first known aboard the ship coming up from New Guinea. Schuster's platoon had the mission of seizing a small, boulder-strewn knoll located maybe half a mile north of the Damortis-Rosario road, and I was overhead to handle general observation and artillery support as called for. As we had begun doing in New Guinea, we habitually carried not only our SCR-610 two-channel artillery radio back on the chart board but also had an SCR-300 radio mounted overhead for communication with the lower echelon infantry units we supported. One limitation, however, was that—for reasons I can't recall—the infantry always insisted that they could not operate their SCR-300 while actually moving, so when they began the attack on the knoll, they shut off their radio.

It was like a scene out of a movie. With Schuster at their head, the platoon charged up the slope, firing from the hip, throwing grenades, moving rapidly to close with the Japanese defenders. And the enemy's nerve gave way. Nipponese fighters began jumping up from their foxholes and running for the rear, bounding over the boulders and down the rear slope with the agility of mountain goats. The Americans chased them, individuals halting occasionally to aim and fire, and several of the enemy were knocked down as they fled.

Down the reverse slope, through a row of banana plants, across a shallow dry creek, and up a slope where stood a thatched Filipino farmhouse, moving toward a large banana grove on the next ridge, the enemy fled in apparent panic. Instead of halting to consolidate his position on the knoll, Lt. Schuster led his men in a wild pursuit to exploit the rout. As they went down the hill, I saw two of the enemy halt behind the farmhouse and set up a machine gun to fire from one corner. I could not talk to Schuster or to his radioman, so I dived over him, gunning the engine and rocking the wings to warn him of the danger. But he paid no heed. His helmet gone and his blonde hair shining in the sun, his carbine held high in one hand, he raced at a dead run, a good fifty yards ahead of his men. As he was passing through the row of banana plants, the machine gun opened on him. He pitched headlong into the bottom of the dry creek and lay still.

Traditionally, it was a glorious way for a soldier to die; nevertheless, I felt heartsick as I looked down at that tow-headed bloody heap in the dusty creek. It was so unnecessary.

Intelligence from various sources, including observations by Vin and me, indicated the probability that the enemy was withdrawing from his positions in front of the 123d, leaving only an outpost line, while he established a new main line of resistance (MLR) somewhere back on the mountains. To help verify that, one Lieutenant Jones was assigned a patrol mission to feel out the enemy line and determine its nature. I didn't know Jones before and never met him afterward, but before he led his reinforced platoon out on the mission, I flew him on a reconnaissance of the area in which he was to operate. Jones was a small, thin, very mild and modest young man with light brown hair and a nervous manner. Upon our return from the recon, I asked him what he thought. He stood with his head down for a few seconds, then looked at me with a worried expression and said, "Kerns, this will be my first time on a mission like this, and it looks very dangerous to me. I don't mind telling you, I'm scared to death."

I could only wish him good luck and silently praise his honesty. Watching over Jones's patrol, I saw them moving down a dry creek between grassy hills in the low range that parallels that part of the Luzon coast a couple of miles inland. Ahead was a junction with a larger dry stream, and beyond that was a hillside that appeared to hold nothing more threatening than dry brown cogon grass waving in the wind. But suddenly that innocent-looking hillside blazed with the fire of numerous Arisakas and two or three Nambu machine guns, and Jones's men hit the ground, taking fullest advantage of every small depression, every rock or tuffet that might stop a bullet. But just a few seconds later, they were up and racing toward the foot of the hill, where a four-foot creek bank offered the only good cover available for hundreds of yards around.

I watched them with serious misgivings. How could they now disengage and get out of the pinned-down situation they were in? Having halted, they turned on their radio, and I asked Jones if he wanted artillery fire on the hillside. He said no, and I thought he was crazy. But soon I saw what he had in mind. At several points along the creek bank, I saw

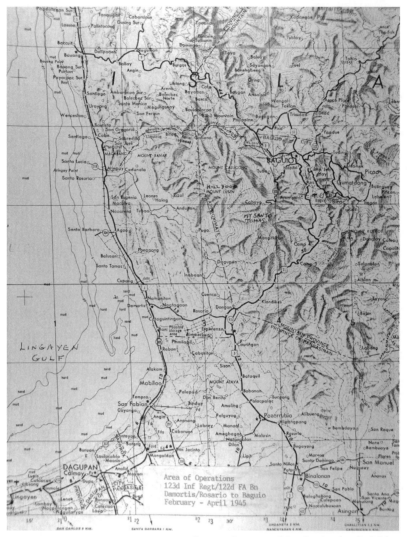

LUZON, PHILIPPINE ISLANDS. Area of operations, 123d Regiment/122d Field Artillery Battalion: Damortis-Rosario to Baguio, February–April 1945.

the men set fire to the cogon grass. The fires quickly spread and joined, and the wind sent a line of raging flame up the hill. Lids of spider holes popped up, and Japanese riflemen ran for their lives as the Americans fired up the hill at whatever they could see. And Lieutenant Jones, the man who was "scared to death," proceeded on his mission.

Moving swiftly, he hit the enemy line at numerous points, sometimes finding nothing, sometimes striking fierce resistance. When he hit resistance, he fought long enough to assess its strength, and he returned to our lines with two captured machine guns, leaving behind at least sixty enemy dead and bringing home two wounded men, his only casualties. He had determined that the enemy was, indeed, withdrawing; only a strong outpost line remained in our immediate front.

The main objective of the 33d Division was the Mountain Province city of Baguio. Baguio, which had a prewar population of about thirty thousand, was established in 1909 and intended by Philippine governor William Howard Taft to become the country's summer capitol, because its mile-high situation in the Cordillera Central made it an ideal place to escape the oppressive heat of Manila. It was now the headquarters of Yamashita's 14th Army. Although the Kennon Road was a paved highway up from the plains of central Luzon, the enemy had practically insuperable advantages for defense on that avenue, and it was pretty much ruled out as the avenue for the division's main effort.

There was supposed to be an ancient road called "the Old Spanish Trail" that led through the mountains from the town of Pugo to a village near Baguio called Tuba (not to be confused with the town of Tubao). It was hoped that this old trail could be used as a route for the main attack on Baguio, and since it lay in the 123d RCT's zone of operations, Vin and I were directed to find it. We tried but with little positive result. If the trail was there, it was long unused and overgrown with trees, brush, vines, or tall grass. Only beyond the crest of the ridge between Mounts Calugong and Santo Tomas was there a clear indication of a trail, although we did spot possible traces at other points. But it was decided that the 123d would seize Pugo and from there would launch its drive into the mountains to take Baguio. Our engineers would build supply roads as we advanced.

The first thing the RCT had to do was take Pugo, and the best routes to that intermediate objective needed to be searched out. Since the ground reconnaissance would have to go far behind the enemy's outposts, the recon force would be in danger of being isolated and destroyed by stronger enemy forces from his main line, the exact location of which

204 ABOVE THE THUNDER

had not yet been established. It was planned as a five-day mission for a company of infantry that would depart the vicinity of Rosario, go north to Pugo, west to Tubao, and through a narrow pass in the coastal hills to Agoo, then south back to our lines at Damortis. The patrol would move fast to minimize the danger of interception.

And who should get the job of commanding this important and hazardous mission but that same rough and tough, bullnecked, red-faced captain who had boasted so much aboard the ship en route to Luzon. Because I don't want to tell you his name, I'll call him Captain Red.

On the morning of the third day of his five-day patrol, Captain Red had still not penetrated the outpost line north of Rosario. In fact, he had veered far to the west, apparently to avoid the outposts, and neither he nor his men had fired a shot. As I went out to relieve Vin in our constant daytime watch over the patrol, I was given a message drop bag containing a written message for Captain Red. On the way out, I took the opportunity to read it, printed boldly in capital letters:

RED:

GET BACK ON YOUR PLANNED ROUTE AND PROCEED WITH YOUR MISSION OR I WILL RELIEVE YOU OF YOUR COMMAND.

SERFF

I dropped the message. About an hour later, I was asked to relay a radio message to the effect that Captain Red had suffered heatstroke and was being evacuated. One of his lieutenants had assumed command and was continuing the mission.

The only account of this patrol that I have ever read makes no mention of Colonel Serff's threat to relieve Red, nor does it mention his evacuation. In fact, it gives him full credit for accomplishing the mission. So maybe I'm wrong, maybe he was just as good a fighter as he claimed to be, and maybe he really did suffer heatstroke. Maybe he wasn't even evacuated. If that is true, I certainly owe him my most abject apologies.

Aerial view of the rugged, mountainous terrain that confronted the U.S. forces in retaking Luzon from the Japanese, and a typical view of the landscape for the pilots of the artillery battalions. The town of Ambuclao is just off the map at left (Photograph from Sanford Winston, *The Golden Cross*).

All things considered, it might be better if I send my apologies by wire from Timbuktu. But this is the way I saw it and the way I still believe it happened.

And so there has existed in my mind a very distinct contrast among three types of officer as represented by Lieutenant Schuster, Lieutenant Jones, and Captain Red: the loner who proved a gallant leader—although a rash one—when sent against the enemy; the modest officer who admitted his fear, then put it aside and led courageously and brilliantly on his first independent combat mission; and the braggart who quailed when the chips were down.

But the adventures of Captain Red's patrol were not yet over. Under his lieutenant (as I believe), the patrol immediately passed through the outpost line and moved toward Pugo, that night digging in somewhere short of that place. In fact, I don't think they ever reached the town itself, but they did pass close to it and probably gained enough information to achieve their purpose.

My first clear memory of them after the heatstroke matter was about noon on the fourth day, I think. They were moving toward Tubao along a narrow gravel road that ran through a wide, open valley. About the time that I came up and relieved Vin, they became engaged in a firefight with a small enemy force that was guarding a stock of ammunition stored in a dry creek just above a little wooden bridge. They killed a few of the enemy but quickly moved on, asking me to destroy the ammunition dump with artillery fire.

I called FDC and asked for precision fire. The creek bed in which the target was located happened to be parallel to the gun-target line, so as the 105 mm rounds came in, one after another, the range dispersion caused some of them to burst in or near the creek, well beyond the ammo dump. These rounds killed or wounded a few of the eight or ten Japs who fled in that direction. Only one man seemed to realize that it was wiser to move away from the creek and the gun-target line, because the lateral dispersion was not so great and, therefore, was less likely to cause him trouble. He ran across a field for about a hundred yards and lay in a ditch. He was perfectly safe from our fire.

The howitzer in the 122d over by Rabon kept dropping the rounds in while I waited for one to hit the right spot and start the ammo blowing up. Meanwhile, I kept an eye on the progress of the patrol as it continued down the road, and I also watched the soldier in the ditch, mentally congratulating him on his wisdom in choosing to get out of the line of fire. I felt glad that he was safe there.

But then I saw him get up out of the ditch and run back toward the creek and the ammunition cache, the center of the pattern of shell bursts. He reached the six-foot-high bank and jumped for the creek bed—but he never hit the ground. At that instant, while he was in midair and I was looking directly at him, the entire ammunition stock went up in one grand explosion, centered right where he was. Anticipating such an explosion, I was flying at almost two thousand feet above the ground. From there I could see a silvery ring of compression that flashed out to a radius of at least half a mile around the target, and a second later I felt an impact as if a giant had hit the propeller hub with a sledgehammer. I'm sure that there was nothing identifiable left of my smart little Nip soldier.

For more than sixty years I've wondered why that fellow went back over there. I've thought of only one probable answer: it may be that there were wounded men still in there, unable to get out of danger, and calling for help. It probably was to help a fellow soldier that our hero went back—and he's one more reason why I say there's nothing finer than a good soldier. Seems to me someone else, too, has said something about a man who lays down his life for his friends. But I don't know the soldier's name, and no other surviving person knew how he died. Some Japanese mother knows only that he never came home from the war.

By the time the ammo had blown up and I was able to catch up with Captain Red's patrol, it had passed Tubao and was entering the pass where a stream cuts out to the coastal flatland. I remember being impressed with the picturesque scene at Tubao, where a tall church steeple stood dominant in the ravaged little town and the wreckage of a U.S. Navy fighter lay in an adjoining field.

The patrol went through the pass at the double-quick and drew not one round from the enemy, so far as I could see. But some distance in its rear was a group of men wounded in the ammo dump fight, escorted by a squad led by a sergeant. They could not go at double time. Neither could Cpl. Alphonso H. DiNunzio of my battery, who had to carry the heavy radio intended for use by our FO team with the patrol. Now the FO was far ahead with the patrol commander, and Al DiNunzio was struggling along with the orphans.

The patrol was out of the pass and still going full tilt toward Agoo when the party with the wounded reached the middle of the danger area. On their right—the north—as they followed the road was a steep hill, on the crest of which, we knew, there must be manned positions of the Jap outpost line. To their left, a high bank dropped off to a rocky creek that had only scattered pools of water in it. Across the creek was a lower bank and a weed-covered bottom that spread about a hundred yards to a line of bushes at the foot of another steep hill—the end of a long ridge—crowned by another enemy position. It was now that the enemy opened fire.

From both hills enemy machine guns rattled, and light mortar rounds dropped about the small party of Americans. They went over the bank and took cover among the large rocks in the creek. I called a fire mission to FDC and tried to get suppressive fire on the enemy but found it impossible. The line of fire was parallel to the ridge, and the nearer position was in dead space for the howitzers. We were firing there at maximum range, and the more northerly hill could not be reached at all.

And then Corporal DiNunzio came on the air and called me.

"Lieutenant, I need help," he said. "The sergeant is dead, and so are several others, and we have the wounded. The company has gone ahead and left us. These men are scared. I'm the senior NCO now, and they're looking to me to get them out of here. Sir, I'm not infantry. I don't know what to do. Can you help us some way?"

I told him to hang on for a minute while I thought about the matter. I figured that the enemy would soon be down with a patrol to finish them off at close range, so we had to do something fast. The enemy would expect them to move down the creek toward the coast so would probably block that route first. The Red patrol was still marching vigorously on down the road and not communicating with me, so there was no help to be expected from that source.

But while I was considering the situation, I noticed a ditch that began at the foot of the south hill and ran across the bottom to the creek, coming out only a few yards upstream from where the men lay. It was covered over by the rank growth of weeds, and I thought it probably couldn't be seen by observers on the ground. I was certain that men crawling through it could not be seen, even from the air.

"Kadi 11 this is Kadi 8. Can you see where a ditch comes into the creek about twenty yards up from you?"

"Yes, I see it."

"OK, listen: leave the dead behind but take the wounded, your weapons, your radio, your water, and your rations. Crawl—I say again crawl—through that ditch until you reach a line of bushes at the foot of the hill. Lie still right there until it gets dark. Then move very carefully around the base of the hill to your left. Don't go to the right, because the Japs may be laying for you that way. Go to the left until you're about two hundred yards back from the nose of the ridge, then go straight up and over and down the other side. Be as silent as possible, no talking, no firing unless you absolutely must fire in self-defense. Do you understand?"

"Yes, sir, I understand."

"When you get well down from the top of the ridge, set up your radio and call Kadi 3 on this frequency. We'll be monitoring and we'll give you instructions from there on. OK?"

"OK, sir."

"Good luck, Corporal. Out."

I hoped I was right about how the enemy would be thinking, and I hoped that there was no manned position on the ridge where I told them to cross. I did not envy the handsome young corporal his task, I pitied the men with him, and I inwardly raged at the commander of the company of American troops disappearing far down the road to Agoo. It was hard to believe. I stayed overhead and watched until the men had disappeared into the weedy ditch, and then I went about my business, hoping the Japs, upon investigation, would think that the four or five bloody bodies among the rocks were the only ones who had not gotten through.

DiNunzio brought out every man to safety. He was promoted to sergeant and awarded the Silver Star "for gallantry in action." As for the remains of the infantry sergeant and the men who died with him in the creek, I have no knowledge. It was a few weeks before we finally secured that pass. The division history does not mention this little episode at all.

Streams of refugees now began coming down the railroad past the airstrip. One day I made the mistake of leaving my brown leather flight jacket in one of the maintenance tents on the side next to the railroad. When I returned no more than five minutes later, it had vanished. A refugee had ducked quickly down the grade and grabbed it.

The nightly harassment by Japanese air continued, and we often sat outside our tents and watched the grand display of fireworks. On a few occasions, while sitting out there, we saw an escaping dive-bomber come

The author, in February 1945, beside the L-4 that was sent to him by the 31st Division to replace the one that sank in Maffin Bay, with mechanic "Wendy" Young lying beneath it. This was at the Rabon strip that was burned off a few nights later. A ship in Lingayen Gulf is faintly visible in the background.

scooting along, following the light strip of beach sand, so low that we could fire straight out at it with our carbines, so near that with better light we could have recognized the pilot. It occurred to us that if we could see the bomber so plainly, he surely couldn't miss seeing our L-4s sitting lined up there, their wings reflecting the moonlight.

It just happened that the day after one of these bombers had buzzed past us in the moonlight we moved from the Rabon strip to a field near a small village on a broad ridge just south of the Damortis-Rosario road. A Japanese artillery unit had been hard hit there by counter-battery fire of the 43d Division only a short time before we relieved them. A number of bodies, including a couple of officers, still lay among the weeds. We could see nice swords, but none of us could stomach the stench of the decaying bodies to recover one.

The nearby village threw a big dance that night and invited us to attend. Except for a few men on guard and telephone watch, all of us went. In the middle of a beaten circle of bare earth hung a lantern on a pole. Around it, the people danced to the music of a small string band playing instruments that resembled guitars if one didn't look too closely at them. I tried to play one until I found that it had only five strings and was tuned unlike any instrument I had ever played. Not being a dancer, I merely watched, as did most of our group.

While the dance was in progress, the nightly visitors from Taiwan arrived over Lingayen Gulf. As soon as they saw the searchlights come on, the Filipinos put out their lantern, and everyone stood in the moonlight and watched. When the guns began to fire, we had a grandstand view of the show, as good a one of its kind as I had ever seen. Then there were flashes much nearer to us than those we had seen before, and the heavy thud of bombs came rolling up to us from about three miles away.

"Those bombs are hitting our old strip!" one of our pilots exclaimed. "Damned good thing we're not there tonight!"

And he was almost right. We guessed later that they probably were aiming at our strip, our planes having undoubtedly been observed the night before. But they hit the division ammo dump over the hill, and they set it off. We watched for a couple of hours as exploding artillery and mortar shells, grenades, demolition explosives, small arms cartridges, and flares put on a sideshow of their own. We went back to our new strip and turned in then, but the fireworks went on most of the night. The next day the old strip was completely burned over and liberally sprinkled with shell casings and cartridge brass. Across the road, the ammo company's tents, those not burned, hung in tatters on their ropes and center poles. The ammo dump hill was gouged, charred, and strewn with brass, and amid the debris were the twisted remains of a couple of antiaircraft guns. There must have been casualties, but we didn't hear of any.

For about two weeks, we had to be very stingy with our ammunition expenditures until the reserve stock could be replaced. Nevertheless, Vin and I—and, I'm sure, our colleagues in the other battalions—fired numerous missions on various small targets of opportunity discovered as we searched every nook and cranny of the coastal hills for the enemy. I remember a tiny village that, on my map, was named Pong Pong. It was just a half dozen shacks that appeared to have been deserted by their

Filipino inhabitants. But under one of the roofs I saw what I thought was a Japanese truck, so I called for fire. I still don't know whether there really was a truck there, but I sure clobbered hell out of Pong Pong.

Around the first of March, the 123d started moving out to take Pugo. During this phase, Vin and I briefly used a forward strip on the southern side of Agoo. Our boys would drive out there in the three-quarter-ton truck and remain until our last refueling of the day, then return to the new Div Arty strip at Rosario.

I made friends there at Agoo with an eleven-year-old Filipino boy named Abelardo Madarang. He came out to the strip, introduced himself, and in a very grave manner presented me with a gift. It was a postcard-size picture of Nuestra Senora de Guadalupe that had on its reverse a Spanish language advertisement for Vicks Vapo-Rub. I wrote his name on it that day, and I still have it. I also have one of two identification tags that Abelardo gave me a little later. He said they belonged to his uncle and his aunt with whom he had lived and who were killed while the Japanese were withdrawing from Agoo when a Japanese soldier tossed a grenade into their home. I understood that such tags were required to be worn by some Filipino adults during the Japanese occupation. The one I still have is a crude, homemade, cloth replica of a Japanese flag and has Japanese characters that I suppose spell the name of a person. This cloth is sewn between two pieces of acetate and has a small loop to facilitate fastening it on a button.

On the day of the big drive to Pugo, Vin and I were quite busy, of course, although I can't recall the specific missions I may have fired that day. We overran the enemy outpost line and pushed on toward his MLR. There was much movement but very little fighting, much territory coming under our control as all the objectives were taken. It extended our artillery observation area of interest into the hills well beyond those objectives, and just before noon I went to our battalion CP, which was still at Rabon, to pick up some new map sections to cover the new areas. General Paxton, the Div Arty commander, was visiting and having lunch with Uncle Bud and the officers. I also stayed for lunch. Afterward, the general's aide took a picture of him standing with Uncle Bud, the staff, and me outside the CP tent. At some point during these proceedings, General Paxton asked me what I'd been doing.

"Flying, sir, watching over the troops, firing whatever targets I can get."

"How's the attack going?"

"Quite well, sir, I believe. Looks to me as if it's moving fast just about everywhere, with only minor holdups. We've started working so far into the mountains now that we ran off our maps. That's why I came down here."

"Well, that's mighty fine, mighty fine. Gittin ahr baws some mighty fine trainin'."

Although he was quite serious, I thought General Paxton's comment was amusing. He was always talking about "getting our boys some training." However, the future would reveal that the 33d Division was one of those scheduled to make the assault landings on Kyushu in the initial invasion of the Japanese home islands in November 1945, had the atomic bombs on Hiroshima and Nagasaki not brought the war to a close before that became necessary. I don't think there is any doubt that whatever previous combat experience our men might have had would have seemed like mere peacetime training exercises in comparison with the fury they would have faced on Kyushu. I suppose Paxton was anticipating that event.

With Pugo secured and the infantry moving into the foothills, the 122d displaced to positions in the valley between the coastal hills and the mountains. Our positions were only a few hundred yards from where I'd blown up the Jap ammo dump, and I walked down to the place, thinking mostly of the little Jap soldier whose compassionate self-sacrifice had so impressed me. I stood there at the crater, where the once vertical creek banks were now just barren slopes, and thought about him. But there was nothing to see.

Div Arty established a new base strip near the beach at Aringay. Our tents were set up in a coconut grove, and our situation was very pleasant. Dick Bortz had scrounged from somewhere a silver Aeronca L-3, and the Div Arty HQ pilots used it for strictly administrative business, no combat flights. But the administrative flights included an occasional one down to Manila to bring back what passed for whiskey—nothing more than water spiked with alcohol and colored with caramel. The taste only vaguely resembled whiskey, but it did have an intoxicating effect on those who drank enough of it. I didn't; however, I did fly the L-3 on the whiskey run one time, stopping at Clark Field en route.

Bortz had the instincts of an Air Force man, as you may already have guessed. He believed in living as comfortably as possible under given circumstances. There at Aringay, he found a rusty old bucket. He'd fill it with sea water and some of the small crabs that swarmed on the nearby beach, and build a fire under it. As soon as the water got hot, the stench would drive the rest of us a hundred yards or so away. And when the crabs were cooked to suit him, he'd make me, at least, sick with the sight of eating them.

And Bortz had built here—using Filipino labor hired with Army funds—a Filipino-style thatched bamboo shack which he named "the Cub Pub." Inside, there was a nice polished bamboo bar equipped with "glasses" of various sizes, from jiggers on up, expertly fashioned of bamboo sections and polished in the Filipino way with banana peels. From somewhere he obtained a monkey-sized ten-gallon hat to be worn by the bartender, and he ran a roster of pilots for bartender duty in the evenings. Of course, the bar was stocked with Manila whiskey, and those bound and determined to be festive sometimes achieved modest success at the Cub Pub.

I must mention my own contribution to the Cub Pub. I had written an absurd verse titled "Purple Petunias," which contained the supposed rambling thoughts of an artillery pilot reclining in the shade of an L-4 wing. Fortunately, it is no longer extant. However, Bortz liked it, and he posted a copy of it behind the bar next to his sign that read: "DON'T FLUB THE DUB IN THE CUB PUB, BUB!"

★

The day our infantry pushed on out of Pugo and into the hills, I observed some preparatory fires for them and watched them assault a fairly open piece of ground not far from the town. The enemy withdrew, leaving a large number of dead and wounded on the ground. As our men moved across the field, I saw them fire several shots from their M-1s into each body, obviously making no attempt to determine whether the Japanese soldier—or marine in this case, I believe—was alive or dead. They took absolutely no unnecessary risks in dealing with the enemy. They shot first and didn't bother with questions.

The generally accepted belief among American troops was that wounded Japanese were suicidal, believing that being made prisoner was a disgrace. And there is no doubt that many of them would, indeed, sacrifice their lives rather than give up. They were dangerous. However, a friend of mine, Kenny Bushong of Findlay, Ohio, who served with occupation forces in Japan after the war, said he spoke with a former Japanese officer who had been a POW. He asked the man how he had reconciled his submission to capture with the bushido warrior code that says suicide is preferable to surrender. The man laughed, and his reply was, "Kill myself? Who? Me? Boo sheet!"

Another story told in those days, but which I am inclined to doubt, concerns an American patrol that surprised a Japanese sentry who was sitting on the ground, his rifle across his knees. When the patrol's point man came into view a few yards away, the sentry leaped to his feet and brought his rifle to his shoulder. Before he could aim and fire, the American merely swung his Garand to the front and triggered several quick shots, never raising the rifle to his shoulder. The Japanese dropped his rifle, and as he sank to the ground he gasped out his last words—in English—"Oh, you hip-shooting Yankee sonofabitch! You've killed me!"

What do you think?

Leaving Pugo, the 123d infantry advanced through a jumble of hills and ravines cluttered with small trees, brush, vines, and cogon grass, that lay between two high, sharp, converging mountain ridges. Ahead, the two ridges came together to form an eminence we called Hill 3000 because its elevation was three thousand feet above sea level—and nearly that far above Pugo. Hill 3000 was our first major intermediate objective on the road to Baguio.

As the infantry worked and fought its way upward through this difficult terrain, it was necessary to control the ridges on the flanks. The tops of those ridges were very narrow, and the Japanese liked to tunnel from the rear side and fire from well-concealed slits. Such positions can use up a lot of artillery ammunition while suffering little damage, since direct target hits are essential, but Vin and I spent hours searching for hidden machine guns along those ridges. We had little success, and our preparatory fires for attacking objectives on the ridges were pretty much in the blind. Infantry units were stopped over and over again by heavy small arms fire and grenades tossed or rolled down the steep slopes by enemy soldiers concealed and protected in the short tunnels through the ridge.

I recall one instance in which an entire company was halted by fire from at least three machine guns. After a delay of several minutes, I saw one man—a staff sergeant, I learned later, but I've forgotten his name—remove his helmet and extra gear and start rolling rapidly to his left. Reaching a shallow wash that led almost to the top of the ridge, he started crawling up it, having just enough cover to keep the machine guns from stopping him. He reached a point almost on the crest, apparently without being seen by the enemy, and now he was so close that they could not see him from their firing slits unless he passed directly in front of one. He crawled along the ridge, then, just below the level of the firing slits. When he got close to a machine-gun slit, he tossed a grenade inside. As soon as it exploded, he grabbed the barrel of the weapon, pulled it out of the position, and slung it down the hill below him. Three times he repeated that performance, and then the company was able to come up and take that section of the ridge.

You see, we had some daring men on our side, too, and very often it was such a man, all alone, who moved us forward.

Among the hills on the approach to Hill 3000 I discovered a village of the mountain people known as Igorots. It was a double row of grass-thatched shacks along a foot trail across a grassy hillside, and a group of the people stood on the trail and watched as I flew over. Thinking of the danger of their being hit by artillery fire or caught in crossfire between American and Japanese infantry, I decided to see if I could get them out of the way. Although Vin and I had no instructions regarding such matters, and although I didn't know whether anyone there could read English, I carefully printed a note:

GO TO PUGO. AMERICANS AND JAPANESE MAY FIGHT WHERE YOU NOW ARE. GO TO PUGO AND YOU WILL BE SAFE.

AMERICAN ARMY

I dropped the note, and they did go to Pugo, the entire population of the village. The note was returned to me through our message center, and I think I still have it somewhere. I was happy to find that the higher command approved of my action.

The Igorots are members of an ethnic group that then inhabited—and, I suppose, still inhabits—the central mountain range of northern Luzon, and that chose to live in the traditional primitive style of their ancestors rather than join mainstream Filipino society. They were handsome, intelligent, and in many cases financially well off, thanks to their mining of gold. In at least one mine, Igorot men had to swim under subterranean water for some distance, then surface and work in a tunnel sealed off by the water. I was told that some Igorot leaders were college graduates, and in later years the tribal peoples slowly started assimilating into the general population.

Although combat engineer troops followed as closely as possible behind the infantry, building a supply road, supplying the most forward elements became a serious problem in the rugged mountain terrain. To help solve the problem, the 33d Division hired a number of Igorot men to serve as water carriers for the troops. That didn't work very well. First, many an Igorot bearer arrived at the front having consumed—or poured out—a good part of his five gallons of water. Worse still, when fired on by the enemy—and ambushes or isolated snipers were not uncommon—the men tended to drop their loads and head for home. They lost the job.

But the Igorot women—the wives and daughters of those same men—now stepped forward and offered to take over the task. And they did. Each carrying an American five-gallon can of water, escorted by a few American riflemen, they became a familiar sight on the trails leading to the most forward positions. They drank only the water designated for their use, and when the bullets started flying, they merely hit the dirt and trusted the soldiers to protect them.

While the Div Arty airstrip remained at Aringay, Vin and I established a new forward strip at Pugo. Since it was at the foot of the rugged terrain in which there was no place to safely land, we operated from there for quite a while. A couple of our boys drove over there daily in the weapons carrier, taking fuel and tools for the day. After the last refueling, the men took off for home, and each pilot terminated his last flight at Aringay. There the men who had rested during the day did our deeper maintenance during the night. I think we almost never had an unflyable plane during daylight hours.

The terrain in this area made maintenance of a continuous line of contact impossible. Instead, the line was composed of a series of defensive perimeters of company or smaller size. In spite of numerous patrols operating between these perimeters, it was not difficult for the Japanese to infiltrate our territory and give us a hard time in a small way. For example, they mined our newly built supply road almost every night. The small antipersonnel mines did little damage to vehicles, but they were a distinct nuisance.

Infiltrated Japanese snipers hiding in bamboo thickets on nearby hills occasionally fired at people, airplanes, and vehicles on our forward airstrips, but although they sometimes kept our ground crew lying in ditches when not busy, they never managed to do us any harm. In fact, it almost seems as if they must have tried not to hit anything important.

At one of our forward strips—I've forgotten which one—I was resting by a tree one day while the men were lying on the ground in deference to one of these snipers. A pilot from I Corps landed his L-4 and walked off a few yards to take care of some personal business, yelling imperious orders at me to refuel his plane. Apparently, he didn't see that I was an officer, but his manner angered me. I never moved, and I told the men to stand fast as well. He turned back toward his plane, looked closely at me, and then helped himself to a tank of gasoline. I don't think he realized that the sniper fired at him a couple of times. We didn't worry about him. The sniper had never hit anything of importance. I think he must have been a volunteer they felt they could well do without up in the lines.

A little later, this same corps pilot—a skinny guy whose appearance reminded me so much of myself that I didn't like him—had an engine failure and crash-landed several miles out in enemy country. He managed to evade capture and spent two weeks making his way through the mountains. During that period, he had nothing to eat but some rations he found on the bodies of Japanese soldiers killed by artillery fire. He finally made contact with a patrol of the 25th Division, far to the east of us, and came home safely. After the war, I became acquainted with an Ohioan named Lynn Jones. Exchanging war stories with him, I learned that he, as a sergeant, had led the patrol that brought in our lost corps pilot.

The bulldozers the engineers used on the road job became prime targets for Japanese suicide squads.[1] That brought trouble for some of the infantry companies within whose perimeters the dozers were parked at night. Enemy soldiers carrying demolition charges would try to sneak into the perimeter, and when discovered they would charge for the bulldozers, creating pandemonium among the defenders. During one of these attacks, my friend Lt. Raymond Utke, firing his carbine at a Jap racing toward him, detonated the demolition charge the man was carrying. The explosion disintegrated the Japanese, of course, and it was just about the last straw for Utke. The concussion left him punchy like a boxer who has taken too many blows to the head. I never saw or heard of him after that; I hope his recovery was complete.

At dawn one morning, I was called up to investigate some kind of enemy activity outside one of the company perimeter. The perimeter was on the nose of a grassy ridge surrounded by ravines except where the ridge continued rising gently toward Hill 3000. Out there about two hundred yards, I spotted a Japanese officer lying on his stomach and looking toward the perimeter with field glasses. He seemed to pay no attention to me as I searched for the troops I thought must be with him. But I could see no one else. I suggested to the company commander that he drop a few light mortar rounds out there and see what developed.

When the first 60 mm mortar round burst, the officer leaped to his feet and headed back up the ridge on the run, and with him went fourteen men who had been perfectly camouflaged in the grass. Not far up, the ridge narrowed to a small peak overgrown with brush, and over that the enemy could not be seen by the Americans on the ground. But I could see that the path they were following led them up to the head of a ravine, then cut back left around a grassy hillside in full view from where they had been when I first saw them.

Anticipating that they would continue to follow that path, crouching low in the grass while crossing the hillside, I suggested to the company commander that he send a machine gun out to where he had fired the mortar rounds and set up to cover a point where the enemy's route would pass around the nose of the hill and, therefore, could be seen from the ground. I would give the gunner the word to open fire when the enemy was most exposed and vulnerable.

A squad of men with rifles and a couple of BARs moved out and, once in position, established radio contact with me. The Japs moved, crouching, across the hillside, then turned the corner to go around and behind the nose of the hill, where they would be safe from our direct fire. As the leading man was almost to safety and the maximum number of them were exposed, I told the infantry to fire. There was an instantaneous hurricane of lead along that pathway, and twelve of the fifteen men fell. Only three got over the hill and kept going.

The officer was among those fallen, and I could see a light machine gun lying in the path among the bodies. The company agreed that it was worthwhile to see what of intelligence value might be found on the officer and started the squad moving around the same route the enemy had used. The route was completely concealed from the enemy line on what I'll call "the giant's footstool," although we didn't call it that then, because it would have made a footstool for a giant seated on Hill 3000 and facing us. Meanwhile, I watched the fallen enemy troopers very closely from very low altitude to try to detect any signs of life. I saw only one.

A soldier who looked young and was tall for a Japanese got up from where he had fallen in the grass just off the path. He drew a knife and began stumbling about, slashing at the air all around him. It was obvious that he was blinded, and I was immediately struck with pity for him. His blind wandering, always fighting imaginary enemies with his knife, took him on around the hill in the general direction they had been going, but he strayed down the hillside until he came up against the bushes along a ravine. He followed the edge of the ravine for a short distance, stabbing and slashing at the bushes. Then, as if his sanity had returned to him, he stopped fighting, walked up the hill a few paces, and sat down. He laid his head back on his pack. Flying over within a few feet of him, I could see that his eyes were just bloody holes in his head, as if a bullet had gone through from side to side and taken both of them out. After a few minutes, he put a white cloth over his face. It was soon discolored with blood.

Meanwhile, the American squad traversed the hillside and arrived at the point where the trail turned and they could see the bodies lying in the path. I had told them about the machine gun and a man I judged to be an NCO who lay near it. I had asked the squad leader to halt and contact me again before turning the corner. He did so, and I told him I had seen no movement other than the one blind man, but I warned him again about the machine gun, which lay pointed back toward the turn. Serving as point for his squad, the sergeant cautiously moved toward the gun.

Quick as a flash, the Jap NCO rolled over and had the gun firing. I could see the grass movement and the dust as the bullets cut through just in front of the American sergeant's feet. He leaped back a step, but the instant the machine-gun burst ceased, he leaped forward again, leading with his tommy gun, and the Japanese gunner slumped in death that this time was not a pretense.

The squad searched the enemy bodies and carried back the weapons, but they did not venture over the hill to get the blinded soldier. He sat there on the hillside all day, the cloth over his face his only protection from the blazing sun. All around him the war went on—infantry firefights, artillery fire here and there—but he could only wait in darkness and what must have been terrible pain. I looked at him several times during the day, and the only movement I saw was when he would occasionally wring out the bloody cloth and put it back over his face. Next morning, he was gone. I wonder whether, somewhere in Japan, that man is still living today. I hope so. I feel responsible for his blindness, and I hope that it has not kept him from enjoying a good life.

American forces came into closer proximity to Baguio, and as the food supply in that city dwindled, General Yamashita permitted many civilians to leave and seek refuge wherever they might. Groups began making their way through the mountains to our lines. It wasn't an easy trek. Besides the possibility of trouble from the combat activity, there was the very serious problem of food and water. For this reason, we pilots were directed, when not flying combat missions, to load our planes with emergency rations and go looking for refugees in the mountains needing help. We were to be especially watchful for any of the Belgian or Filipina nuns from the convent at Baguio.

One day I sighted a group of refugees that included several of the nuns. Their position in a small vale between steep mountain walls, on a trail surrounded by forest, made getting into position for the drop a difficult proposition. I had to go into a diving turn, then pull level at the last minute and drop the rations. During the turn, I heard a loud noise, like a round of light antiaircraft artillery bursting close by. I wondered how that could be, in this remote situation, but I heard no more, so I soon forgot about it.

Arriving back at the Aringay strip, I approached in our usual steep slipping turn and landed. As I rolled up to the tie-down spot, all the men came running out to the plane. As usual, Wendell Young was first on the spot. He dashed up with a very concerned look on his face.

"Are you OK, sir? What happened?"

I didn't know what he was talking about, and I said, "Nothing happened. Why? What's wrong?"

"Well, how did you get that big hole in your left wing?"

When I made my slipping turn, they had seen it, and they thought the plane had been hit by artillery. All the fabric had been torn off the top of the outer three feet of the left wing. That's why I said earlier that the Dixie Division certainly didn't send me the best plane they could dig up.[2]

Vin really did get hit by artillery about that time—our own, in fact, artillery he was adjusting. He came in from a mission looking just slightly pale, and he called me into our tent. He showed me a hole in the right hip pocket of his trousers, a mangled handkerchief that had been in the pocket, another hole through his shorts, and a blistering red burn on his hip. Then he showed me a shell fragment that had come through the bottom of his L-4, through his canvas seat, and—well, you've heard the rest.

"Crash, do you think I should report this?"

"Why, certainly you should report it, Vin. Technically—and actually— you're wounded. I wouldn't hesitate a minute."

And he did report it.

Getting hit by fragments of our own shells was not at all uncommon for us pilots. I've already mentioned it happening to me—to my plane, that is. And it had happened to Vin before, too. Fred Hoffman had his aileron cable cut by a fragment and had to use rudder only for bank control on the way home. A fellow I knew later, Capt. Sidney Richardson, was flying an observer in Europe when a 155 mm shell passed through his L-5 without exploding; however, the bourrelet—a ridge on the shoulder of a projectile that centers it in the tube of the weapon— grazed the observer's back and killed him. On many occasions, usually when the sun was low in the sky, I have been able to see the yellow HE projectiles zip past my plane on the way to my target. Thinking about it now, I'm astounded to recall that we gave little regard to the danger at the time, but we normally tried to fly a little to one side of gun-target line, a little beyond the target, or at a higher or lower altitude that we thought would keep us clear of the trajectory. But some targets required us to get in very close.[3]

There was another hazard of which the L-4 pilot needed to be careful, but only when he carried an observer or passenger. I learned of it one day when I was carrying Lt. Keith F. Kirkbride, a very nice young officer of HQ Btry. The mountain winds were boisterous, as they often are, but Kirk was all business and made no complaint. And then I was shocked to feel a blow squarely between my shoulders, and something hot flooding down my back. Good Lord! I'd been hit, I thought. Funny, it didn't hurt a bit. Must be a temporary numbing effect. Before I got further along in my thoughts than that, I heard the strangled voice of Kirkbride.

"Oh-h-h. I'm sorry, Kerns, I'm sorry. I thought I could hold it back, but it came on all of a sudden. I've ruined your shirt. I'm sorry."

When we landed, Kirk insisted on giving me one of his clean khaki shirts, and I had it for many years.

Kirkbride needn't have been so concerned about my shirt. I was probably about the grungiest looking pilot in the entire Army. I wore the same uniform as the others but had only an almost fleshless and ill-proportioned skeleton to give it shape. When I took my flight physical in 1944 in New Guinea, the doctor said I was three pounds under the minimum weight for my age and height and should not be on flying duty. But then he asked me whether I wore combat boots when I flew. I said I did, and he said that since my boots must weigh about three pounds he would pass me.

There were a couple of exceptions to the uniformity of my attire. One was that I habitually wore a shapeless old HBT field cap, although I had a baseball-type cap that had written under the visor the name of Maj. Sanford Wolff, one of our infantry officers, who had used it when he went along as an observer at the taking of Kwajalein Atoll. The other exception was that I had traded my pistol to CWO Rudy Krevolt, our personnel officer, for his carbine, because I couldn't hit the side of a barn with a .45 automatic. But most of the boys carried their .45s in shoulder holsters and wore baseball caps.

One day when I was tooling around up in the mountains, looking for something worthwhile to shoot at, I was told to knock off and head back to the Aringay strip immediately. When I got there, Vin said I'd have to get into a clean khaki uniform, wear a baseball cap, and carry a .45 in a shoulder holster. General Clarkson was to be there in a short time and there would be a formation. I had a clean uniform but I couldn't find my Wolff cap, so I borrowed an extra from one of the other pilots. With Vineyard's shoulder holster and pistol, I was all set.

The pilots who were to receive awards lined up between my plane and Vin's. Dick Bortz, who was in charge, stood a little ahead of us. The

Lieutenant Kerns receives an Air Medal from Maj. Gen. Percy W. Clarkson, commanding general of 33d Infantry Division.

general presented Air Medals to all of us except Bortz, Mossman, and Vineyard, mine being for the New Guinea activities. Vin had already received one for New Guinea, and I think Bortz and Mossman had theirs presented at the general's office. For the rest of us, unless we had received the Purple Heart this was our first decoration, and that made it a red-letter day.

– Six –

OVER THE HILLS
TO BAGUIO

The nearer we came to Hill 3000, the harder the enemy resisted our advance. We got the Footstool, and there we sat. Assault after assault met with defeat, in spite of heroic efforts by some of the best of Colonel Serff's infantrymen. Army Air Force P-38s clobbered the knob with bombs and napalm until it was just a scorched and desolate pile of dirt into which the 122d poured tons of HE shell, and yet the stubborn Japanese defenders hung on and held us off. But until we took Hill 3000, our progress toward Baguio by the Pugo-Tuba route could get nowhere.

Uncle Bud Carlson considered the problem carefully and came up with a suggestion for Colonel Serff: why not try a night attack? No big fuss about it, no special artillery preparation that might reveal our intentions, just get up some night around 2200 hours and walk up there. The enemy would not be expecting us to attack at night—we never had—and it was a good bet that we'd find his forward positions very lightly held while his men were sleeping snug and warm back in their tunnels to avoid our harassing artillery fires.

Under pressure from General Clarkson to get things rolling at this critical point, Colonel Serff bought the idea, and it was carried out without a hitch, just as our brilliant Uncle Bud had envisioned it. After a sharp but brief fight with a few surprised Japanese defenders, a battalion of the 123d Infantry occupied the enemy's positions on Hill 3000 with few friendly casualties.

In the predawn darkness, Lt. Lorne Stanley of HQ Btry, 122d FA Bn, an FO with the troops on Hill 3000, crawled forward alone, dragging a field wire-remote connection to his radio. When the Japanese troops came swarming back to reclaim their positions on Hill 3000, it was Stanley who was first to meet them and to greet them with crashing volleys of 105 mm artillery fire that caused great consternation in their ranks. Most of the enemy were halted by the fire, dead, wounded, or forced to take cover; but some raced forward, trying to reach their old positions. Two of the latter happened to run directly toward the spot where Stanley lay hidden, flat on his belly, adjusting the artillery fire. In his excitement, the heroic Stanley momentarily forgot himself and opened fire with his carbine, killing one and stopping the other's advance. But that disclosed his position to the enemy, and he immediately became the focal point of a lot of rifle fire. Realizing that the better part of valor was to withdraw to his own line, Stanley pushed up on his hands to rise. As he did so, a bullet clipped a path through the thick hair all the way down his chest and abdomen without breaking the skin. He made it back safely, and the fire he had brought to bear with such surprise to the Japanese effectively prevented their return to Hill 3000. The infantry had little to do.

Stanley—who was called "Burrhead" by his friends in that outfit—was a medium-size guy as hairy as an ape, and he was quite proud of that depilated streak left by the Jap bullet down the front elevation of his hirsute self. He was also grateful for the impulse to rise just before the bullet appeared. And just to be sure that I don't leave you with a wrong impression of Burrhead Stanley, let me add that he was an intelligent, Stanford-educated son of a corporate lawyer and a professional opera singer who made his home in San Francisco and was as bold and clever a fighter as the United States ever sent to the field. For his heroism on Hill 3000, he was awarded the Distinguished Service Cross, and we in the 122d were quite proud of him. It was only the highest of numerous decorations he received for bravery and achievement.

Gen. Walter Krueger, commanding general of the Sixth Army, came out to visit the 123d one day during our approach to Hill 3000, and I got to meet him. I left our Pugo forward strip driving a jeep, heading up into the hills along our new supply road, having in mind a visit to Uncle Bud's CP and lunch in Uncle Bud's mess tent. Shortly after leaving the strip, it was necessary to ford a stream. It wasn't very deep, but it was wide, its banks were steep and muddy, and its bottom was covered with rounded boulders slick with slime. In short, it would have been very easy to get a jeep stuck in that stream. You had to hit it pretty fast and keep on going. As I bounced up over the bank on the opposite shore, around a clump of willows just ahead of me came speeding another jeep, bearing General Krueger with his four stars, and standing up in the rear seat, swinging his arm and yelling at me, "Get out of the way! Get out of the way!" was no less a person than Colonel Serff. The only way I could get out of the way was to go full speed straight ahead, off the outside of the curve and into the boonies. And that's what I did, while the General's jeep, its velocity unchecked, went bounding and splashing on across the stream.

Come to think of it, I did not salute General Krueger.

After Hill 3000, our next major terrain objective was Mount Calugong, which, as I recall, is more than forty-seven hundred feet in elevation. The way was rough, and the enemy was tough, and it was a pretty hard row to hoe. Vin and I were busy every day, searching out the enemy and bringing fire on him wherever we could see him or reasonably suppose him to be. The 33d Division historian estimated after the war that 95 percent of the observed artillery fire in the division was either adjusted by, or under the surveillance of, one of the eleven field artillery pilot observers. Vin and I certainly did our share of it.

Searching the terrain on the approaches to Mount Calugong one day, far ahead of our troops, I spotted one solitary Japanese soldier. He was sitting on a log seat above an open pit latrine, surprisingly located right out in the open, although there was a tree-lined ravine only fifty yards away. The chilly winds were blowing up there in the mountains that day, and he was wearing a long overcoat, but the coattails were thrown up over his shoulders and his bare behind was fully exposed to the wind— and to the enemy. Nevertheless, true to his training, he froze—probably almost literally froze—right where he was while I surveyed the area and tried to figure out what else was in the vicinity.

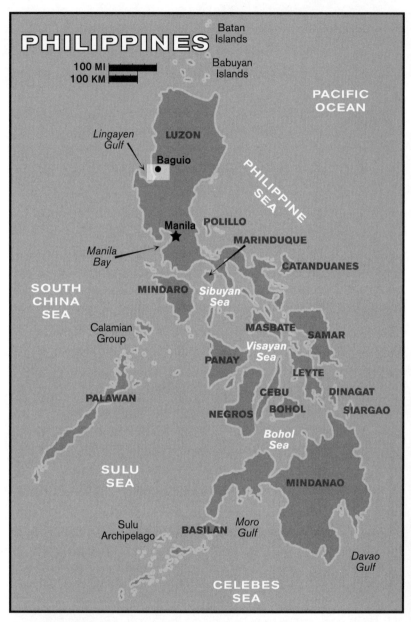

Map of the Philippine Islands, showing where the 33d Division operated on Luzon during the drive to capture the summer capitol of Baguio (Map by Carol Kerns).

This map fits into the rectangle on the upper left of the adjacent map of the Philippine Islands, on the island of Luzon, and shows the various objectives of the 33d Division in the battle for Baguio. Note Hill 3000, Mount Calugong, and other terrain features that had to be wrested from the Japanese on the approach to the city (Map from Sanford Winston, *The Golden Cross*).

Considering the terrain and the location relative to other enemy activities of which we knew, I came to the conclusion that there was a regimental CP located in that wooded ravine. But it was in an area where I had not worked closely before and which, as a matter of fact, was off the maps I had with me, so I looked around for something from which to transfer fire. Far away among the hills I could identify an old concentration that I had plotted on my map, so I called in my fire mission something like this:

"Kadi 3, this is Kadi 8. Fire mission. Over."

"Kadi 8, send your mission. Over."

"This is Kadi 8. Concentration 261 is one thousand right, two thousand short. Suspected regimental CP. Request Willie Peter. Will adjust. Over."

After the usual preliminaries, the round of white phosphorus was on the way, and I watched carefully, expecting nothing more than that I'd spot it somewhere within several hundred yards of the target area. Astonishingly, the fearsome burst of fire and white smoke appeared among the trees in the ravine at precisely the point at which I had supposed the CP was probably located. It was hard to believe, fantastically lucky, and I'll bet it made quite a reputation for American artillery among the local Japanese population.

The most immediate effect, I think, was one of great relief for the poor soldier on the latrine. Relieved now of his obligation to remain immobile to avoid detection, he leaped up from the log, pulled up his britches, and headed for parts unknown. I'll bet that overcoat felt good to his chilled posterior.

The next effect I saw was a hasty evacuation of a large group of Japanese personnel, heavy with officers, flapping the tails of their long coats as they hightailed it around the gentle slope leading away from that smoky hollow. Of course, I had already given the word to FDC:

"Repeat range. Request HE. Fire for effect. Over."

They switched to HE and fired the entire battery three rounds in effect. It was rather exhilarating to me at the time—such a lucky guess at the target, such a lucky shot with the WP, so much fun with the guy on the latrine, and now—well, I feel kind of sad now to say that several of the fleeing enemy officers and men fell on that hillside. It's too bad that when a war is over the dead and the wounded cannot rise up smiling, whole and happy, and go home to their families.

But who was so foolish as to put that latrine right out in plain view of the whole world when everything else about the place was perfectly concealed? Well, our troops captured a letter addressed by a superior commander to the officer who had allowed Hill 3000 to be taken while he slept. Among other pleasantries, it included the Japanese equivalent of "You damned fools!" So that officer is probably the same one who put the latrine out in the open. Maybe he died there that day for his poor judgment.

But lucky shots happen more frequently than it seems they should. I recall a time when a platoon was working its way up a very narrow ridge, following a path through the tall grass that covered it. They came to a screeching halt when a machine gun began kicking up a fuss every time they tried to pass a certain point. There was no way around, nor could they determine exactly where the gun was located. I was called over to try to find it, but I could see nothing. Nevertheless, I asked for one piece to fire a few rounds on the little ridge to see whether I could uncover or flush out anything. The transfer distance was not great, so we fired HE shell from the start. The very first round fired burst directly in a shallow hole at the base of a solitary tree that stood on the ridge. A machine gun was flung out to the front, and I could see the gunner lying back against the tree, dead. Our platoon walked on up the ridge without opposition.

The all-time world champion lucky artillery round, of course, was one of the first rounds fired by the 33d Div Arty after relieving the 43d on the highway between Damortis and Rosario (see the lower left corner of the map of of 33d Division objectives, p. 231). That was the one that hit the highway, tore up a chunk of pavement, and uncovered about half a million dollars worth of Philippine coin that had been concealed there before the Japanese invasion. They dipped it up in steel helmets and hauled it away in quarter-ton trailers. But I didn't see that round burst, so my personal candidate for champion was . . . well, one day I was informed by our S-2 that the enemy had a light artillery piece concealed in a tunnel through a small knoll on top of the mountain ridge not far west of Mount Calugong. That perfect little circle contour line on the map was the origin, he believed, of the interdicting time-fused rounds that kept bursting periodically over a certain curve in our road just below the batteries. I was asked to adjust fire on it and see whether we could discourage such rude conduct by the Japanese artillerymen.

I got into position to observe the knoll and was soon told that my first adjusting round was on the way, and it was white phosphorus, of course, because it would be easy to lose anything else in those mountains. For a few seconds after the round should have burst, I saw nothing, and I thought it must have gone beyond the ridge and down into the Asin Valley. But then I saw white smoke billowing out of the little knoll, and then explosions blasted out fore and aft, and I knew that the round, fired with only corrected map data from FDC, had gone directly through the camouflaged firing opening in the knoll and burst inside. The explosions that followed must have been ammunition set off by the fire. I doubt that anyone who was inside the position survived.

In contrast to that luck, I was sent to adjust a 155 mm howitzer on a large corrugated metal warehouse located just north of the Naguilian-Baguio road and being used by the enemy. Although partially protected by having been built into the side of a slope, the building should have been very easy to hit and destroy. But I fired up all the ammunition they could spare for the mission and was never able to get a direct hit or any detectable damage to the target. Why? Don't ask me!

While actually engaged in one of the dangerous actions that occasionally involved us fair-haired boys, I seldom was conscious of fear or nervous tension, and I think that was true of all the boys. Nevertheless, the stress factor was pretty high much of the time. I can recall times after coming out of a dangerous situation when I would become conscious of an aching in my jaw muscles, and I'd realize then that my teeth were tightly clenched and must have been so for some time. While we were still in New Guinea, I developed a habit of opening my eyes quite wide at frequent intervals—the "nervous tic" that people joke about. And many times, when relieved from patrol over the mountains there in Luzon, I would get down into some narrow ravine and dive my L-4 down the mountain at its top speed, deliberately courting collision with the trees or the ground, while I'd shake the controls violently and yell and curse to relax myself. I don't know whether anyone else did such things.

About the middle of April, the 123d was closing in on the summit of Calugong, and the enemy was resisting with all he had. The rainy season was due, and our commanders wanted to get to Baguio before the mountain trails became slick with mud. Uncle Bud Carlson happened to be with Major Wolff when Wolff's advancing battalion of infantry ground to a halt in a heavy exchange of gunfire with well-covered Japanese defenders. Bypassing them in the steep and wooded terrain would be costly in time, while direct assault would cost many lives. The leaders were hesitant to use artillery, or even the infantry's mortars, the troops being in such close quarters and in great danger of being hit by tree bursts of our own shells. Withdrawal of the troops to a safe distance would also be difficult and time-consuming.

Uncle Bud discussed the problems with Wolff and offered to try to reduce the enemy position with artillery if he'd pull his troops back two hundred yards. Wolff agreed, and Uncle Bud called FDC and asked Major Hadfield to send Vineyard up. (Yes, incredibly, Uncle Bud asked for Vineyard, even though he knew that I was somewhere around.) Using a smoke grenade as a reference point, Uncle Bud described the problem and the general area involved, and while Vin was studying the target, the infantry pulled back about 150 yards. Uncle Bud, with Wolff and Capt. Raymond Rush, a company commander, remained out in front of the lead squad of Rush's company, communicating by SCR-609 radio.

Bud called Vin then, and Vin reported:

"OK, Bud, I see you. Have spotted four machine-gun positions and many spider holes around them. The one where the smoke grenade fell is in the center—one other emplacement west of it and two east. Where are our leading troops?"

That description tallied with what the infantry officers had observed, and they nodded their agreement.

"Foremost elements at this spot," replied Uncle Bud. "Start shooting. Watch the tree bursts, we're mighty close."

Vin objected that they were too close, but after consultation with Wolff, Uncle Bud told him to get going, they were not moving any more.

Vin said, "Roger. Kadi 3, this is Kadi 7. Fire mission: Jap strongpoint, machine guns emplaced, riflemen. Concentration 264 is two hundred left, four hundred short. Request battalion. Will adjust. Bud will designate volleys for effect. Over."

Uncle Bud told Wolff that fire for effect would be five volleys, then a three-minute silence to let the Japs get their heads up again, then six more volleys. After the last six, Bud would call out, "Rounds complete," and then the infantry should wait ten seconds for time of flight of the last round before jumping off.

When the first adjusting rounds burst, Number 4 was very close to Uncle Bud and party, so Vin moved it forward a hundred yards. After the next battery salvo, he reported:

"Effect excellent. Short rounds are getting the machine-gun positions, long rounds the spider holes behind. Are they safe, Bud?"

Uncle Bud, speaking directly to Hadfield at FDC, called for fire for effect as he had told Wolff to expect it, and he added, "Bill, tell the cannoneers to level the bubbles carefully. Anything short will hurt us badly."

Uncle Bud knew that cannoneers in the 122d FA Bn did not have to be cautioned to level the bubbles carefully. They always did. But he was being extra careful. The fire from his eleven volleys stunned and decimated the enemy troops, and Wolff's men quickly overran their position. Only two Americans were hit by our own shell fragments. One of them was Uncle Bud—but it was only a scratch.

I told you before that Lt. Col. Roland "Bud" Carlson was a fine artilleryman, but did I mention Lt. Dolman Winston "Don" Vineyard? He was a pretty good one, too. And he was a lucky one, because also present up there on the slope of Mount Calugong that day was Col. Andrew T. McAnsh, chief of staff, 33d Infantry Division. McAnsh apparently took careful notes on all that went on, and he wrote a detailed account of it for the *Infantry Journal.* That account was later quoted in the division history. It was an excellent illustration of the close coordination that was needed and possible between artillery and its supported elements, and of the highly valuable contribution the L-4 pilot-observer made to the effort. Reading it, I can still hear the voices of those men, although today Uncle Bud, Don Vineyard, and most of the others have gone on to better worlds.[1] But I still don't understand why Uncle Bud *called for Vineyard by name!*

(Well, yeah, I do.)

From the top of Calugong, our path turned sharply eastward along the serrated ridge toward Mount Santo Tomas. On the south, deep, wooded ravines defined more thinly forested knolls and grassy slopes, while the north side dropped very steeply far down into the Asin Valley, offering no possibility of traverse even by foot soldiers.

The first terrain objective east of Calugong was a wide place in the main ridge that we called Machine-gun Hill. About a mile from the top of Calugong, Machine-gun Hill was separated by a hollow from Hill Charlie immediately to the south, and both hills were at about thirty-five hundred feet elevation.

Company L, commanded by Capt. William Crenshaw, walked onto

Machine-gun Hill to find it wide open, no enemy present at all, and I was overhead watching as they prepared it for defense, improving on old Japanese works. I was talking with our field observer, Keith Kirkbride, who was lying on his back in a shallow hole and had spread his handkerchief out on his chest so I could identify him. As I was telling Kirk I had spotted him, he suddenly was blotted out of my view by a shell explosion that appeared to me to be right on top of him.

"Kirk! Kirk! Are you OK?"

I honestly did not expect him to reply, but his voice came back, cool and unconcerned.

"Sure, I'm OK. Why?"

"Good Lord! It looked like that was a direct hit on you!"

"Oh, no," he replied casually. "That was over in the next hole—a good six feet away."

While I marveled at Kirkbride's composure, the Japanese batteries poured in on Company L a concentration of artillery that obviously had been preregistered. Casualties were light, but the company was withdrawn by higher command. The enemy reclaimed the position.

Cutting across the corner of the Mount Calugong summit route, two companies assaulted Hill Charlie. The situation developed to a point where one company had to hold position while the other made the final attack. I was overhead and adjusted their preparatory artillery fires as they twice attacked and twice were repulsed by machine guns and heavy rifle fire from a line of foxholes around the forward slope of the knoll. Each time, they withdrew behind the crest of a lower rise to the south. For the third assault, we fired a heavy preparation, ending it with smoke that signaled "rounds complete." The infantrymen were immediately on their feet, charging across the ravine and up to the line of foxholes as fast as they could negotiate the steep terrain, firing as they ran.

This time the enemy's reaction was weak. Stunned by three heavy bombardments within the hour and partially blinded by thick white smoke, he began to withdraw in some disorder, running back across the unusually open hilltop, some halting occasionally to fire at the American riflemen who followed rapidly, ducking from cover to cover, firing as they came.

Two very courageous Japanese machine-gunners brought up the rear of the enemy retreat. They carried their weapon back a few yards at a time, halting to sweep the approaching Americans with its fire, then pulling farther back when threatened with being surrounded. They were the last to be seen on the hill when, their ammo gone, they removed the breech mechanism from their weapon, flung it far away into a gully, and ran after their already vanished comrades.

Colonel Carlson required each of his firing battery commanders to serve at least one tour of FO duty, and thus it was that Capt. Perry Jones, commander of Btry C, was the FO with the company that took Hill Charlie. Perry was a chunky, quiet Southerner with a large blonde mustache—a dangerous distinguishing feature in the presence of the enemy—and he was the only Regular Army officer in the 122d. As the victorious infantry company was digging in on Hill Charlie, Perry called me and asked if I would help him adjust the night protective concentrations around the new position. Of course, I told him I would, but that I would have to refuel first. Then I said:

"Perry, it looks as if there are lots of good souvenirs lying around down there. If you get a chance to pick up something for me, I'd appreciate it."

"OK, Crash, I'll see what I can do."

I made my usual dive down the mountain, and five minutes later I was on short final at the Pugo strip when I heard Captain Rowland, CO of the company on Hill Charlie, come on Perry's radio, call Kadi 3, and ask to speak to "Bud." When Uncle Bud responded, Rowland said, "Bud, I hate to have to tell you this, but Perry just got it—right between the eyes."

A few minutes later I was back over Hill Charlie, helping Rowland and Perry's radio operator adjust the night fires. While thus engaged, I noticed movement in a hole left by the roots of a large fallen tree in the middle of the position where our men were still busily digging in. Although I couldn't see him very well, I knew that the man there was Japanese, so I informed Captain Rowland. He sent two sergeants armed with tommy guns to take care of the matter. They approached along each side of the tree trunk, guns at the ready. When he realized that he had been discovered, the Japanese lieutenant—as he proved to be—leaped out of the hole and charged toward Sgt. Jack Van Assen, his sword in one hand, his pistol in the other. Van Assen riddled him with .45-caliber slugs before he had taken half a dozen steps.

A few days later I received through message center a bullet-torn leather holster containing a small automatic pistol made in Herstal, Belgium, on a Browning patent. One ammo magazine was in the weapon, the other ruined and made fast in its pouch on the holster by the passage of a bullet. With this souvenir was a note that read:

THIS IS OFF THE BASTARD THAT WAS UNDER THE ROOTS OF THAT BIG TREE. THANKS.

Jack Van Assen
Sgt., Co. G, 123rd Inf.

Only one week later, Sergeant Van Assen, his face shot away, joined Perry Jones and the Japanese lieutenant in that long, long line of brave men who have given their lives for their respective flags. But I still have the pistol—probably the weapon that killed Perry Jones—and it's just as deadly as ever.

Back in the early days of our fighting on Luzon, two platoons had been sent out on patrols along separate routes. With one platoon went some mortars, and with the other went one of our artillery lieutenants as FO. During the course of their movements, the officer leading the patrol with the mortars saw the other patrol and, mistaking it for enemy troops, opened fire with the mortars. The FO saw where the mortar fire was coming from and, believing it to be enemy fire, brought an artillery concentration down on the other patrol. In this exchange, several infantrymen were killed, including the lieutenant in charge of the mortars, and others were wounded, including our FO. Fortunately, our lieutenant was able to return to duty within about six weeks.

One night I happened to be in our battalion CP when one of our infantry positions far up in the mountains came under heavy enemy artillery fire. The FO at the position was that same lieutenant, and he again was able to spot the source of the incoming shells. He requested a fire mission and was told to send it, but as he began to transmit the essential data he suddenly broke into weeping, his transmission unreadable. Uncle Bud got on the radio and, sounding like a father speaking to a small boy, said, "Now, son, get ahold of yourself. Calm down and give us the data and we'll soon get those people off your back." But it was useless. The sensitive young officer had to be evacuated, and he never returned to combat duty, so far as I know.

But he was not by any means the only man who could not indefinitely endure the stresses of combat. They called it "combat fatigue," and it got the best of many a strong man. Sometimes they were sent down to our strip to be evacuated in Stinson L-5s flown by some AAF unit. Other times their transport to the strip would be a three-quarter-ton truck with the muddy boots of two or three tarp-covered dead soldiers bouncing on the tailgate. And while they waited to be flown out, these haggard, dead-eyed men would stand in silence, gazing at the ground, giving no heed to those who might speak to them or offer them a cigarette.

Of all the dreadful, nerve-racking, heartbreaking tasks that fall to men in warfare, it seems to me that the duty of an infantry rifleman is the worst. He's been called "doughboy," "gravel agitator," "dogface," and many other names, the latest being one that burns me with anger: "grunt." The fact is that he is the very epitome of a soldier, the bravest of the brave, the toughest of the tough, the most miserable of the miserable. And no fighter is more to be admired than the one who is not brave, is not tough, but who overcomes his fears and weaknesses by sheer force of will and does the job anyway. Silver wings and crushed caps and the romance of the wild blue, gallant sea captains on flaming ships, the traditional heroes of the nation, all pale in my estimation before the tired, dirty, miserable infantry private with a rifle in his hand and no plans for tonight or tomorrow. He's the guy who does most of the dying for the country—and gets the least reward.

The second assault on Machine-gun Hill bogged down in the face of at least nine machine guns and numerous rifles covering a field so narrow that only one platoon could be deployed in the attack. The infantrymen were lying flat in the shallow washes of the trail, hugging the ground, unable to move forward or back. Fifteen yards ahead two or three American bodies hung in barbed wire barricades only a few feet from slits where bunkered machine gun muzzles spurted fire every time another American moved.

My first job was to help them get clear and withdraw. Anticipating that task, I had loaded my L-4 with smoke grenades, and just above the trees, I set up a tight orbit to the left, dropping a grenade each time around, gradually building up a fog to blind the Japanese gunners. While I was doing this, one of the officers on the ground called and said, "Kadi 8, be advised that they're firing at you with rifles every time you come around." I thanked him but made no change in procedure—partly because there was no other way to do the job and partly because we didn't worry too much about Japanese rifle fire. They fired at us just about every day, but seldom did we find bullet holes in our aircraft, so as long as they didn't use machine guns, we didn't worry much.

Concealed by the smoke screen, the American platoon was finally able to move back. At this point, the Cannon Company took over. The 123d's Cannon Company, equipped with M-7 self-propelled 105s, had served as "Btry D" of the 122d FA Bn in New Guinea but now was back under direct control of the infantry. They had been brought to the very peak of Mount Calugong, and from there they were trained on Machine-gun Hill for direct fire. In the course of a series of bombardments and unsuccessful infantry attacks, they fired approximately a thousand 105 mm shells into the Jap positions on Machine-gun.

At some point in these proceedings, the 122d, firing from its positions on Hill 3000, also plastered Machine-gun Hill quite thoroughly, after which I dropped a bunch of "surrender" leaflets over the position. A few minutes later, FDC asked me whether I could see any of the enemy troops now that much foliage and a number of trees had been knocked down and, if so, what they were doing. I replied that I could see a number of the riflemen "hunkered down in their holes and looking at the leaflets" I had dropped. Next time I was at the CP I took a lot of ribbing about that word "hunkered." I had to find a dictionary and prove to my colleagues that it was a legitimate word and that I had used it correctly. (Strange, isn't it, the things one remembers from a war?)

The M-7s, using delay fuse so their shells would penetrate the soil before exploding, finally cut the Japanese defense on Machine-gun Hill down to size, and the 123d continued its march along the ridge toward the east.

★

Smoking is a terrible habit of which I have long since broken myself, but in 1945 I had it bad. Although the L-4 had no ash receptacle and was, in fact, a rather dangerous place in which to smoke, I regularly lit up while flying. The hazards of that practice were brought home to me one day when I dropped a lighted cigarette down through the opening in the floorboards around the control stick, where there was nothing to stop it except linen cloth treated with highly flammable airplane dope. I was suddenly acutely aware that I had no fire extinguisher, no parachute, and was over rugged mountains infested with thousands of men who would gleefully cut out my gizzard if they got the chance. I sweated, but nothing happened—except that I thought I heard an ominous voice say, "That's once!"

Finishing a long and uneventful patrol one afternoon, I happened to see one Japanese soldier out in a patch of grass extending south of the ridge and east of Machine-gun Hill, a little west of Hill 4980. I figured he probably was not alone, so, without adjusting, I asked for battery one round, and four 105s burst in the grassy area. Looking the area over, I could see nothing but four shell craters, so I reported that results could not be determined. But next day one of our infantry units moved through the place and reported finding twenty-four dead Japanese, "killed by artillery within the last twenty-four hours." The little field must have been crowded with enemy troops, lying on top of the ground and camouflaged with grass, and besides the dead there must have been a number only wounded.

Seldom do four rounds of light artillery produce such results. However, there was a place between Machine-gun Hill and Hill 4980 where Vin and I often were able to see movement under the trees on or very near the trail, sometimes including pack horses. Many times we dropped a few rounds into the spot but never were able to see positive results. But after our infantry moved through there, they reported that scores of enemy bodies littered both sides of the trail, and nearby ravines were choked with shell-torn bodies. Our battalion commander's policy of placing confidence in the judgment of his observers and giving them fire when they asked for it definitely paid off.

There was some fighting around Hill 4980, but Machine-gun Hill had been the last major obstacle to our advance to Tuba. When we reached that village, Captain Rowland's Company G was sent to have a look at Mount Santo Tomas, the dominant terrain feature southwest of Baguio. I happened to be watching when, on the northern approaches to the mountain, they ran into a fight in which the eighty-eight men present for duty in Company G killed seventy-five of the enemy. I had little to do but watch the exciting action on fairly open ground—and that was appropriate, since it was 26 April, my twenty-fourth birthday.

When the 123d turned to the east from Mount Calugong, another regiment of the 33d Division, the 130th, had swept around our left flank. For the final drive on Baguio, the line was farther extended to the left by elements of the 37th Infantry Division, and the entire line had swung eastward like a gate hinged on Mount Santo Tomas.

A preliminary to the final assault on Baguio was the forward displacement of the artillery. The 122d leapfrogged its batteries from Hill 3000 back down through Pugo, Agoo, and Naguilian, to positions west of Baguio and south of the Naguilian Road. The 124th FA Bn, the direct support unit for the 130th Infantry, which was now positioned on our left flank, also took new positions in the same vicinity. The 124th was commanded by a younger brother of our Uncle Bud Carlson.

Late that afternoon, I had just finished registering our batteries from the new positions when I was directed to contact the 124th on the Div Arty liaison channel to perform a mission for them. I was informed that the 124th was unable to get observers into position in time to register its batteries before dark, and they wanted me to register on their base point. They gave me map coordinates of the base point they had selected.

Checking the location on the ground, I found that it was the site of two brick apartment buildings near the eastern edge of Baguio. As I flew over, a group of Filipinos—men, women, and children—quickly formed between the two buildings, and some of them waved white cloths to indicate that they were friendly. I looked the place over very carefully and could see no sign of enemy presence.

With memories of Check Point #6 at Maffin Bay in my mind, I informed the 124th's FDC of the facts and suggested that we register on a rock formation on top of a prominent knoll about two hundred yards north of the apartments. The reply came back, "Negative. Register on the point originally designated."

In my mind, I could transfer the bloody splotches from the New Guinea jungle to suburban Baguio, from the poor ignorant Melanesians to the friendly and trusting Filipinos, and I could not accept the thought of firing on these noncombatants and their homes when there was no sufficient reason for doing so. And so I again remonstrated with the FDC, urging that a different base point be used. There was a vacant knoll nearby that would serve the purpose just fine. This time, I recognized the voice that came into my earphones.

"Lieutenant, this is the battalion commander. Will you register my battalion as directed or must I report to your battalion commander that you have refused to obey my direct order?"

Through my mind flashed the thought that no one could see where I would register for the 124th and that in this case there was practically no risk of harm to American personnel from misplaced unobserved fires due to wrong registration of data. Unobserved fires in those mountains, with their rough terrain and highly variable winds, were quite unreliable at best. Anyway, a bird in the hand is worth a couple in the bush, so after only a couple of seconds delay I replied to Colonel Carlson:

"Kadi 8, ready to observe."

I proceeded to register on the knoll, and there was no harm done to the Filipinos, no damage to the apartment buildings. I never mentioned that fact to anyone until many years later. Better yet, no one ever mentioned it to me.[2]

And then our infantry was faced with the rim of the huge "punch bowl" in which lay the mile-high city of Baguio. The whole picture is quite complicated, so I'll discuss just the part in which I personally had a role and which has not faded from my memory.

I remember a line of men hugging the ground behind a fencerow just at the foot of one of the major terrain features, called Hill 24-A and otherwise known as Dominican Hill, under fire from the enemy. It was too late in the day for them to start an advance, and Vineyard and I dropped rations to them, close behind their line. A few men crawled

Machine gunners of Company C, 123d Infantry, on top of Hill 24-A on the approach to Baguio (Photograph from Sanford Winston, *The Golden Cross*).

back to retrieve them. There was a problem of water for the troops, but I don't recall how it was solved. My memory is blank until the next day.

Positioned hull down near the top of Dominican Hill were five Japanese tanks in support of the defending infantry. In their immediate vicinity were a number of very beautiful residences, giving the appearance of an elite neighborhood. A tunnel on the back side of that hill—the city side—had been the location of General Yamashita's army headquarters until only a day or two earlier. My immediate task was to knock out the five tanks, employing the 155 mm howitzers of the 123d FA Bn, our general support unit.

I can't say much here in terms of artillery artistry. I adjusted on the tanks and the batteries fired while I watched and reported the results. The only significant result that I could see was the destruction and burning of most of those fine houses. So I was surprised when I saw the crews of the tanks swarm out of the turrets, spread out battle flags on the front cowls, and run down the hill to the rear.

I pondered over those flags, and I still don't know why they did it. I was told later that all five tanks were immobilized and generally disabled, not able to continue the fight. The division history says that they seemed to symbolize the condition of the entire Yamashita force at that juncture.

With the tanks out of the way, I expected to see our men of the 1st Bn, 123d Infantry, come swarming up the hill, but it didn't happen. They started, but the assault seemed to fizzle in the face of the relentless small arms fire coming from tunnels scattered over the hillside. And then there emerged one of those heroes who seem to be in every outfit and who like to go bareheaded. I don't know who he was, but this time he was a dark-haired fellow. All alone, he went up the hillside, ducking swiftly from tunnel to tunnel, tossing in a grenade or two at each and following with fire from his tommy gun. To and fro across the broad hillside, always moving upward, hitting tunnel after tunnel, seeming to lead a charmed life, he breached the enemy defense that had stopped a battalion cold. I thought I was seeing a man earn the Medal of Honor, but I never heard of his getting it.

Dominican Hill was the key to the defense of Baguio, and when it fell the Americans swarmed into the mountain city.

On the left of the 123d was the 130th Infantry on Mount Mirador, and left of them, orienting on the Naguilian Road just north of Observatory Hill, was a regiment of the 37th Infantry Division, augmenting the 33d for this final assault. Out on the extreme left flank were some tanks belonging to this regiment, and I saw a couple of them parked over there on the hill north of the Naguilian Road and firing their cannon at the gray, barracklike buildings of the convent in Baguio where several nuns could be seen standing out on the lawn. There was no indication of enemy activity there, and certainly the unnecessary fire seriously endangered the nuns' lives.

I got just a bit hysterical about that, I guess, raising hell on the airwaves, trying to get the firing stopped. But we had no direct radio communication with those tanks, and so, in desperation, I got down in their line of fire and flew toward them, making violent S-turns with my L-4. Whether I stopped them or someone else did, I know not, but they did cease.

Aerial view of war-shattered Baguio, the once beautiful summer capitol, in its picturesque mountain bowl after its capture by U.S. forces. The city park with a lake in it, where two L-4s met their end trying to land, is at upper right (Photograph from Sanford Winston, *The Golden Cross*).

Baguio had had a prewar population of about thirty thousand. It was then a beautiful city, situated in a mountain bowl at an elevation of about five thousand feet. In the middle of town, at the lowest part of the bowl, was a small lake around which was a wide street running through a park with large trees (see the aerial photograph of Baguio on page 247). While the infantry patrols were still advancing through the now devastated city, "Speedy" Spendlove decided that the time had come when he could realize the dream of all 33d Div pilots, which was to be first to land in Baguio. He set his L-4 down on the street beside the lake. Then he looked about him and decided it would be much wiser to get a truck and haul it out rather than try to fly it out. He pulled it off under a tree and went to look for a truck.

And now along came that same corps pilot who had once tried to get me to fuel his plane. He didn't see Speedy's plane, so he, too, decided to be first to land in Baguio. He landed, saw the other L-4 parked there, and, disappointed, took off.

Unfortunately, he was unable to climb out of the bowl, crashed into a hillside, and burned up his plane. He escaped alive, though minus eyebrows and lashes.

The next L-4 to come humming along was none other than our old and honored friend, the *Arizona Keed*. Unaware of the two angels already fallen, Vin made an approach to land beside the lake, but, at the last minute, experience whispered that if he did so he would never fly out. So he aborted the landing and started climbing out. Sad to say, he didn't make it either. Vin escaped with hardly a scratch, but the *Arizona Keed* found a final resting place on a hillside in Baguio.[3]

Blissfully unaware of this sudden loss of 30 percent of our air strength, I was busy watching over the 3d Bn, 123d Infantry, as it moved southeast from the vicinity of Dominican Hill to secure Loacan Field, Baguio's airport. Lorne Stanley was with one of the companies, and when they had the field pretty well in hand he asked me to pick him up for an aerial look around the countryside. I approached the sod strip from east to west, and noted the sound of rifle fire at the east end as I came in, so I dragged it well down the strip before I touched down. Then I rolled along wondering whether the Japs had mined the runway.

Pilot's view of Loacan Field, Baguio's airport (Photograph from Sanford Winston, *The Golden Cross*).

Having made the first landing on the newly liberated Loacan Field, I immediately proceeded to share with Stanley the first takeoff. We headed eastward, three or four miles on the Japanese side of the line of contact with American forces still facing north. To our right, the mountains rose well above our altitude, and to our left front, open ridges broken by wooded ravines sloped far down to the valley of the Agno River. At the head of one of those ravines, where the trees dwindled out to mere bushes, a brief flash of sunlight on shiny metal caught our attention.

I swung the plane around and we saw two Japanese soldiers frozen in their tracks. A closer look revealed that they had been digging, and an entrenching shovel probably had made the flash we saw. We reasoned that it was not at all probable that the two were alone, so after brief discussion we called FDC and asked for fire.

They copied our request, but the S-3 got on the radio himself and said that there would be a delay until he could get a clearance from Div Arty to fire outside our sector. While this communication was in progress, the Japanese realized that they had been discovered, and they began to disperse, making our suspected target a very definite but rapidly dissipating one as the enemy troops began moving out of the ravine in both directions along the open slopes. We so advised the S-3 and assured him that there was no doubt as to identification, no question of the safety of friendly troops. We urged him to open fire at once, but he would not.

And then, from some unknown location, there came the familiar voice of Uncle Bud Carlson.

"Damn it, Bill! Fire that mission! I'll take the responsibility!"

"On the way!" replied the S-3.

We had requested "battalion three rounds in effect," and the ravine boiled with fire and smoke, dust and leaves, as the shells came in. From our aerial OP, we could only imagine the crashing thunder of the explosions, the squalling fragments, the yells of men. The enemy had been walking briskly, and now he ran.

"This is Kadi 8, roger, wait . . . Bravo repeat range, repeat fire for effect. Alpha left one hundred, repeat range, repeat fire for effect. Charlie right one hundred, repeat range, repeat fire for effect. Over."

"Roger, Kadi 8, wait . . . Bravo on the way . . . Alpha on the way, Charlie on the way, over."

Thus we shifted one battery to the right and one to the left, leaving the third firing into the still well-populated ravine.

Out on the hillside, the running soldiers were knocked down all over the place as the vicious missiles burst among them. We walked the batteries out and then back to the gully, and when we stopped firing, the few Japanese left on their feet were too widely dispersed to be considered a target. In the ravine, the leafy concealment had been blasted away. In the dusty debris of leaves and shattered branches there were red splotches, bodies, and a few living binding their own wounds.

"Kadi 3, Kadi 8. Cease fire, mission accomplished. Estimate eighty-five enemy killed, remainder dispersed. Over."

"Roger, Kadi 8. Cease fire, mission accomplished. Out."

This was one of the few occasions when I had two pairs of eyes in my L-4, and it had been a very productive mission. I dropped Stanley back at Loacan to rejoin the company. Later that day, returning to the scene, I found considerable activity as the enemy engaged in evacuating wounded and recovering materiel from the field. I really felt sorry for them, but war is hell, and so I brought down several more volleys on their bloodied heads. Afterward, I reported an estimated twenty-five more enemy killed and recovery activities disrupted.

Three days elapsed before an American patrol reached the area of that target. They found 167 bodies the enemy had left on the field, and they hauled away three truckloads of supplies and equipment worth salvaging. Considering a reasonable ratio of killed to wounded, it was estimated that our fire mission had essentially destroyed a battalion of infantry. Whether the battalion had been withdrawing from the line or en route to reinforce it is a moot question, but I suspect the latter.

Without my beat-up old L-4, that mission would not have been fired, and that enemy battalion would have gone into combat somewhere against our infantry, to be vanquished only at the probable cost of many American casualties. I think the event went a long way toward supporting the conclusion reached by some postwar study that proclaimed, in essence, that the most cost-effective piece of materiel in the U.S. Army in World War II was the Piper L-4 airplane used by field artillery units. In 1943, the cost to the government of an L-4 was only $2,800.

While our troops were searching the field and recovering the abandoned Japanese equipment and supplies, I was keeping an eye on them. Well down the ridge beyond the main area of the search, I saw a Japanese officer lying in the shadow of the trunk of a lone tree a few yards off the dirt road. As an hour passed, the shadow moved, of course, but I noticed that it did not move off of the officer. Very cleverly, he was imperceptibly inching sideways just enough to remain in the shadow, which he probably thought would keep him from being seen. But it was his very cleverness that exposed him as not dead, just wounded.

When I notified the commander of our patrol on the ground, he sent one sergeant down the road to take care of the enemy officer—by capturing him, I had supposed. But I should have known better.

Crouched below a bank along the road, the sergeant moved down until he was directly opposite the tree. Then he suddenly leaped up the bank, his rifle blazing. After that, the shadow moved slowly away from the clever captain. I was informed that his sword, an exceptionally nice one, was being sent to me, but I never received it.

★

Somewhere back up the line I threatened to tell a funny story about Fred Hoffman. Here it is:

When we were advancing on Baguio, we heard strong rumors of a new Japanese air defense weapon called the "barrage mortar" that was now in the hands of the troops opposing the 33d Division. Supposedly, batteries of barrage mortars would put up a barrage of shells ahead of and above approaching enemy planes. Each shell would descend on a parachute, and its proximity fuse would detonate the shell upon the near approach of a plane. We were advised to be on the lookout for these barrage mortars. I guess even the top G-2 people were not sure about the truth of the matter.

This rumor made us a little apprehensive for a few days. On one of those days, Fred was out flying just below a broken layer of cloud, intent upon his reconnaissance duties. Unknown to him, Dick Bortz was flying just above the same overcast, dropping propaganda leaflets. Fred glanced up and saw the air immediately ahead of him filled with fluttering white objects that he took to be parachutes, with more of them still descending out of the clouds. They said that his voice on the radio was high-pitched and frantic:

"Barrage mortars! Barrage mortars! I can't possibly avoid them! The sky is full of . . ."

He broke off and was silent for a few seconds. When he spoke again he was very quiet and sounded embarrassed.

"Disregard. It's just sheets of paper."

– Seven –

SASHAYING AROUND
UP NORTH

General Clarkson set up his headquarters in the old Baguio Country Club building, and for the first time since Hawaii the air section people got inside a real house. It was a small frame schoolhouse near the Kennon Road and within a couple of hundred yards of the west end of Loacan Field. A shell had collapsed one corner, and the roof there touched the floor, but we made ourselves at home with great pleasure, thanking our stars that we were not infantrymen out there in the hills in the chilly wind and rain.

Over in the corner where the roof was down sat a young Filipino man holding in his arms a very small baby. A little girl of about three also huddled against him, coughing almost constantly, and the baby had cried until its voice was nearly gone. Seldom have I seen so pitiful a little group. I wondered what had happened to the mother, and I was glad they had found even this poor shelter, for thousands of local citizens were homeless, living in tunnels left by the Japanese along the roads or huddling under trees and in the wreckage of buildings.

And then in strode an officer who, with a wave of his hand, told me, "Get them out of here." I tried to defend them, arguing that the baby, at least, was obviously sick and probably would die if taken out into the cold rain. I realized, of course, that it was not good to have civilians inside billets occupied by troops, but we had tents we could quickly pitch, leaving the building to this poor family and others wandering in the night. The Filipino listened hopefully, but my arguments were futile. When the officer saw that I was not going to send the people away, he did so himself, coldly, without apology or apparent sympathy.

One night during the late stages of the Baguio campaign, I visited a POW interrogation station. One of the men I saw questioned was a very young Japanese soldier who had been captured when flushed out of a small tunnel by a white phosphorous grenade only hours before. He was quite pale, obviously ill, coughing frequently, his lungs probably pretty well seared by the heat and fumes of the grenade. He looked as if he could barely stand, as he was required to do while being questioned. He said that he was a truck driver.

Although I knew a few words of Japanese, I could not understand the questioning or the replies, but I did gather that something unusual was going on. The POW seemed to be extremely frightened, while the interrogators were searching for something in a book. After he was taken away, I asked what the problem was and was told that the interrogators had suspected that the leather belt the prisoner wore was not an authorized item of Japanese uniform. If it had not been, even though the rest of his uniform was regulation, he would have been accused of being a spy and taken to Manila to be shot, in which case the escort would have been able to bring back some whiskey for the interrogation unit. Unfortunately, they said, the belt had proven to be an issue item for cadets at the Japanese military academy. They were disappointed.

I think General Sherman was not entirely correct when he said that war is hell and you cannot refine it. War certainly is hell, but there are some respects that we *can* refine—if our hearts are so inclined. Nevertheless, so long as leaders and nations remain ambitious, greedy, callous, uncaring about human beings, the wars, with all their inhuman cruelties, will come. As Sherman further observed, "You might as well appeal against the thunderstorm."

We tied down our planes and set up a few tents in a space at the northwest corner of Loacan, and after that first night we moved the pilots into new billets in Baguio proper. The new place was the former summer residence of the U.S. commissioner, a fine big frame house with a fireplace in the living room and a screened porch off the kitchen. Out by our front gate lay one of the hundreds of dead Japanese soldiers that were scattered all over Baguio and had already become very hard to handle. Our "gatekeeper," whom we called George, of course, was with us for several days. We never failed to speak to him politely each time we came in or went out.

Our first night in the commissioner's house, Bortz got a big fire going, and it felt good as it dispelled the damp chill of the mountain air. All the pilots gathered around, talking and joking, some of us looking through a small library left there by representatives of the Japanese Domei News Agency, who had been the previous occupants of the premises. We couldn't read the Japanese language, but the illustrations—such as a photo of General Wainwright and General King surrendering to General Homma—gave clues to the nature of the contents.

While we were thus engaged, there was a knock at the door. When I opened it, there stood out in the rainy night a well-dressed young Filipino bearing a large bouquet of flowers. As Dick Bortz came up behind me, the Filipino held out the bouquet to us, bowed deeply, and said, "Gardenias for you, sir. A group of local young ladies has sent these flowers to the brave American officers."

Although we joked about it, I think all of us were touched by this totally unexpected visit. Thinking of Baguio as it appeared to us that night, it was hard to envision the presence of young ladies and gardenias and a young man to carry their message of appreciation to us. We thanked the man as well as was possible and asked him to convey our gratitude to the young ladies. Again bowing, he retreated into the darkness.

I don't think it occurred to any of us that the young ladies may have been waiting nearby in the cold, rainy night, hoping to be asked to come inside our warm, dry house. (Virtue is such a burden!)

The liberation of Baguio did not finish the mountain operations of the 33d, but it opened a new and final phase in our campaign against Yamashita. There seemed to be a kind of relaxation on the part of some of the senior officers, and there was even a social event or two that involved some of us pilots. I remember being at a GI-ration dinner in a large but rather dingy room in northern Baguio at which the division chief of staff had as guests of honor a British mining engineer and his daughter who had been held by the Japanese throughout the war and liberated when we took Baguio. There were two main topics of conversation that I recall. One was Gen. George C. Marshall, of whom the chief of staff told several interesting tales as he made his main point about the general's powerful personality and brilliant conversation.

The other topic was one on which there was general agreement among the officers present. We had recently fired a celebratory barrage on our local enemy with all available weapons: the war in Europe was over! With that out of the way, we had available in Europe the most powerful war machine ever seen, and the consensus was that we should keep it rolling—toward Moscow. In retrospect, I'm convinced that not only would such a move have resulted in disaster for all nations involved but it would have been morally indefensible. The Soviet Union had been one of our allies through the long hard years of the war, and no other had suffered so much nor contributed so much to the defeat of the Nazis. To have turned on them in the moment of victory would have been a terrible thing, yet I joined then with those who favored the idea.

Not so the men in Europe who constituted that "great war machine." To the melody of the bittersweet German wartime song, "Lili Marlene," my brothers, Bob and Gerald, in Europe were singing:

Oh, Mister Truman, why can't we go home?
We've liberated Paris and we have conquered Rome.
We have defeated the "Master Race,"
Now why is there no shipping space?
Oh, why can't we go home?
Oh, why can't we go home?

Despite their combative natures, President Truman and Prime Minister Churchill had the character and good sense to resist whatever temptation they may have felt. To the joy of American motherhood and several other categories of interest, Truman scraped up the shipping space as fast as he could and began dismantling the great armies—although some of the less fortunate men were sent to reinforce the Pacific forces.

I took advantage of a lull in the action to fly east to where the 25th Division was fighting at Balete Pass and visit my friend Bill Gibson, in the 8th FA Bn, and friends in my old outfit, the 89th. I found a place to land along a dirt trail where a few blasted snags of trees gave the landscape the look of a Hollywood war movie set, and then I found someone who could direct me to the 8th. After a good talk with Bill, I borrowed a jeep from his battery commander and went over to the 89th. I spent an hour or so with several of the men from my old radio section, which now was headed by Ralph Park. Leroy Ryder, Ralph's erstwhile "damned handcuffed volunteer," smiled modestly as I congratulated him on his new gold bar, evidence of a field commission. One of the men I had most wanted to see, Burnis Williamson, was up forward somewhere with an FO party, so I missed him. Some of the boys had gone home or on to other assignments. My former battery commander, John Ferris, had become a lieutenant colonel and commander of the battalion.

But the tragic news was that Carl Bunn, the old beer drinker and orange lover from Columbus Grove, was no more. He had been radio operator for an FO party with the 161st Infantry when it became engaged with a Japanese tank unit in the town of Binalonan. Under fire from a tank, Bunn lay on the ground beside a jeep, his microphone in hand, when a shell struck a nearby tree and blasted splinters into his body. At the same time, a shell fragment punctured a fuel container and burning gasoline poured down onto the wounded man. No one could help him. He died there before the night was done.

Up there on the highest mountain ridge on Luzon we got some extremely bad winds. We had flown our L-4s at Fort Sill in winds that made us actually drift backward while in flight, but the turbulence in the mountain winds was something else. Somewhere a few miles generally north of Baguio there was a broad ridge that terminated in a very high, almost vertical bluff. One day when the wind was howling down that ridge and burbling off the bluff, I foolishly ventured into the worst of it—just to see what it was like.

One second I was flying along in pretty rough air, and the next second I wasn't flying at all. I was simply being slung about inside a crate over which I had absolutely no control. Totally disoriented and unable even to keep hands and feet on the controls, I just tried to keep from being battered against parts of the plane or thrown completely out of it. I had a vague sensation of rapidly losing altitude, but there was nothing I could do about it. How long that condition lasted I cannot say, but while it seemed like a long time it couldn't have been more than twenty or thirty seconds.

When the gyrations eased enough for me to get back on the stick and regain control, I was fifteen hundred feet lower than when I started and was headed in the opposite direction. Believe me, I was thoroughly frightened and most thankful for several things, including the fact that the L-4 was a sturdy little airplane.

Just before dark one day, I was coming around one of those high bluffs in the Cordillera Central. On a narrow shelf cut into it was a hair-raising mountain trail such as Donald Duck and his nephews used to travel on some mission in the Andes for Uncle Scrooge McDuck. Rounding a curve, with the high wall close on my right, I saw ahead of me a Japanese patrol of about fifteen men. Evidently they were getting an early start on their mission of the night.

The only place for the Japanese to hide was on a small, brush-covered knoll that jutted out about forty yards from the cliff. It was connected to the cliff by a slim neck of earth, and it formed the top of a cone-shaped slide area that dropped about two hundred feet to a jumble of boulders and dirt in the edge of the forest below. The brushy top was no more than fifteen yards across, but the patrol members dashed out there and concealed themselves in the brush. I suppose they hoped I hadn't already seen them.

It would have been quite difficult to hit the men with artillery even if I'd had time to do it before dark, so I decided not to ask for fire. But there was that matter of pride that made it necessary for me to show them they had not escaped my eagle eye, so I swooped across the knoll and dropped a yellow smoke grenade into their midst.

As the evil-looking yellow smoke billowed up through the bushes, Japanese soldiers erupted from their cover like a covey of quail out of a patch of weeds. I guess they thought it was toxic gas of some kind, for it panicked them in an instant, and they went in all directions. The trouble was, they couldn't stop going, for the moment they left the brush they were on that long, steep slide of dirt and rock, and they went skidding and tumbling all the way to the bottom. Among them, I saw falling the usual light Nambu machine gun, and, like the men, it vanished into the maze of rocks and debris far below. Only one man ran back across the path to the cliff trail. The others were scattered widely around the base of the slide cone, some of them undoubtedly injured. Their equipment likewise was scattered and lost, and I feel certain that they accomplished little that night except to get themselves together and salvage their gear. I flew on to Loacan, quite pleased with myself.

You know, it occurs to me now that such incidents as this were seldom reported to our headquarters. Many were the times Vin or I got in a lick or two against the enemy and never even mentioned it to Uncle Bud or his staff. We had no standing operating procedure covering such matters, as far as I can recall, and unless we called for fire or had been asked to look for some certain thing, it was unlikely that we'd bother to mention anything outside our own little circle of aviators.

Yamashita's troops in our front were getting to be pretty hard up for rations by this time. I recall flying around a cliff one day, looking into its caves, when I saw two or three enemy soldiers sitting up there on a ledge and gnawing the last shreds of meat off of what I judged to be the leg bones of a carabao, a draft animal similar to a water buffalo. The poor devils looked like wild animals as they crouched there, holding the bones, momentarily ceasing to chew as they watched me go by only a few feet away.

Another day, I saw in a little mountain cove something I first thought was a red blanket spread on the ground. On closer inspection, I saw that it was the laid-open carcass of a carabao, and still closer examination of the scene disclosed at least twenty Japanese troops lying in the weeds around it.

Having evaluated this as a target worth a fire mission, I was coming around just below some scattered clouds and checking my map for the location's coordinates when I became aware of a flock of tracers going by my plane, most of them a little in front. It took a second for me to realize that they were not coming up, they were going down. Just as I came out from under the edge of the cloud, a P-51 Mustang flashed downward from left to right close in front of me, his guns spraying tracers toward the "red blanket" target. I doubt he ever saw me, but he very nearly scored an aerial victory that day.

I happened to be the only pilot at the Loacan strip when Dwight Mossman phoned and said G-2 needed a volunteer for an unusual and risky mission. What could I do but volunteer? The job was to deliver some radio equipment to a guerrilla force located about forty miles north-northeast of Baguio and, at that time, nearly that far behind enemy lines. On the return trip I was to bring out a particularly valuable prisoner, an interpreter/translator from Yamashita's intelligence staff. The guerrillas would temporarily secure a small area where landing was possible and mark it with white panels. My timely arrival was critical, since they could not count on being able to hold the place very long before having to withdraw to their mountain stronghold. Because of the difficulty of communication, another rendezvous would be hard to set up.

The radio gear didn't make it to Loacan before I had to take off to keep the date, so I went without it. Carefully following terrain features on my map, I located the little field, a weedy path among low bushes beside a ravine emerging from between two mountains on the west side of the Agno River Valley. There were no buildings or other signs of life or recent activity in the vicinity—but no panels to indicate that the guerrillas were in control. I flew about in the valley for about ten minutes, trying not to draw attention to the vicinity of my intended landing, but still there was no sign from the guerrillas.

At length, I decided to go in anyway. I landed toward the mountain, slightly uphill, blasted the tail around, ready for takeoff, and sat there with the engine at a fast idle, my hand on the throttle, fidgeting, trying to look in all directions at once. After about five minutes, I was extremely uneasy and was about to take off when I saw a movement in the bushes on the edge of the ravine to my left.

The first identifiable thing I saw as a man emerged from the bushes was a Japanese field cap with a yellow star in front. I started the throttle forward, but the man stepped on out, waving his arms in a negative signal, and I could see that he was not Japanese, so I held my position.

He was unusually tall for a Filipino, spare and angular in build, and his hard, brown face below his Japanese field cap bore a long slash scar. Heavy ammunition belts were crossed over his chest à la Nelson Eddy, and at his waist hung a machete and a large revolver. He wore what appeared to be a faded American khaki shirt minus sleeves, and the matching trousers were roughly cut off at the knees. He sported a Japanese officer's brown boots. I'm not sure I correctly recall his name, but I think he said he was Lieutenant Ramos, commander of the local guerrilla band.

Ramos assured me that the strip was safe for the time being, and he apologized for being late. The prisoner would be there very shortly. He told me that the POW had been very cooperative and should be treated well, especially since he was suffering severely from malaria. I assured him that, at least while he was in my custody, he would not be mistreated. While we waited, I removed the front control stick and installed the rear one. I did not want even a sick and cooperative Japanese POW sitting behind me in the airplane.

Soon the prisoner appeared, escorted by about a dozen ragged Filipinos, some of them with Japanese rifles, others with only machetes. The Japanese was a stocky soldier with a heavy shock of stiff black hair. Although he was powerfully built, his movements were shaky and he appeared to be quite ill. His hands and feet were free, and he climbed into the front seat of my L-4. I fastened the safety belt for him, shook hands with Ramos, and got into the backseat. Remembering that Japanese prisoners sometimes were suicidal, I stuck my .45 in my belt in front. And off we went for Loacan.

During the thirty-minute flight the POW looked neither to right nor left, made no sound, and moved not a muscle, so far as I could see. At Loacan I turned him over to two MPs who came in a jeep to pick him up. I told them he was sick and fully cooperative, but they were peremptory and tough with him, and I could see that it made him nervous. I heard nothing more about him.

So my great volunteer mission turned out to be interesting but tame, as far as action was concerned; however, a day or two later it had a sequel that gave me the worst scare I ever had in my life, I believe.

One of the division's infantry patrols had been sent into enemy territory, had gotten involved in unexpected troubles that delayed its return, and had run out of rations. Requests for a supply drop by AAF C-47s was, for some reason, denied, so four L-4s were sent to drop cases of C rations.

We found the patrol on a very narrow spur that sloped steeply down from a high mountain ridge, and on both sides of the spur were the usual deep ravines choked with masses of vines and bushes that made them practically impassable. To be reasonably sure of getting the rations to stay on top of the spur, we had to fly parallel to it, straight toward the side of the main ridge until we dropped, and then pull up and turn away along the side of the mountain, since we could not climb over it.

Bill Brisley dropped the first case, followed by Speedy Spendlove, Don Vineyard, and me. On the rear seat I had two of the wooden or cardboard cases bound with wire, sitting one on top of the other. I opened the door, reached back with my right hand, and slid the top box over to the door ledge. I balanced it there while, with throttle reduced and the stick in my left hand, I glided in for my drop. At the right instant, I shoved the box out and pulled up and away.

The other pilots made their second drops in good shape, and I followed them in. As before, I reached back to move the box over to the door ledge—but I couldn't get it to move. In those days I only had about 140 pounds on my six-foot physique and I was not very strong. This case of rations was not on top of another, like the first one was, but was sitting down on the seat itself, and there was a slight lip at the front of the seat that prevented it from sliding. I was getting close to the drop point, and so, holding to the wire binding, I made a supreme effort to lift the box over the ledge. It came over, but not to the door ledge. In spite of my best efforts, it dropped off the front of the seat—and hit that control stick I had installed when I hauled the POW. The C rations jammed the stick hard forward, I could not move it in any direction, and the plane went into a dive toward the mountainside that was much too close below me.

As slow as I usually am, I am quite amazed at how fast I moved then. I knew the rations had to go without delay or else the war—and everything else—would end for me within five seconds. I flipped loose my safety belt and whirled around and up onto my knees in the seat, my rear end up into the windshield. I grabbed that box with both hands and heaved with the strength of desperation. The stick grip popped off, the box came up, and I hurled it out the door. It bounced off the wing struts and fell as I reached around behind me and hauled hard back on the stick. As the plane pulled out of its dive, the G-forces pulled me down onto the back of the seat, but I managed to advance the throttle and go skimming across the mountainside, barely clearing the terrain. And then I was able to sit down again and follow the other boys toward home.

Vin called me then. "What happened, Crash? That last case went into the ravine. They'll never get that."

I didn't reply.

"Crash, this is Vin. Do you read?"

I didn't reply.

"Kadi 8, this is Kadi 7. Do you read me, Crash? Over."

He didn't call any more. After about ten minutes, when I had recovered enough that I could keep the tremor out of my voice, I called him and explained.[1]

Back in the early months of 1942, when General MacArthur's beleaguered forces on Bataan were surrendered to the Japanese, certain American and Filipino personnel were authorized not to surrender but to withdraw into the mountains, evade the enemy, and carry out against him such irregular warfare as might be within their capabilities. Others had been cut off in the northern Luzon mountains by the swift-moving Japanese invasion of the island and remained there for the duration. Among the latter was an American infantry officer named Russell Volckmann.

By the time of the American landings at Lingayen in January 1945, Volckmann was a guerilla organizer and leader of long experience and considerable success. His numerous narrow escapes from death or capture had given rise to a saying: "Volckmann walks with God." His guerilla command had grown to regimental strength, and as the command had grown he had provisionally promoted himself and his subordinates to commensurate grades. Soon after the Americans returned to Luzon, Colonel Volckmann's force secured a position at Tagudin, on the west coast of the island in Ilocos Sur Province, and there received an issue of American supplies and equipment. He was given a mission of attacking inland toward the high mountain town of Bontoc, a movement that would threaten the lines of communication of Yamashita's forces opposing the American divisions pounding on the south gates of the Cagayan Valley.

With the 33d Division's responsibilities somewhat reduced after the capture of Baguio, the 122d FA Bn was detached and sent to Ilocos Sur Province to give artillery support to Volckmann's guerrillas. As a preliminary to our move, Colonel Carlson had me fly him to Volckmann's headquarters at Tagudin for a planning conference.

Volckmann already had some artillery—four mismatched Japanese field pieces and a few assorted rounds of ammunition for them. He even had a Filipino major designated as his chief of artillery. That officer and an American major, who, I believe, was Volckmann's second in command, seemed to constitute the top level of the staff, but there were a number of other officers in the headquarters, all Filipino as I recall. All these officers, including Colonel Volckmann, proudly wore U.S. Army insignia, much of which had been handmade by their own troopers.

The CP tent and the artillery officer's tent, new American issue, were neatly set up quite near the beach, but I don't recall seeing many other tents nearby. We were taken to lunch in a mess hall in an old factory building of some kind, and there Colonel Volckmann displayed considerable pride as well as pleasure in showing us that his men had not only managed to obtain but had learned to use a commercial ice cream machine. It was the first ice cream Uncle Bud and I had seen since Hawaii, except while we were aboard ship.

Volckmann and several of his officers barely touched their food in the mess hall, and they soon politely excused themselves, urging us to enjoy our meal at leisure. We finished and returned to the CP area, and soon I saw the reason for their behavior. A couple of hundred yards up on the slope of a pleasant little hill stood a row of neat huts, and from these huts began emerging the guerrilla officers. In each doorway appeared a wife—or girlfriend—saying goodbye. A very lovely young woman walked most of the way down toward the CP with Colonel Volckmann and then returned to the cabin.

Nothing wrong with that, of course—in fact, I believe that the young woman with the colonel became Mrs. Volckmann soon thereafter—but to Uncle Bud and me, accustomed to the field army environment with its essential austerity, this seemed a pretty plush way to fight a war. I'm sure that a few years of hiding in the mountains and fighting a guerrilla-style war would have changed our outlook considerably. In retrospect, their situation seems very romantic, indeed, in every sense of the word.

Vin and I flew our planes to a new landing spot near Tagudin, and our ground crew drove up in our three-quarter-ton truck. We were there a day ahead of the battalion and, pending their arrival, had nothing in particular to do but set up our tents and drive tie-down stakes for the two planes. Once that was done, Vin and I got into the truck and set out for a short drive to become acquainted with the immediate locale. Expecting to be gone only a few minutes, we didn't even tell the boys we were going.

A short distance up the road, we came upon six Filipino guerrillas and two volunteer nurses who had been serving with Volckmann. They were walking, so we offered them a ride. They told us that they were on leave; this was their first chance in three years to go home, and they were hoofing it in that direction. Home for all of them was in the town of Laoag, Ilocos Norte, roughly a hundred miles to the north. Having nothing better to do, we decided to give them a lift a few miles up the road. It was a little risky, maybe, since there were still small bands of Japanese in the coastal areas who had been left behind when their main forces hastily withdrew into the mountains, and they had occasionally attacked small parties along this highway. But we had the six stalwart guerrillas, so we were bold. We decided to take them as far as we could before dark, then turn back.

We were still trudging slowly northward when it began to rain. It was still raining when darkness fell, and we didn't have the heart to put the Filipinos out in the rain, so we kept going. At about 2100, some fifty miles from Tagudin, we were approaching a long highway bridge over the Abra River when several Filipinos standing in the dark beside the road hailed us—the first sign of life we had seen since we picked up the guerrillas.

They told us that the bridge was down, thanks to the bombers, and they led us off to the left down a narrow, wet trail to the edge of the broad river. The headlights of the truck showed only an endless expanse of surging muddy water in which the presence of much driftwood indicated a flood condition. At the edge of the water floated a raft of bamboo, perhaps thirty feet from end to end and just wide enough for the length of the truck, crosswise to the raft. The loaded truck sank the center of the raft about a foot below the surface, although the ends stuck out of the water on either side.

Out there at the ends were about a dozen Filipino men, all dressed in straw raincoats that made them look like small haystacks with bare legs, each topped with one of the wide, conical straw hats common all over southeast Asia. Each had a long bamboo pole. With our headlights showing the way, they poled the raft out onto the flood.

On the way over, as the rain poured down and the river seethed around us, the raftsmen, one by one, came to the truck and asked Vin and me for cigarettes. We gave each a cigarette—and that was the fare for the ferry ride. Before long, we began to see the opposite shore, and we soon grounded some distance downstream from where we had started. In response to our questions, the ferry men told us that the only place they knew where we might find gasoline was a government radio communications station near Vigan, which they told us how to find.

The radio station was a small, isolated white frame building in the middle of a field. All was dark—in fact, the whole countryside was dark except for the lights of our truck—and it was a long time before anyone responded to our knocks and shouts. Finally, a nervous young man in U.S. Army HBT uniform opened the door a little. He told us that we might be able to get some gas from a certain American civilian who could be found at a hotel in Vigan.

The sizable town of Vigan was dark—totally dark, not a soul in sight—but we found the hotel, a Spanish-style stucco building that was reminiscent of California. Inside, we saw the dull glow of a candle behind the desk, and a skittish Filipino man asked what we wanted. When we asked to see the American who was staying there, he denied any knowledge of an American having ever been there, and he refused to change his story. However, while we were still insisting that we knew there was an American there, a voice spoke from a western movie–style balcony that overlooked the lobby—and there was our tall and very businesslike American civilian. Who he was I do not know, but he arranged for us to get some gasoline—although I don't recall just where it was.

We pulled out of Vigan shortly after midnight, still with our guerrillas, still heading north, despite advice from the mysterious civilian that we wait until daylight and join some convoy if we were going toward Laoag. And that's where we had now decided to go—all the way.

It was a long, slow, lonely, and difficult trip, during which we neither saw nor heard any indication of the presence of other people of any kind. Not one bridge on the route was serviceable, but, fortunately, none of the streams was large. We'd find loose planks and lay them across the impossible places, inching the small truck across on those. In many places the blacktop road was cratered, if not by bombs or shells then by lots of heavy wartime traffic with little or no maintenance. We half expected to come up against a road barrier and be fired on by Japanese stragglers, but no such excitement came. Even the rain had stopped. Just at daylight, we came to a place where flimsy barracks along both sides of the road had been hastily set up as a recuperation hospital for sick or wounded guerrillas, and we felt safer from there on. It was the first sign of life we had seen since Vigan.

One more hurdle remained, however. The town of Laoag lay on the north side of the Laoag River, and—you guessed it—the bridge was out. It would carry only pedestrian traffic. Just above the bridge, U.S. Army trucks were fording the stream, which was rather wide but not too deep. Not too deep, that is, for a two-and-a-half-by-six truck. It was just a bit much for our weapons carrier, but we were not convinced of that until it drowned out in midstream.

With polite but rather hasty apologies and most sincere thanks, all of our eight passengers hopped out and waded on across the river. Vin and I sat there with our feet soaking in the muddy water and saw all the invitations to family breakfasts of fried eggs—something we hadn't seen in more than a year—go sloshing and dripping into the realm of memory.

An accommodating six-by-six driver soon towed us out to the south bank once more and pointed us toward an Army engineer unit where we got breakfast and all the gasoline we could carry in our tank and five-gallon cans. Then we headed back south, posthaste, now hoping we could get back to Tagudin before Uncle Bud arrived there and called for us.

The trip home was much faster and easier during the dry and sunny daytime. We didn't need to stop for fuel, we hit the ferry just right, and the only people who had worried about us were the air section men. They were not used to having their officers go AWOL, and they had no idea what had happened to us. Vin and I were pretty well exhausted, but we believed we had done a good service for some deserving young people. In later years, our daughter said that my story of the trip to Laoag sounded like a scenario for the TV adventure series *Tales of the Gold Monkey,* and it does appear that an excellent setting for a truly swashbuckling adventure was largely wasted.

And then it was back to the mountains for Vin and me, flying up narrow valleys between spines so thin that the Japanese easily dug through nearly anywhere they wished, and where the nervy little Filipino guerrillas, now equipped like American GIs, fought them at close quarters in some actions as spectacular as any I ever saw. Clouds roofed over the valleys, making them tunnels from whose sides machine guns lashed out at us as we flew our L-4s along just beneath the ceiling. From a tunnel position in a sharp ridge just at our altitude, a gun would send out a spray of bullets and wait for us to fly into them. We quickly became quite proficient at rapid 180-degree turns. Getting artillery hits on the narrow ridges was most difficult, so the well-protected enemy gunners were not afraid to cut loose on us.

As Volckmann's men worked their way from Cervantes toward the region of Bontoc and the 122d gave them fire support, there came a day when Uncle Bud wanted to personally recon the terrain over which they would have to fight. He wanted to go all the way up until he could see the final objective area, and then to Baguio, where the 33d Division headquarters were still located.

I told him we would have to refuel after the reconnaissance in order to make it to Baguio, but he suggested that we shorten the trip by going straight down the high mountain route without returning to the coast, thus saving time and obviating a need to refuel. Of course, we would be over enemy territory all the way, but he was willing to risk that if I was. I thought it would be kind of fun to surprise the enemy and see some areas we hadn't looked at before, so I agreed.

From where we finished the recon, it was about sixty miles almost straight south to Baguio, and that made about forty-five to fifty minutes of flying for the L-4. The farther south we flew, the lower came the bases of the towering cumulus clouds to the rolling plateau over which we were flying, and on both sides they were already clinging to the ridges and peaks that rimmed the plateau. I didn't like it much, but we soon had reached a point from which it was impossible to return to Tagudin on the fuel we had, so we had to go on toward Baguio.

The clouds kept rearing higher and higher, crowding nearer together, and lowering their wispy bottoms closer and closer to the ground, and that surface was nearly six thousand feet above the sea. With the colonel and me and our two radios with power packs, the plane could not hope to top those clouds, so we had to either stay below them or wend our way between them. It became increasingly difficult to do either, and very often we had no choice. During one of the times when we were passing under one of them with no more than a hundred feet of clear air in which to operate, we suddenly realized that we were flying right down the runway of a Japanese-occupied airfield. We saw only one or two planes, a few buildings, and, finally, a machine gun that sprayed a few tracers at us just before we got out of range.

It had gotten so bad that I no longer even consulted the wildly gyrating magnetic compass that was our only directional reference. I just flew where I could—and by that time I was convinced that finding Baguio was a forlorn hope. I could only hope that when we finally either piled in or ran out of gas we would have gotten out of the enemy area. I just searched the murky atmosphere for the place where I could see farthest, and I flew that way.

At last that procedure led me to a dead end. There appeared to be no place to go, no way to get over a ridge that suddenly came into view just ahead. I supposed that I would have to just head up the slope, look for the clearest place I could reach, and then cut the ignition and set it down, for better or worse. But as I flew closer and closer, the bottom of the clouds kept following up the slope, leaving me just enough room to keep climbing. I was encouraged—until the clouds stopped rising with the ground. Ground and clouds came together no more than a quarter of a mile ahead of us. But then I spied one small place where the crest of the ridge was barely visible, and I thought maybe I could slip through. But into what? I had no idea, but maybe the land beyond would lead us downward and out of the high mountains, so I headed for that thin spot.

We passed over the ridge no more than twenty-five feet above the ground, and flying in the cloudy mists at that. Ahead, for the first time in half an hour, there was good, clear air and sunshine in the distance, and—I could hardly believe my eyes—dead ahead, spread out there in its bowl of hills, was Baguio! I had never seen anything so beautiful as that poor, beaten-up city. In a few more minutes, we landed at Loacan Field.

As he climbed out of the plane, Uncle Bud said, "Crash, that was great, but don't you ever take me on a trip like that again!"

"Sir," I replied, "I'll be very happy to comply with that order."

On the night of 4 June 1945, Rudy Krevolt called me at the Tagudin strip and told me that Lt. Bill Swift would be flying down next morning from Div Arty to take my place in the battalion. I should be prepared to fly his plane back to Baguio. I was going back to the States!

It was a shock, since I'd had no inkling that such a thing might happen. But I learned that after VE-Day—the end of the war in Europe—a rotation plan for troops in the Pacific theater had been instituted, selections being made on the basis of points awarded for such factors as time overseas, time in combat, decorations, and number of dependents. I was to be in the first group of rotatees from the 33d.

I was up at the battalion CP bright and early next morning, turning in my weapon, watch, blankets, and a few other issue items, picking up my orders, and saying goodbye to the people I knew, from Uncle Bud on down. And then I was back at the airstrip, watching for Bill Swift. Vin shook hands with me and went off on a mission, expecting that I'd be gone by the time he returned.

But Swift was late, and the next thing that happened was a telephone call from Colonel Carlson himself.

"Crash, you've got your orders, and I don't like to expose you to any further danger, so I'm not going to order you to fly another mission. But Vineyard is about out of gas, and we badly need someone up there to relieve him. If you should volunteer to go, I'd be grateful. But if you don't volunteer, I won't think the less of you."

Those were just about his words. What could anyone do but volunteer? So off I went for my last combat mission in World War II. It was just the same thing we'd been dealing with up there before—the tunnel-like clouded valleys and the horizontal machine-gun fire. Only it seemed to me they were worse that morning than ever before. But I returned to Tagudin unscathed and turned my old 31st Division plane over to Swift, who, a short time later, got a bullet through its fuel tank and made an emergency landing with gasoline all over his legs and the cockpit. If the bullet had been a tracer, I suppose there'd have been no more Swifty.

I stayed at Loacan that night. Dwight Mossman took me up to division headquarters, and General Clarkson, in his office, pinned a Silver Star on me—another surprise. Mossman gave me copies of two classified G-2 reports that covered the big target Stanley and I had fired and my earlier twenty-four-at-one-blow mission near Hill 4980. And on 6 June, someone—I think it was Mossman again—flew me to a strip near the replacement depot at Manila.

The "repl depl," as those addicted to slangy terms called a replacement depot, was a huge tent camp spread over a large and gently sloping hill somewhere outside Manila. I was assigned a cot, put down my duffel bag, and went to the showers that a latrine screen sheltered from general view. When I finished my ablutions, I wrapped a towel around my middle and walked back to the tent, where I started putting on clean clothing.

In the midst of dressing, I was suddenly confronted by a second lieutenant of the Quartermaster Corps whom I had never met before but who, I learned, was commandant of the repl depl. He strode into the tent and literally shouted at me in a rage.

"Have you no respect for decent American womanhood?"

And he went on from there, a tirade such as I could never reconstruct here. I could only stand and gape at him, because I had not the slightest idea in the world what might have brought on his outraged assault. Man, I hadn't seen anything even faintly resembling decent American womanhood in many long months, and I don't think there was a more respectful fellow in all Luzon than I was, whether the decent womanhood was American or otherwise.

While I continued to stare at him, stupefied, a captain who occupied a nearby cot came to my defense. He stopped the chivalrous lieutenant and turned the tables on him, raising hell with him for raising hell with me. And then, he continued in a loud voice to point out that the fault lay with field grade officers from MacArthur's headquarters who lacked the sense not to bring female personnel into the middle of the replacement depot without warning. As he said that, I noticed a major who was just putting his duffel down in the tent. He got red in the face but said not a word. And the captain then explained to me that the major's driver—sitting outside in a jeep, dressed in GI fatigue clothes and steel helmet, back toward us—was a WAC, a female soldier of the Women's Army Corps.

I had never seen a WAC before. I certainly hadn't expected to see one there—or to be seen by one.

Our processing in Manila was brief. There was a short lecture about security matters, and the same fellow who'd delivered it told us that our baggage would be thoroughly checked before departure for the dock. Any weapons and any maps, notebooks, or other items containing information of possible value to the enemy would be confiscated and the holder would be scratched from the shipping list, he said. Reluctantly, I took from my baggage the soiled map on which I had marked many a target concentration and burned it. But I couldn't bring myself to dispose of the pistol Sergeant Van Assen had sent to me, so I concealed it. When the time came for the inspection of baggage—there was no inspection at all. We just left the wonderful repl depl and were hauled through the ruins of Manila to where a gray ship waited beside a long quay.

A short time after leaving Manila, the vessel stopped off the shore of Leyte in the vicinity of Tacloban, and there she took aboard about four hundred serious casualties of the fighting then going on in Okinawa. It was just about that time that I began to have severe headaches from a wisdom tooth breaking through. My efforts to obtain aspirin were futile; all the medics were too busy with the casualties to worry about some lieutenant's headache. And the odors associated with the large number of casts on arms, legs, and torsos of the wounded men discouraged me from spending much unnecessary time in their area of the ship.

And so I suffered with severe headache during most of the thirty-day trip to San Francisco. Being one of three lieutenants in charge of troop security, with seventy-two sentry posts to be manned, relieved, and inspected several times during each eight-hour shift, I came to sincerely appreciate the big, shiny coffee urn in the troop galley, and its twenty-four-hour access granted to troop security officers on duty. I must say I've never had better coffee than I had there. And I got cussed out plenty, too, because in the sweltering nights the outer decks were always covered with men sleeping there to escape the suffocating heat below. Making my rounds in the darkness—blackout being enforced—I often accidentally stepped on or kicked some sleeping soldier, and seldom did he wake up in a good mood.

Wendell Young was on the same ship with me, and I managed to talk with him occasionally. His mind was already in Chicago with his wife and stepdaughter.

Aboard the ship, I became acquainted with Lt. Anthony Malik, formerly of the 37th Infantry Division, who had led the platoon in which Pvt. Rodger Young, the Medal of Honor soldier made famous in song, had performed his heroic deeds. The first thing Malik and I did when we hit the streets of San Francisco was stop at the first tavern we came to and order ice-cold beer! I was not really a beer drinker, but it seemed that the thing every soldier was dreaming of was ice-cold beer, and I caught the fever. The fever quickly cooled, because the ice-cold Miller High Life had no more taste than water on our palates, long unaccustomed as we were to cold drinks of any kind.

Both Malik and I were going initially to Camp Atterbury, Indiana, and we were placed in charge of a carload of troops going to Chicago

The author's beautiful wife, Dorothy, with him on leave in Xenia, Ohio, 1 May 1952. He left for Japan shortly after this picture, and Dorie sailed over on the *President Cleveland* to join him.

and Camp Atterbury. When came the first halt where the troops had a chance to leave the train, we feared they'd come back with liquor and beer and we'd have problems. And they did bring back a large number of bottles, but as far as we could determine, every one of them was a bottle of milk—real, pasteurized, whole milk! They hadn't had it for many months or even years, and they wanted it far more than they wanted beer or whiskey. So did Malik and I.

I said goodbye to Wendy Young when he detrained at Chicago.

At Atterbury, I filled out a form to indicate that I wanted to be relieved from active duty but retain a commission in the Organized Reserve. I was given thirty days' leave with orders to report at the Field Artillery Replacement Center, Fort Bragg, North Carolina, on 14 August for duty as assistant troop movement officer.

Dorie met me in Indianapolis, and we caught a bus for her folks' home in Ohio. My homecoming was saddened by the word they had recently received that Dorie's brother, Fay Clifford Lane, Company K, 17th Infantry, 7th Infantry Division, had died 28 April of bullet wounds sustained 27 April on the Shuri Line on Okinawa.

I worked a half day at Fort Bragg. When I came in at noon, there was a note on my new desk directing that I see the personnel officer. He had a War Department TWX message authorizing my release from active duty and commissioning me in the Organized Reserve. I started out-processing immediately.

Driving back to Fayetteville late that afternoon, Dorie and I noticed lots of people sounding automobile horns, yelling, laughing, waving, crying, and so on. We soon learned the war had ended. Two days later, I was on terminal leave, and we headed west.

EPILOGUE

At least until Mikhail Gorbachev's ascension to power in the Soviet Union, the Cold War dominated international affairs after the end of World War II. Twice it escalated into shooting wars involving the United States, and in those wars many veterans went back to combat zones in Korea and Vietnam. I was one of those.

When I landed after my first combat flight in the Korean War, I was greeted by D. W. Vineyard, my old flying partner from the 122d FA Bn. He was then detailed as pilot for a Korean corps commander. Later, we both transferred to Yokohama, where we served together again, flying and carrying out various other duties for Headquarters, Army Forces, Far East. In 1966, Vin retired from the Army. Later, retired again from a successful career as a farmer, he became a realtor in Mansfield, Missouri. He has since passed away.

My own further experience in the service was varied, interesting—to me, at least—and brought me into contact with some widely known people, both military and civilian. I graduated from the Artillery Officers Advanced Course at Fort Sill and from the Command and General Staff College at Fort Leavenworth. I served in both artillery and aviation command assignments in the United States and in Germany and for several years was involved in managing research, testing, and evaluating equipment, organization, and operational concepts. For about a year, I was proud to serve as chief of doctrine in the Artillery Agency of the Combat Developments Command.

I was in Vietnam, too, but I won't brag about that. I didn't like that war, and I especially didn't like some of my superiors. Added to my age and expanding waistline—and maybe I had reached my last plateau, anyway—that put the quietus on any hope I may have had for an eagle.

Dorie and I were stationed in Yokohama, Japan, in the late fifties, as Vin was. While there, Vin and I corresponded with Uncle Bud Carlson, who was then commander of Fort Slocum, New York. We heard many years ago that he had died. His former S-3 and later commander of the 122d, Major Bill Hadfield, retired as a colonel and became a bank vice president in Lawton, Oklahoma, adjacent to Fort Sill, where I met him in the sixties. He later died in San Antonio.

Going still further into the past, let me mention the pride of the 89th FA Bn, Jay D. Vanderpool. When I finished Army basic training and joined the radio section in HQ Btry, 8th FA Regt, Staff Sergeant Vanderpool was the section chief. By the time the war began, he was Second Lieutenant Vanderpool, serving as battalion adjutant. His career during the war proved him one of the most able and daring soldiers in the U.S. Army, and he ended the war as Lieutenant Colonel Vanderpool, G-2, 25th Infantry Division. I met him in 1962 when he was Colonel Vanderpool, G-4, Seventh Army, at Stuttgart. I met him again at the battalion reunion in Florida. He now lives in Sarasota.

Col. John W. Ferris died in Florida years ago. He was my first battery commander and one of the best officers I ever knew. Every man of the old battalion, which he eventually commanded, cherishes his memory. I think it was his training and example that enabled several of the ordinary soldiers who served under him in HQ Btry to become successful officers and senior NCOs, and contributed far more to this nation than the general citizenry will ever know.

Lt. Col. William Bledsoe, first commander of the 89th FA Bn, became a brigadier general before the war ended, but an untimely death ended the career of that irascible old veteran of the First World War.

My very close friend, Bill Gibson, served through the war as a gunner in the 8th FA Bn. I saw him a few times in the seventies and talked to him by phone occasionally before his too-early death.

Of my friends in the radio section of the 89th, Carl Bunn, was killed in action as described, and Mulherin and Crupi have faded away, as all old soldiers eventually must do. Pappy Downs became radio chief when I left for OCS, and later he moved up to become first sergeant of the battery. And then, sad to relate, he died of tuberculosis while still a young man. But Ralph Park, who became radio chief when Pappy moved up, Williamson, Willy Cancro, Leroy Ryder, and Shea were all together again with me at our 1988 reunion.

Also at the 1988 reunion I saw Warren Harriman, who advised us that the Japanese were firing real bullets that morning at Pearl Harbor, and Claude Phipps, who got two of them through his body—which is why he was lying on the floor when I stepped over him en route to the Supply Room on 7 December 1941. And there were others, like Williamson, Park, Cancro, and Rider.

It would be great to see all the old bunch from the 122d, too, but it takes a dedicated fellow like L. W. LeGrand of Bronson, Florida, to find people and organize a reunion after over half a century, and I guess the 122d doesn't have one like him. Phil Ryan could do it if he's still alive, but I haven't seen or heard of him since I met him at El Paso Municipal Airport in 1965 when he was managing a couple of car rental agencies there. Are Allen, Young, Kinsch, and Janes still living? I wish I knew. And all the pilots from the 33d—Brisley, Spendlove, Eder, Hoffman, Swift, Donaldson, Pickett, Mossman, and Bortz—where are they now?

Hal Davis, the daring pilot who used to fly rings around the rest of us, is alive and well in Virginia, and it has been a pleasure catching up with him by phone. Hal and I and our friends were not the first, but we were within a few months of being the first pilots organic to field artillery combat units, and we were the simple beginning of an Army Aviation branch that today is extremely complex and highly technical, that now carries and uses its guns and rockets with deadly effect, that flies the infantry to remote and isolated battle areas and flies them back again, alive or dead. It picks up the artillery's heavy cannon, rockets, trucks, ammunition, fuel, and rations, and sets them down beyond the beach, across the river, or far away among the pathless mountains and jungles, where they could never go under their own power. Today's Army pilots still watch above the thunder of the battlefield—and they can even see in the dark.

But it's an expensive proposition. Back in the sixties I officially opposed abandonment of light airplanes in favor of the light observation helicopter, and I had serious reservations about the viability of airmobile forces against even a modestly equipped enemy like the Viet Cong and the North Vietnamese regulars. Although air mobility certainly showed its worth in that affair, I think the high rate of helicopter losses at least partially justified my fears. And, aside from the personnel casualties associated with aircraft losses, the cost of helicopters is extremely high. The price of one Vietnam War light observation helicopter would have paid for the ten L-4s of a World War II division artillery and probably for the flight training of their crews as well. In its expensive complexity, Army Aviation is right in line with the overall current U.S. military trend. As Henry David Thoreau said, we need to simplify, simplify, simplify.

Although I loved the Army—especially in my earlier days with it—there are a few things about it that distress me now. One of the most trivial is the nose-to-nose, top-of-the-lungs, git-down-and-give-me-ten style of handling soldiers. I've found it to be true that when a man is treated like a man—with respect—he generally responds like a man, and he feels much better about being a soldier. He must be toughened, true, and he must learn to respond instantly to orders, but I believe this can be accomplished by treating him as an intelligent human being, not a dumb animal, and I think he will be more dependable when he has to think and take responsibility for his own decisions. Only twice in my entire Army experience did I ever feel myself maltreated, and each time the offender was a smart-aleck brigadier general.

I get angry when I hear anyone belittle the Army uniform, or those who wear or have worn it. It's a uniform that has been honored by the service and sacrifice of hundreds of thousands of men, some famous, most unknown, but all of them as deserving of honor as any of those who disparage it. My wife's brother, Fay Lane, was in Army uniform when he died in a hail of machine-gun bullets on a little hill on Okinawa. My brother Gerald was wearing it when he and Bryant Hicks, another 82d Airborne trooper, using a captured gun, held out alone for two days and nights in the face of a German panzer attack that swept away everything around them. They destroyed one tank, surrounded their foxhole with the equivalent of a platoon of dead and wounded enemy, and held their position until a counterattack uncovered them. Gerald was wearing it when a German artillery shell burst hurled him against a tree, broke his legs, knocked him into a coma for six days, and left him lying in the snowy darkness of the Ardennes until his hands and feet were frozen. My brother Bob was wearing that uniform when he drove a half-track recon vehicle with a cavalry reconnaissance squadron that led or screened Patton's famous Third Army in its great drive out of the Normandy hedgerows and on across Europe until the victory. They fought numerous small actions, many of them desperate, as they "either rescued or had to be rescued."

In a presidential campaign during the First Gulf War, one of the candidates publicly observed that the men manning our ships in the Persian Gulf are "the finest sailors our Navy has ever had." What did he mean by "finest?" If he implied that they were the tallest, handsomest, healthiest, best educated, best dressed, best equipped, best trained, best fed, best entertained, and best paid, then he may have had a point. But if he was saying that they were the most worthy, most courageous, most devoted to duty, most truly patriotic and willing to sacrifice all for home and country, then his statement is an affront to the memory of thousands of faithful American sailors whose bones are strewn in the briny deep from the North Sea grave of the *Bonhomme Richard* to Pearl Harbor and Savo Island, wherever the oceans roll. And I have heard other politicians make similar statements regarding today's soldiers, with equal affront to the ghosts of hundreds of thousands of soldiers who, like John Durant and his men whose bones lie in the alien sands of Maffin Bay, have been sacrificed to preserve our nation's sovereignty and liberty—and, sometimes, for its greater power and glory.

Those men will never grow old.

Some years ago I stood alone in the summer sun in a little cemetery at Columbus Grove, Ohio, and watched as a soft breeze ruffled a decorative

American soldiers who made the supreme sacrifice during World War II
lie in thousands of cemeteries throughout the world, like this one in the
Philippines where many of the dead of the 33d Division were buried. This is
Cemetery #1 at Santa Barbara on Luzon (Photograph from Sanford Winston,
The Golden Cross).

shrub growing beside a red granite tombstone. The marker reminded
me that Carl Bunn had been dead for more than forty-one years, and it
was hard to believe. In my memory, I could see him walking across the
Schofield street from the mess hall to the barracks, the pockets of his
khakis bulging with oranges.

Someone yells, "Hey, Bunn, let me have an orange!"

And Carl's young voice comes back, clear and fresh, "To hell with
you, bud! Didn't the government issue you an orange this morning?"

—Appendix—

HISTORY AND SPECIFICATIONS OF THE J-3 PIPER CUB

TOM BAKER

The story of the J-3 Piper Cub began in 1926 with C. Gilbert and Gordon Taylor, brothers and partners in the very small Taylor Brothers Aircraft Company of Rochester, New York. Onetime barnstormers, the Taylor brothers had designed, and were attempting to market, a two-seat monoplane they named the Chummy, when Gordon was killed in a crash.

Gilbert Taylor then moved the operation to Bradford, Pennsylvania, where community leaders, anxious to promote new local industries, provided $50,000 to capitalize the new Taylor Aircraft Company. One of the stockholders was a Pennsylvania oilman named William T. Piper, who was interested in aviation but believed that the Chummy was too expensive and inefficient a design. Piper offered to sponsor the development of a small plane to sell for half the Chummy's $3,985 price tag. The resulting aircraft, designated the E-2, was completed in late 1930 and fitted with a twenty-horsepower, two-cylinder Brownbach "Tiger Kitten" engine. The airplane was named the "Cub" to go along with the Kitten engine. The diminutive motor proved too weak to fly the airplane and was soon abandoned, but the name "Cub" stuck.

In 1931, with no suitable engine available for the Taylor Cub, the company was forced to declare bankruptcy. Piper bought up the assets,

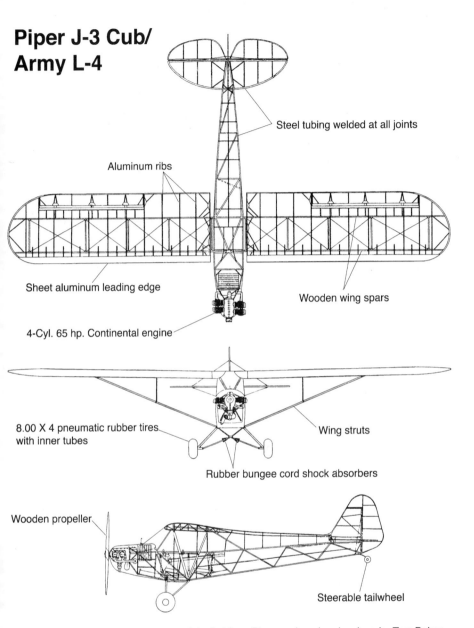

Piper J-3 Cub/
Army L-4

Steel tubing welded at all joints

Aluminum ribs

Sheet aluminum leading edge

Wooden wing spars

4-Cyl. 65 hp. Continental engine

8.00 X 4 pneumatic rubber tires
with inner tubes

Wing struts

Rubber bungee cord shock absorbers

Wooden propeller

Steerable tailwheel

Adapted from Piper engineering drawings by Tom Baker

A three-view diagram of the Piper Cub airplane.

retaining C. G. Taylor as chief engineer. Continental Motors Corporation provided a solution to the engine problem that same year when it came out with the thirty-seven-horsepower A-40 aircraft engine, and the Taylor E-2 Cub was placed on the market with it. Piper sold twenty-two Cubs that year, with sales growing tenfold by 1935.

In 1936, William Piper hired a young aeronautical engineer named Walter Jamouneau, who redesigned the airplane (hence the J in J-3), among other changes, rounding off its square wings and tail. The irascible C. G. Taylor had been quarreling with William Piper over various matters anyway, and to him the unwelcome redesign of his Cub by Jamouneau was the last straw. Taylor quit the company to establish the competing Taylorcraft Aviation Company in Alliance, Ohio.

When the Piper plant at Bradford burned down in 1937, W. T. Piper moved his manufacturing equipment and more than two hundred employees to a roomy, abandoned silk mill in Lock Haven, Pennsylvania, and resumed production under the name Piper Aircraft Corporation. By the end of that year, the company had built 687 Piper Cubs.

In 1938 Piper introduced the improved J-3 Cub, powered by forty-horsepower Continental, Lycoming or Franklin engines, which sold for $1,300. Engine horsepower was soon raised to fifty, and by 1940 it reached sixty-five (which it would retain throughout World War II, with the Continental engine). Piper also standardized a color scheme; just as Henry Ford's Model Ts were all black, so William Piper's Cubs were all bright yellow with black trim. When Piper began producing Cubs for the Army during World War II (see the introduction), the Cub was designated the L-4 (L for liaison) and received extra Plexiglas panels at the rear of the cockpit for better visibility, along with an olive-drab color scheme. Minor modifications resulted in such designations as L-4A (the original model), L-4B (no radio), L-4H (improved brakes and tail wheel), and L-4H (adjustable-pitch propeller).

Immediately before the U.S. entry into World War II, sales of the Cub were spurred by the government's Civilian Pilot Training Program, organized to develop a pool of pilots for the U.S. military. Seventy-five percent of all pilots in this program were trained in Cubs, many going on to more advanced training in the military. In 1940, 3,016 Cubs were built, and peak wartime production saw a new L-4 emerge from the factory every twenty minutes. Between 1941 and 1945, the Army procured nearly six thousand Cubs, and they were flown in all theaters of the war. These L-4s (also known as the Army O-59 and Navy NE-1) rendered invaluable service training pilots, directing artillery fire, evacuating wounded, carrying and dropping supplies, and doing courier service, aerial photography, and frontline liaison.

Production of the J-3 Cub ended in 1947, by which time a total of 14,125 civilian and 5,703 military Piper Cubs had been built. The J-3 was succeeded by the PA-18 Super Cub, basically the same airplane with a bigger engine (up to 150 horsepower) and wing flaps, which was produced up into the 1980s. In Army use, it became the L-21 and saw service in the Korean War.

Today the J-3 is finding ever-increasing popularity among antique airplane buffs. It has been estimated that perhaps forty of the original Army L-4s are still flying in the United States and Europe, along with hundreds of J-3s. Still an excellent trainer and an enjoyable sport plane, the Cub remains simple, economical, slow, and safe to fly, and the demand for J-3 Cubs remains high today, with corresponding prices. The Piper Aircraft Company is still in business, but no longer makes the Cub.

PIPER J-3/ARMY L-4 SPECIFICATIONS

Wingspan:	35 feet 2.5 inches
Length:	22 feet 4.5 inches
Height:	6 feet 8 inches
Wing area:	178.5 square feet
Wing chord:	5 feet 3 inches
Empty weight:	680 pounds
Useful load:	540 pounds
Gross weight:	1,220 pounds
Engine:	Continental O-170-3 (A-65-8)
Horsepower:	65 at 2,300 rotations per minute
Fuel capacity:	12 U.S. gallons

Fuel consumption:	4.08 gallons per hour
Top speed:	87 miles per hour
Cruising speed:	73 miles per hour
Stalling speed:	38 miles per hour
Rate of climb:	450 feet per minute
Cruising range:	220 miles
Service ceiling:	11,500 feet
L-4 armament:	None
Cost (during WWII):	$2,800

NOTES

TOM BAKER

Introduction

1. Sanford Winston, *The Golden Cross, A History of the 33rd Infantry Division in World War II* (Nashville, Tenn.: Battery Press), 353–44.

2. Bulldozers were tremendous assets to the American forces, hence Gen. A. D. Bruce's famous comment: "The secret weapons of the South Pacific War were the Piper Cub L-4 and the bulldozer," and thus there was good reason for Japanese suicide squads to target them. The Japanese had no earthmoving equipment equivalent to the American bulldozer, instead employing large gangs of human laborers—often prisoners or slaves—for the same purposes. With bulldozers, the Americans could quickly create roads, level obstacles to tanks and other vehicles, seal off enemy-occupied caves and pillboxes, build and repair airstrips, and generally accomplish earthmoving tasks much more quickly than the Japanese could. Bulldozers could do things in a few days that took Japanese laborers months to accomplish.

3. Devon Francis, *Mr. Piper and His Cubs* (Ames: Iowa State Univ. Press, 1987), 104.

4. Ibid., 99.

5. Ibid., 115.

6. Ibid., 82.

7. Ibid., 92.

8. Joseph Furbee Gordon, *Flying Low, and Shot Down Twice during World War II in a Spotter Plane* (Middletown, Conn.: Southfarm Press, 2001), 159–60.

9. Ken Wakefield with Wesley Kyle, *The Fighting Grasshoppers: U.S. Liaison Aircraft Operations in Europe, 1942–1945* (Stillwater, Minn.: Specialty Press, 1999), 19.

10. Francis, *Mr. Piper and His Cubs,* 115.

11. Julian William Cummings with Gwendolyn Kay Cummings, *Grasshopper Pilot: A Memoir* (Kent, Ohio: Kent State Univ. Press, 2005), 35–44.

12. A good friend of my father's, Lt. Gerald Middleton, tried flying an L-4 in the dark once at Fort Sill but got lost and had to light matches to see the compass on his instrument panel. Afterward, he told my father that he could not recommend this type of flying.

13. Cummings, *Grasshopper Pilot,* 65.

14. Ibid., 49.

15. Bill Stratton, *Box Seat over Hell,* vol. 2, (San Antonio, Tex.: International Liaison Pilots and Aircraft Association, 1985), 107–10.

16. Francis, *Mr. Piper and His Cubs,* ix, 101–2.

17. Heckmann Wolf, *Rommel's War in Africa* (New York: Doubleday, 1981), 40, 60, 227.

18. Cornelius Ryan, *The Last Battle* (New York: Simon and Schuster, 1966), 310–12.

19. Francis, *Mr. Piper and His Cubs,* 108; Cummings, *Grasshopper Pilot,* 56.

20. Gordon, *Flying Low,* 211.

1. THE PINEAPPLE SOLDIER

1. One witness thought that the white uniforms of the cooks made them highly visible targets to pilots of Japanese planes. (Ray Glazer, quoted in *Thunder* 16 [Jan. 1988]: 5).

2. A number of women and children ran out of the family quarters at Schofield Barracks onto the parade ground near the artillery barracks, where they were in grave danger in the open. Carl B. Mett was one of a number of soldiers detailed to round them up and get them back under cover again. In the process, one woman went into labor, and Mett helped place her on a pool table in one of the dayrooms where a medic delivered her baby. In 1991 Pearl Harbor veteran Ray Glaser also mentioned the incident but could only remember that it was an officer's wife. Carl Mett wondered who that baby was—and is, today (*Thunder* 3 [1991]: 6–7 and 16 [1998]: 5).

3. This miniature submarine, known as the HA-19, is now on display in the Admiral Nimitz National Museum of the Pacific War in Fredericksburg, Texas. It had been unsuccessful in its attempts to penetrate Pearl Harbor to participate in the attack and had then drifted around to the east coast of Oahu and become stuck on a reef, where it was captured the next day and salvaged. One of its two crewmen drowned on the reef, and the other, Ensign Kazuo Sakamaki, was captured and became the United States' first prisoner of the war. The submarine subsequently toured the United States on a trailer in a war bond drive.

Phil Grimes, a fellow artilleryman in the author's 89th FA, remembered the miniature submarine in 1997: "About 10 AM on the 8th, a call came to send a howitzer to Waimanalo Bay to shoot a miniature sub caught in the reef. We sent the first section and could see the periscope swaying back and forth, so we bore-sighted on it and wanted to shoot but they held up for a long time and finally said it was permanently caught and they were going to try to salvage it. We returned, fully realizing that we could have won the war right then and there if they had let us fire. The next day or so they did salvage it and bring it up on shore to be moved away. Later, it was taken to the US and was moved all over the country on a flatcar in the efforts to sell war bonds. There were two officers on it. One got killed on the reef, but the other survived and was captured by the Air Force and abused a bit, if I'm not mistaken. There was no love for the Japs at that time." "Me and the Army," *Thunder* 14 (Jan. 1997): 16.

The Japanese Navy sent five battery-powered midget submarines into the Pearl Harbor attack. Each was seventy-eight feet long, six feet in diameter, weighed forty-six tons, and carried two men and two torpedoes. Transported piggyback on large I-type submarines, the midgets were launched near the entrance to Pearl Harbor five or six hours before the aerial attack began. Four of the five have now been accounted for, and three recovered. Studies of photography taken during the Pearl Harbor attack have led some observers to argue that the fifth of the midgets was in place off Battleship Row as the Japanese torpedo planes came in and may have fired its torpedoes at the USS *Oklahoma* or *West Virginia*. If true, it may yet lie undiscovered on the seabed inside Pearl Harbor.

4. Phil Grimes described Colonel Bledsoe's mobile guns in 1997 ("Me and the Army," 17):

After being in position for about a month, Col. Bledsoe came and asked if I thought we could put a 75 mm howitzer in the back of a 2½ ton truck with enough protection to absorb the recoil and not destroy the truck. He said he thought we could and wanted my opinion. After a brief discussion, we decided to try it, and he asked me to do it and let him know when ready. I discussed this with the Motor Sergeant and the Chief of Section One, and then we loaded the howitzer pointing to the rear. We put a big timber to absorb the recoil with sandbags and soil behind the board. We put a cable around the axle to hold the howitzer, and some ⅜ inch armor plate in front of the sights and other parts to protect the gunner and crew. It looked good, and we called Col. Bledsoe, who came and said, "Let's try it out." We did, and it worked fine.

About that time a Major from Island Ordnance came and confronted Col. Bledsoe with the remark that the trucks were the property of Ordnance and that using them for mounting a howitzer was not authorized and it would have to be dismounted. Upon hearing this, and with his neck getting redder all the time, Col. Bledsoe said, "Major, we are at war. This is not peacetime. We are expecting and preparing for an attack by the Japs. We do not have a mobile gun, and we need one badly to move up and down the beach to help defend our sector. We have it mounted and it has been tested and it works. We don't think it will destroy the truck. We are going to leave it as it is and prepare to use it in our defense. Will you please go and report this to your commander." We used it for gunnery practice several times, using Rabbit Island as our target. We trained a driver how to handle the driving and getting into position quickly and accurately. Nothing further was ever heard from Island Ordnance.

5. Major Devereaux was taken prisoner and survived the war in a Japanese POW camp. After the war he became a brigadier general and then a member of Congress. He died in 1988. As the author mentioned, the valiant and stubborn defense of the island by the Americans until they were overwhelmed by a vastly superior enemy force was a source of pride to the nation at a time when it sorely needed a boost to morale in the face of so many Japanese victories. Wake Island became known as the Alamo of the Pacific.

Wake Island itself is a small coral atoll 2,300 miles west of Hawaii, and was attacked by the Japanese on 8 December 1941, the day after the Pearl Harbor raid. It was captured after a fifteen-day siege by Japanese bombers and warships, culminating in an amphibious landing by 1,500 Japanese troops. Their first landing attempt was repulsed by the Americans—the only failed Japanese landing of the war. The island was defended by the First Marine Defense Battalion, totaling 449 officers and men, commanded by Cdr. Winfield Scott Cunningham. Others on the island were 68 U.S. Naval personnel and about 1,221 civilian workers. U.S. Marine pilots flying from Wake's airfield in four Grumman Wildcat fighter planes attacked incoming Japanese aircraft as well as surface ships and a submarine until their aircraft were destroyed.

It was famously reported that the embattled Marines on Wake, when asked by radio if there was anything they wanted, replied defiantly: "Yes, send more Japs." Forty-nine of the 449 U.S. Marines were killed in the battle, along with 3 U.S. Navy personnel and at least 70 civilians. The Japanese retained 98 of the remaining civilians on the island for forced labor, then executed them all in 1943 when the Japanese commander feared they were plotting rebellion (he was hanged for the atrocity after the war). Japanese losses while capturing Wake were recorded at between seven and nine hundred killed, with at least a thousand more wounded, in addition to two destroyers sunk in the first invasion attempt, as well as at least twenty land-based and carrier aircraft shot down. Wake Island was surrendered to the United States by the Japanese garrison at the end of the war in 1945.

6. The Battle of Midway, fought over and near the tiny U.S. mid-Pacific base at Midway atoll 4–7 June 1942, was the turning point in the Pacific war. Prior to this action, Japan possessed general naval superiority over the United States and could usually choose where and when to attack. After Midway, the Japanese Pacific offensive was derailed, the two opposing fleets were approximately equal, and the United States soon took the offensive and kept it from then on. The Japanese lost four irreplaceable aircraft carriers at Midway and were demoralized.

7. Lindbergh, an Army Air Corps reserve pilot and mail flier, at age twenty-five became the most famous man in the world and probably of the twentieth century in May 1927 when he made the first nonstop crossing of the Atlantic by air in a monoplane called *The Spirit of St. Louis* (named for his St. Louis

financial backers), to win the Raymond Orteig prize of $25,000 for being the first pilot to do so. It was a solo flight of 3,612 miles from New York to Paris, which took thirty-three and a half hours. He followed the transatlantic flight with a triumphant flying tour of the United States and Mexico, and it was on this national tour that six-year-old Raymond Kerns in Kentucky saw his airplane and its two-plane Army escort pass overhead.

2. Ninety-Day Wonders and Fair-Haired Boys

1. Fort Sill military reservation covers 148 square miles in southwest Oklahoma and is home to the U.S. Army Artillery and Missile Center. The site of Fort Sill was chosen on 8 January 1869 by Maj. Gen. Philip H. Sheridan during a winter campaign into Indian Territory to stop hostile tribes from raiding border settlements in Texas and Kansas. The six regiments of cavalry were accompanied by such famous frontier scouts as "Buffalo Bill" Cody, "Wild Bill" Hickok, Ben Clark, and Jack Stilwell. Sheridan named the post in honor of Brig. Gen. Joshua W. Sill, a West Point classmate and friend of his who was killed in the Civil War. Some of the fort's original stone buildings are still present around the post quadrangle, and the post maintains museums open to the public (there are forty-eight designated historic sites in the area).

The U.S. Army Field Artillery School was founded at Fort Sill in 1911 and continues to operate today, having graduated generations of artillerymen as well as Army artillery officers in its Officer Candidate School (OCS). Today, Fort Sill remains the only active Army installation of all the forts on the South Plains built during the Indian Wars. It serves as a national historic landmark and home of the Field Artillery for the free world.

2. Signal Mountain at Fort Sill has been a landmark to generations of artillery students, so named because a heliograph, or sun-signaling device, was once emplaced there during the early days of the fort to signal the approach of Indians or other news. The concrete base of a heliograph is still visible on the summit.

3. Henry Post Army Airfield at Fort Sill, Oklahoma, was the first home of Army Aviation and is still in use today. It was named after Lt. Henry Burnet Post, an early Army aviator who became famous for setting an altitude record of 12,120 feet. He died in an airplane crash in 1914. This airfield was the original home of all Army Aviation training, and since it began before there was a separate Air Force, it is the first home of Air Force aviation also. The first aircraft in the Army Air Corps were assigned to Post Field, and before that, balloons were flown from it; in fact, there is still a balloon hangar beside the field, now listed as a historic landmark and slated to become an aviation museum. The first rotating beacon was used at Post Field.

3. Kauai to Fortification Point

1. Above ten thousand feet, the air is so thin that pilots flying without supplemental oxygen soon begin to experience hypoxia, with symptoms of euphoria similar to being drunk.

2. Ancestors of the Robinson family bought the island (twenty-three miles long and three to six miles wide) in 1864 from the Hawaiian King Kamehameha V for $10,000 in gold. Today it is managed by Keith and Bruce Robinson, who try to protect it from modern influences and preserve the traditional Hawaiian way of life.

3. A Japanese pilot from the Pearl Harbor raid took over Niihau, one of the Hawaiian islands, with the collaboration of Japanese Americans living there. The incident is not well remembered today but is seen by some as a contributing factor to why Japanese Americans were distrusted by the government and interned during the war.

Two Japanese fighter planes (Zeros) became too damaged in the Pearl Harbor attack to make it the two hundred miles back to their carrier, and instead, according to a prearranged plan, headed for the remote westernmost Hawaiian island of Niihau, eighty miles northwest of Oahu. Japanese intelligence had thought the island to be uninhabited, and a submarine was to pick up any such stragglers there. One of the planes didn't make it and dove into the sea, but the other, piloted by Shigenori Nishikaichi, crash-landed in a field on the island. However, far from being uninhabited, Niihau was (and still is) home to a small group of the last purely ethnic Hawaiians—at that time around two hundred Hawaiians plus three people of Japanese descent. Unaware of the Pearl Harbor attack, but suspicious of an obviously foreign warplane, one of the Hawaiians disarmed the pilot before he could get out of his aircraft, taking his pistol and papers, which included maps of Pearl Harbor, radio codes, and attack plans.

Once he had regained his senses from the crash-landing, the Japanese pilot took back his pistol and demanded the papers back also, but by this time they had been hidden. Two of the three Japanese Americans on the island were a man and his wife, Yoshio and Irene Harada, who had been born in Hawaii and were thus U.S. citizens, Yoshio having also lived in California for seven years. Speaking in Japanese, which none of the Hawaiians could understand, Nishikaichi won the Japanese Americans over to his side, and, with the pistol plus a shotgun taken from a ranch house, the three instigated a brief reign of terror on the island. They threatened the rest of the islanders with death if they did not hand over the papers taken from the airplane, burned down the home of the man who had taken the papers, and then Nishikaichi and the Haradas entered the home of Hawaiian Ben Kanahele and threatened to kill Kanahele's wife if he did not produce the papers. Instead Kanahele lunged for the shotgun. Nishikaichi shot him three times with the pistol, but despite his injuries Kanahele picked the pilot up and threw him against a stone wall, killing him. Yoshio Harada then killed himself with the shotgun (Irene Harada was later arrested and imprisoned in Honolulu). Ben Kanahele recovered from his wounds and was proclaimed a hero by the government and press, and a song, titled "They Couldn't Take Niihau Nohow," was written about him and became popular during the war. This was the man whom Kerns and Vineyard hoped to meet when they flew their L-4s to the island.

The Niihau incident was investigated by the Army and a report forwarded to Washington. In the atmosphere of near hysteria in the United States following the Pearl Harbor attack, with the large numbers of ethnic Japanese on the U.S. west coast, the fact that the traitor Yoshio Harada had lived in California as well, and fears that a Japanese invasion of California might be imminent, President Roosevelt and others in government viewed it as reason to believe that Japanese Americans might ally themselves with the invaders just as they had so readily done on the island. As a result, Japanese Americans in the United States were interned in camps and kept under supervision for the duration of the war. The Niihau episode is detailed in a book by Michelle Malkin titled *In Defense of Internment: The Case for Racial Profiling in World War II and the War on Terror* (New York: Regnery, 2004).

4. After its recapture from the Japanese, Finschhafen became a big World War II resupply and staging area for the retaking of New Guinea and then the Philippines as the Allies island-hopped toward Japan. Aircraft shipped to the airfield at Finschhafen were assembled and flown to other airfields in the area. At the end of the war, there was so much war materiel left at Finschhafen that much of it was simply bulldozed into big holes in the ground and abandoned, and generations of salvagers have made a living from recovering it. Aircraft left parked on the field were initially cut up and melted down for scrap, but some partial or nearly complete aircraft have recently been dug up and exported to museums or restorers, their rarity today making them more valuable as historical artifacts than as scrap metal.

5. Lieutenant Kerns had undoubtedly stumbled upon the former home of one of the many German Lutheran missionaries in New Guinea. In the late 1800s Germany made attempts to colonize New Guinea and convert the natives to Christianity, and the port town of Finschhafen had been first occupied and settled by Lutheran missionaries. Before the outbreak of war there were some eighty of them at Finschhafen running several missions, schools, the port, and a large radio station in the town. They even bought some airplanes and constructed their own airfield. Their missionary work was made difficult by the malaria and tropical diseases prevalent on the island. All these Germans abandoned New Guinea at the outbreak of the war, and when the Japanese invaded the island in March 1942, they used the Lutheran missionary buildings at Finschhafen as their headquarters. After the war the Lutherans returned to the area, and there are Lutheran missionaries on New Guinea again today.

6. Colonel Truxton never made it home with his seashells. He was later killed by a sniper on Luzon Island in the Philippines.

4. Tornado Task Force

1. The 33d Division history states that the next day Captain Marchant returned to the scene of the fight with a group of volunteers, hoping to bring the third Japanese tank back to their camp as a war trophy, since it was only lightly damaged. However, he found that the bazooka rounds he had fired at it the previous day had destroyed its ignition system, and it wouldn't start. With no way to move it, they decided instead to destroy it with incendiary grenades. (Winston, *The Golden Cross,* 60.)

5. Luzon: Lingayen to the Hills

1. On the strategic use of bulldozers by the American forces, see the introduction, note 2.

2. There were other incidents of Cubs losing fabric from their wings in flight. The humid jungle climate apparently weakened or rotted the cotton cloth covering, and/or the thread used to stitch it to the wing structure, and the suction of lift while flying then pulled it off. Don Moore wrote in his book *Low and Slow:* "The fabric situation got so bad that, one day when I was flying my commanding officer, Col. Knowlton, from the battalion strip to the main strip in Bacolod, fabric ripped off of the upper surface of the right wing. Two sections, each about three feet in width, came off and blew away. The Colonel, Stewart Knowlton, understandably, was a little nervous, as he saw the fabric fluttering down to earth. The Cub, or L-4, has so much excess wing surface for its weight that I was able to fly tolerably well with that much surface gone. A lot of cross controlling got us into the base without difficulty. Our excellent ground crew had an adequate patch on it before the day was out" (143).

3. Artillery-spotting aircraft were indeed occasionally hit by their own artillery shells. L-4 pilot Ernest Kowalik described how an L-4 had its tail shot off by a 105 mm shell in Italy (pilot and observer were both wearing parachutes and survived), and war correspondent Ernie Pyle once wrote from Italy about another incident that did not end so happily: "One of the worst strokes of fate I ever heard about happened to a Cub there on the Fifth Army beachhead. A 'Long Tom'—or 155 rifle—was the unwitting instrument. This certain gun fired only one shell that entire day—but that one shell, with all the sky to travel in, made a direct hit on one of our Cubs in the air and blew it to bits." Over Stolberg, Germany, Capt. Francis P. Farrel was killed when his L-4 was hit by an American shell, and Lt. Thomas Turner had a 105 mm shell pass through the tail of his Cub without detonating. See Ernest Kowalik, with John R. Baylor, *Alone and Unarmed: An Army Pilot Sharing the Skies with Artillery Fire in WWII Italy* (1968; rpt., Seminole, Fla.: Glenn Curtiss Press, 2005), 249; Ernie Pyle, *Brave Men* (New York: Holt & Co., 1944), 240; and Stratton, *Box Seat over Hell,* 2:79.

6. Over the Hills to Baguio

1. Winston, *The Golden Cross,* 214–19.

2. Just as Lieutenant Kerns saved the civilians from being fired on by making adjustments to the artillery fire unknown to his commander, so did a firing battery apparently deliberately aim wide to avoid shooting at a Japanese hospital on Luzon. In the latter incident, much to the confusion of the aerial observer, Lt. Don Moore (who resented the order to shoot at a hospital as much as the cannoneers did), the widely scattered shells burst everywhere except on the target. Thinking about it later, however, he realized that the artillerymen must have been aware of the nature of the target, since the fire direction center always had to be informed of what they were shooting at in order to select the correct fuses for the job, and

not wanting to fire on a hospital—even one of the enemy's—they had deliberately shot wide. See Moore, *Low and Slow,* 162–66.

3. Undoubtedly the thin air at Baguio's nearly mile-high elevation was to blame for these crashes by significantly reducing both the lift of the wings and the horsepower of the engines (because there is less oxygen for combustion). Each of these pilots knew exactly what his aircraft could do under normal circumstances but probably had little previous experience with takeoffs and landings at such a high altitude. Loss of aircraft performance at high altitudes, especially on hot, humid days, can be dramatic for low-horsepower aircraft like the L-4.

7. Sashaying Around Up North

1. A Cub in Italy crashed for the same reason Lieutenant Kerns's nearly did: something jamming the second control stick in the rear seat (and it has also happened occasionally to civilian Cubs). During the Italian campaign, pilot Ernest Kowalik watched an L-4 Cub sideslip all the way down to the ground and crash. He wrote, "I looked up to see a sideslipping Piper Cub a scant fifty feet overhead. Fascinated, I watched it continue its downward plunge until it crashed, right wing first, into a terrace about two hundred feet away." When Kowalik reached the scene, he found the pilot, a Sergeant Maschmann, standing beside the wreck of his airplane, only slightly injured, and asked him the reason he had crashed. "A package fell off the back seat and jammed the stick-stub to full right aileron. All I could do was cut the throttle and give full left rudder," Maschmann told him. Sergeant Maschmann did not have the backseat's control stick installed like Kerns did, yet the socket for mounting the stick was still enough to cause the jam. Smart Piper Cub pilots today always strap anything set on the backseat securely in place with the seat belt before flying (Kowalik, *Alone and Unarmed,* 117–18).

FURTHER READING

Beers, Clyde. *A Balcony Seat at the E.T.O.* N.p.: C(NMI)B, 1991.

Cannon, Hardy D. *Box Seat over Hell.* Volume 1: *The True Story of America's Liaison Pilots and Their Light Planes in World War II.* San Antonio, Tex.: International Liaison Pilots and Aircraft Association, 1985.

Cummings, Julian William, with Gwendolyn Kay Cummings. *Grasshopper Pilot: A Memoir.* Kent, Ohio: Kent State Univ. Press, 2005.

Francis, Devon. *Mr. Piper and His Cubs.* 1973. Second edition, Lock Haven, Penn.: Sentimental Journeys, 1987.

Gordon, Joseph Furbee. *Flying Low, and Shot Down Twice during World War II in a Spotter Plane.* Middletown, Conn.: Southfarm Press, 2001.

Kowalik, Ernest E., with John R. Baylor. *Alone and Unarmed: An Army Pilot Sharing the Skies with Artillery Fire in WWII Italy.* 1968; reprint, Seminole, Fla. Glenn Curtiss Press, 2005.

Moore, Don. *Low and Slow: The Liberation of the Philippines as Viewed from Eight Hundred Feet above the Ground.* Upland, Calif.: San Antonio Heights, 1999.

Schultz, Alfred W., with Kirk Neff. *Janey: A Little Plane in a Big War.* Middletown, Conn.: Southfarm Press, 1998.

Stratton, Bill. *Box Seat over Hell.* Volume 2. San Antonio, Tex.: International Liaison Pilots and Aircraft Association, 1985

Wakefield, Ken. *Lightplanes at War: U.S. Liaison Aircraft in Europe, 1942–1947.* Charleston, S.C.: Tempus, 1999.

Wakefield, Ken, with Wesley Kyle. *The Fighting Grasshoppers: U.S. Liaison Aircraft Operations in Europe, 1942–1945.* Stillwater, Minn.: Specialty Press, 1999.

Winston, Sanford. *The Golden Cross: A History of the 33rd Infantry Division in World War II.* Nashville, Tenn.: Battery Press, 2000.

INDEX